INVADERS

ORIGINAL SIN

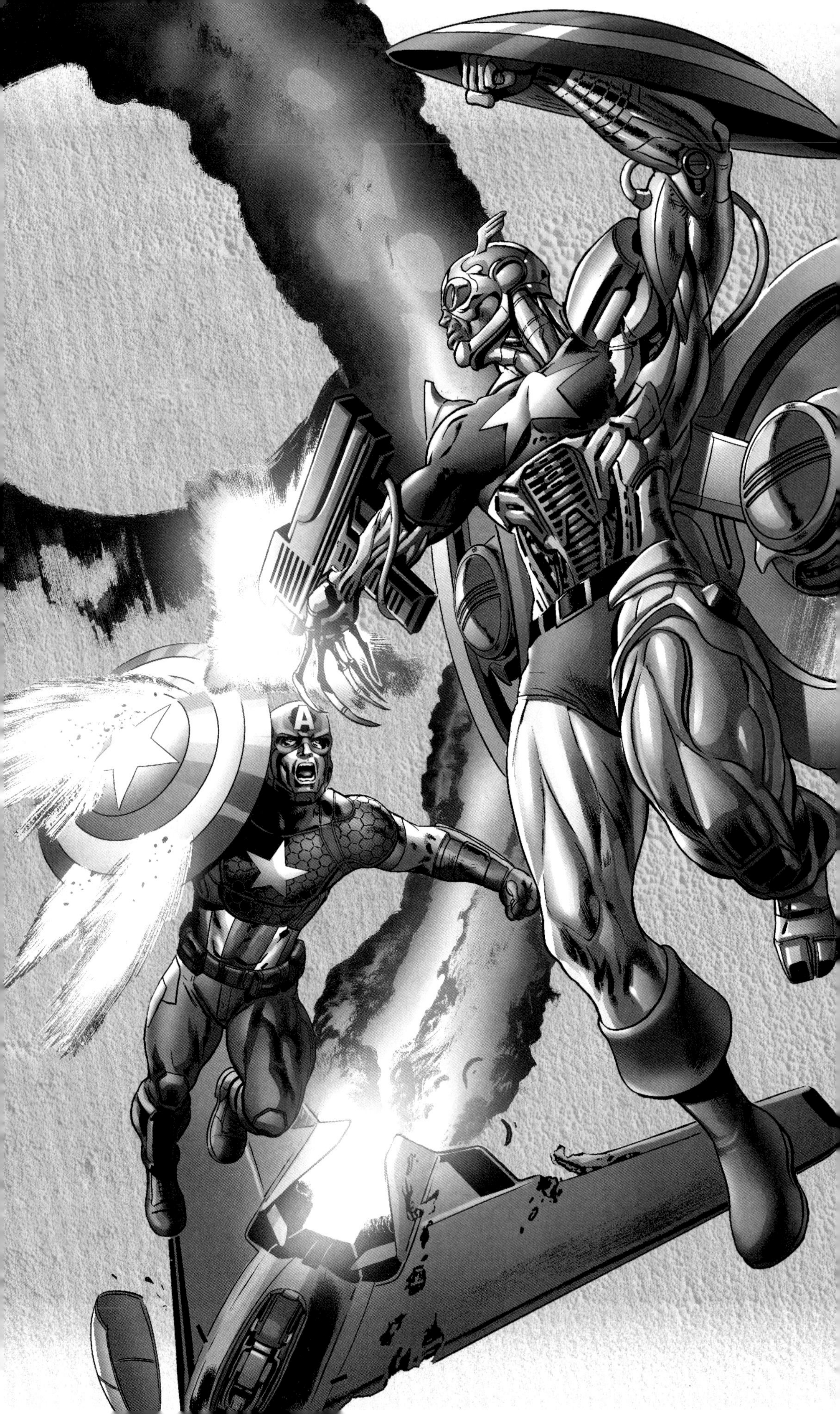

WRITER
JAMES ROBINSON

ARTISTS
MARC LAMING (#6-7),
STEVE PUGH (#8-10)

COLOR ARTIST
GURU-eFX

LETTERER
VC'S CORY PETIT

COVER ART
GREG LAND & NOLAN WOODARD (#6 & #8),
MUKESH SINGH (#7), MICHAEL KOMARCK (#9)
AND SCOTT KOLINS & GURU-eFX (#10)

ASSISTANT EDITOR
EMILY SHAW

EDITOR
MARK PANICCIA

COLLECTION EDITOR
JENNIFER GRÜNWALD

ASSISTANT EDITOR
SARAH BRUNSTAD

ASSOCIATE MANAGING EDITOR
ALEX STARBUCK

EDITOR, SPECIAL PROJECTS
MARK D. BEAZLEY

SENIOR EDITOR, SPECIAL PROJECTS
JEFF YOUNGQUIST

SVP PRINT, SALES & MARKETING
DAVID GABRIEL

BOOK DESIGN
NELSON RIBEIRO

EDITOR IN CHIEF
AXEL ALONSO

CHIEF CREATIVE OFFICER
JOE QUESADA

PUBLISHER
DAN BUCKLEY

EXECUTIVE PRODUCER
ALAN FINE

ALL-NEW INVADERS VOL. 2: ORIGINAL SIN. Contains material originally published in magazine form as ALL-NEW INVADERS #6-10. First printing 2014. ISBN# 978-0-7851-8915-2. Published by MARVEL WORLDWIDE, INC., a subsidiary of MARVEL ENTERTAINMENT, LLC. OFFICE OF PUBLICATION: 135 West 50th Street, New York, NY 10020. Copyright © 2014 Marvel Characters, Inc. All rights reserved. All characters featured in this issue and the distinctive names and likenesses thereof, and all related indicia are trademarks of Marvel Characters, Inc. No similarity between any of the names, characters, persons, and/or institutions in this magazine with those of any living or dead person or institution is intended, and any such similarity which may exist is purely coincidental. **Printed in Canada.** ALAN FINE, EVP - Office of the President, Marvel Worldwide, Inc. and EVP & CMO Marvel Characters B.V.; DAN BUCKLEY, Publisher & President - Print, Animation & Digital Divisions; JOE QUESADA, Chief Creative Officer; TOM BREVOORT, SVP of Publishing; DAVID BOGART, SVP of Operations & Procurement, Publishing; C.B. CEBULSKI, SVP of Creator & Content Development; DAVID GABRIEL, SVP Print, Sales & Marketing; JIM O'KEEFE, VP of Operations & Logistics; DAN CARR, Executive Director of Publishing Technology; SUSAN CRESPI, Editorial Operations Manager; ALEX MORALES, Publishing Operations Manager; STAN LEE, Chairman Emeritus. For information regarding advertising in Marvel Comics or on Marvel.com, please contact Niza Disla, Director of Marvel Partnerships, at ndisla@marvel.com. For Marvel subscription inquiries, please call 800-217-9158. **Manufactured between 10/3/2014 and 11/10/2014 by SOLISCO PRINTERS, SCOTT, QC, CANADA.**

10 9 8 7 6 5 4 3 2 1

PREVIOUSLY...

Jim Hammond, the original Human Torch, android, and member of the Invaders during World War II, was adjusting to life in present day Blaketon, Illinois. His quiet life was interrupted, however, when the Invaders were re-formed to deal with a threat from their past.

When this threat was resolved, Jim was invited to be a S.H.I.E.L.D. agent by Captain America. Jim cautiously accepted.

Meanwhile, the Watcher — a godlike alien being who sees all in the Marvel Universe — has been murdered, sending out a psychic blast across the Earth, revealing sins and secrets that have long been hidden...

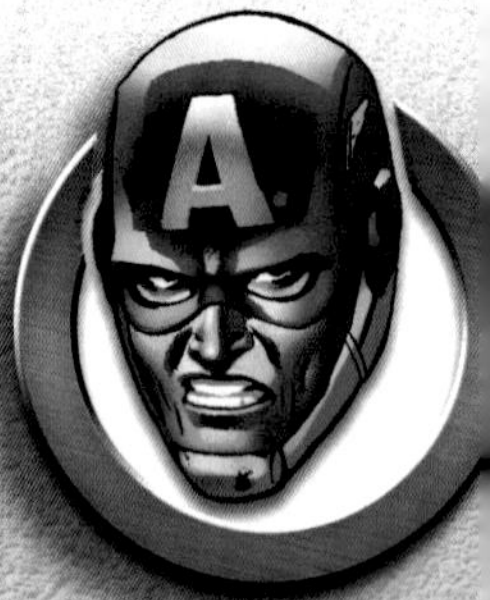

CAPTAIN AMERICA, the super-soldier, living legend, and sentinel of liberty remains the epitome of a national/world hero, with links to both the Avengers and S.H.I.E.L.D. and a continued history of doing good.

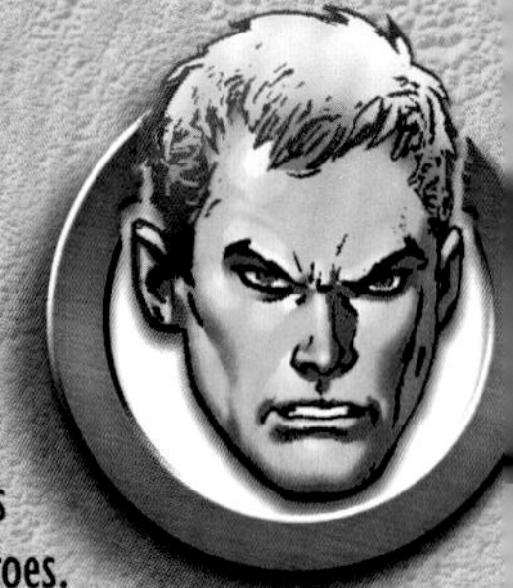

JIM HAMMOND, THE ORIGINAL HUMAN TORCH and the world's first synthetic human, is perhaps the least known of the heroes. Recently a cadre of robots and androids planned to take over Earth, a plan that Jim betrayed and helped defeat for the sake of humanity.

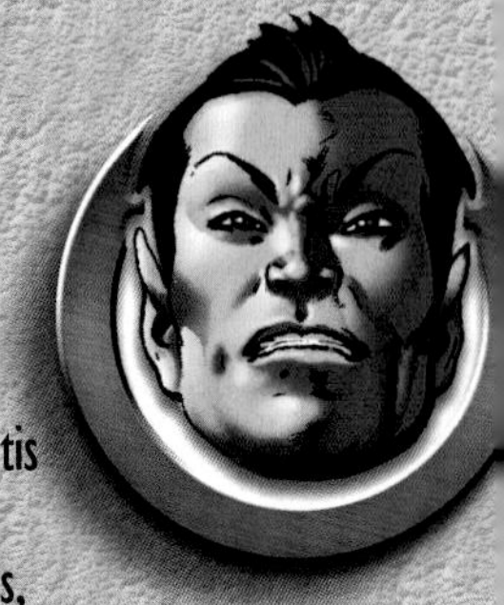

NAMOR, THE SUB-MARINER, aquatic ruler of the undersea kingdom of Atlantis has been a hero too since the war, but at other times, humanity's greatest foe. Currently his place in the world is somewhere between the two.

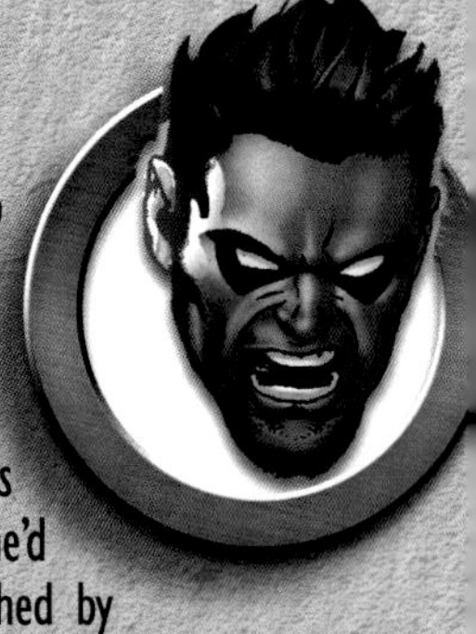

JAMES "BUCKY" BARNES, one-time sidekick of Captain America, was long thought to have died in the closing months of the war. Actually he'd survived and was brainwashed by the Russians into becoming the assassin and super-s known as the Winter Soldier. He remains a wanted m for his crimes as a Russian killer and was forced to fa his death. The Winter Soldier now lives in the shadow

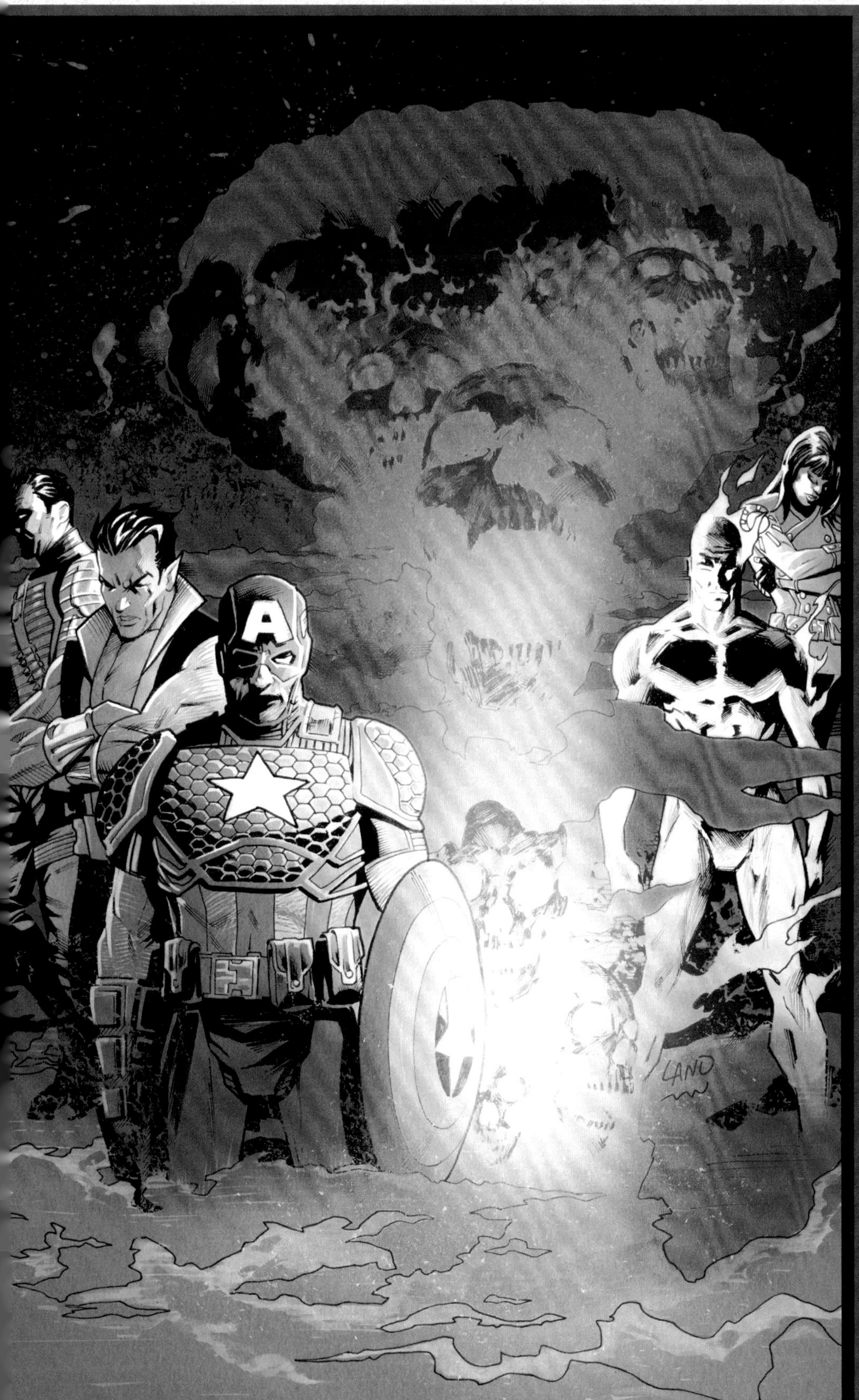
LAND

#6

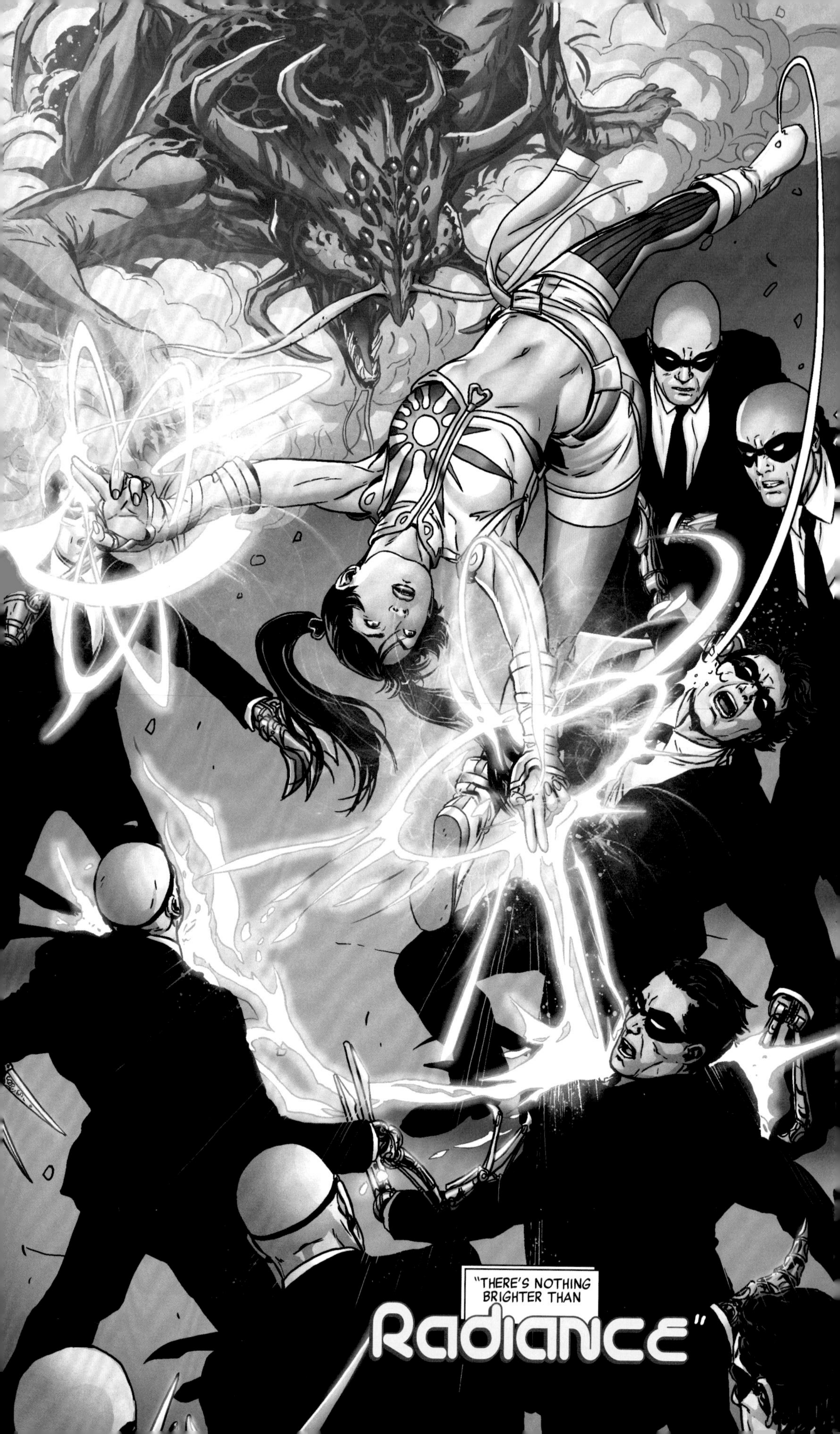
"THERE'S NOTHING BRIGHTER THAN
Radiance"

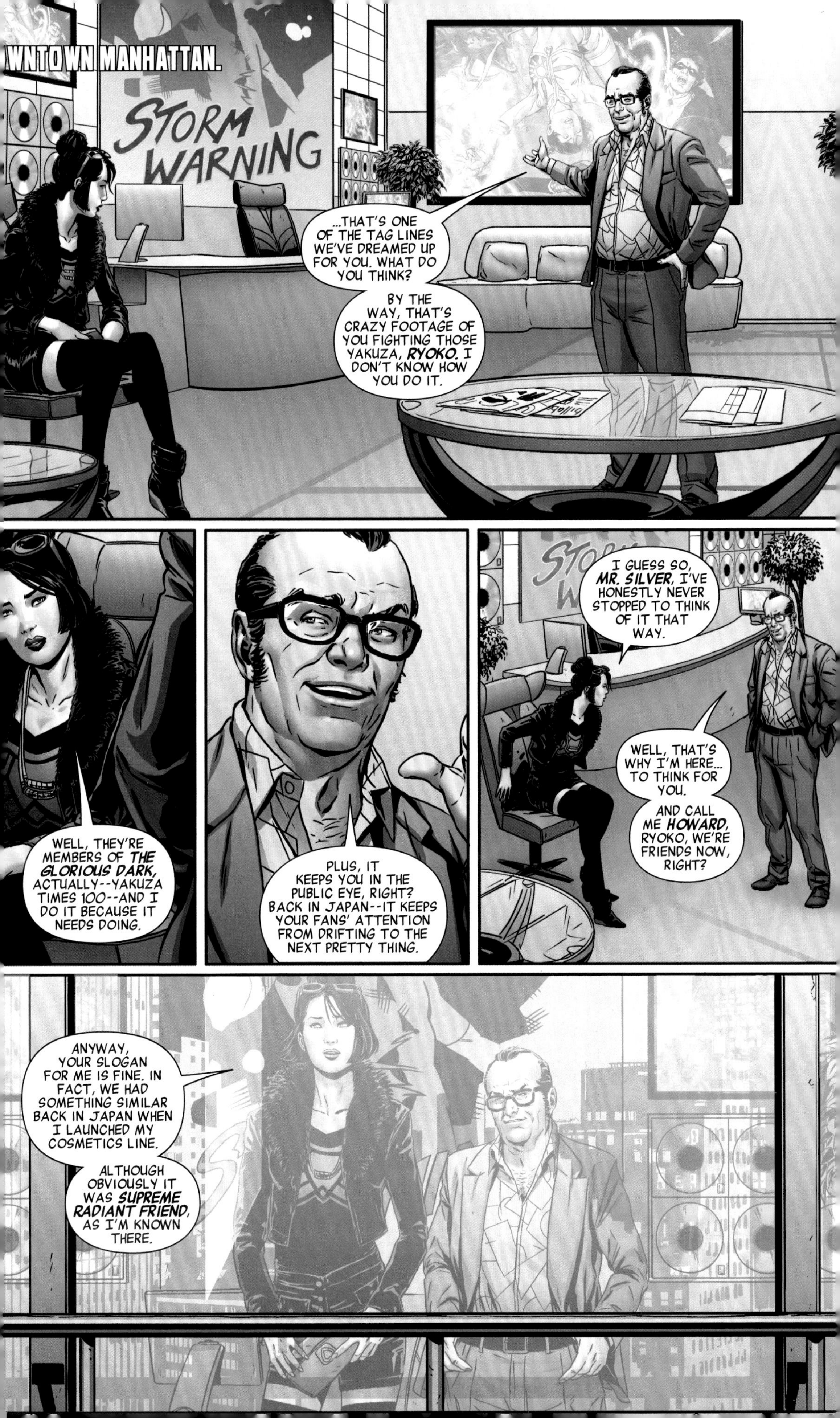
WNTOWN MANHATTAN.
STORM WARNING
...THAT'S ONE OF THE TAG LINES WE'VE DREAMED UP FOR YOU. WHAT DO YOU THINK?
BY THE WAY, THAT'S CRAZY FOOTAGE OF YOU FIGHTING THOSE YAKUZA, RYOKO. I DON'T KNOW HOW YOU DO IT.
WELL, THEY'RE MEMBERS OF THE GLORIOUS DARK, ACTUALLY--YAKUZA TIMES 100--AND I DO IT BECAUSE IT NEEDS DOING.
PLUS, IT KEEPS YOU IN THE PUBLIC EYE, RIGHT? BACK IN JAPAN--IT KEEPS YOUR FANS' ATTENTION FROM DRIFTING TO THE NEXT PRETTY THING.
I GUESS SO, MR. SILVER, I'VE HONESTLY NEVER STOPPED TO THINK OF IT THAT WAY.
WELL, THAT'S WHY I'M HERE... TO THINK FOR YOU.
AND CALL ME HOWARD, RYOKO, WE'RE FRIENDS NOW, RIGHT?
ANYWAY, YOUR SLOGAN FOR ME IS FINE. IN FACT, WE HAD SOMETHING SIMILAR BACK IN JAPAN WHEN I LAUNCHED MY COSMETICS LINE.
ALTHOUGH OBVIOUSLY IT WAS SUPREME RADIANT FRIEND, AS I'M KNOWN THERE.

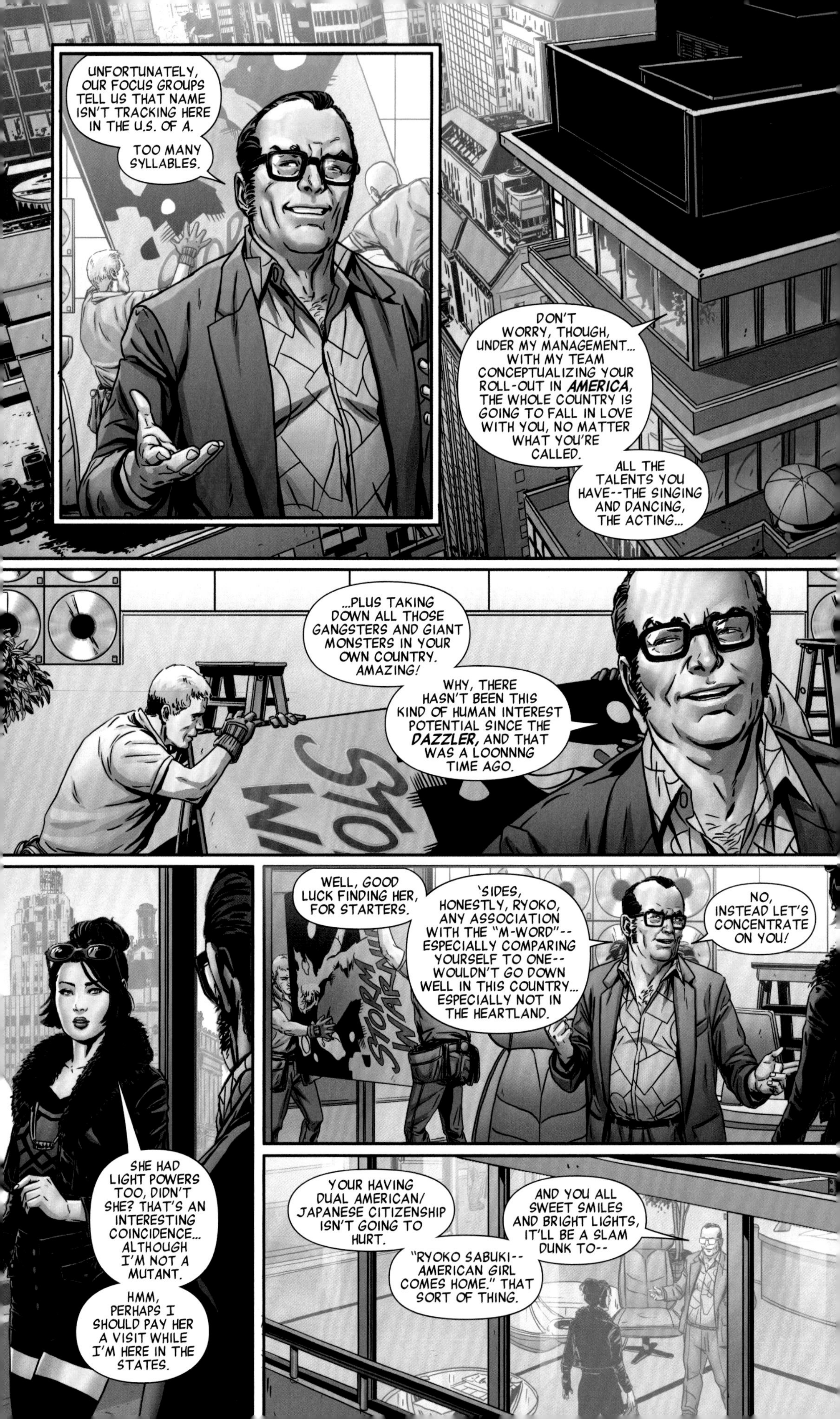
UNFORTUNATELY, OUR FOCUS GROUPS TELL US THAT NAME ISN'T TRACKING HERE IN THE U.S. OF A.
TOO MANY SYLLABLES.
DON'T WORRY, THOUGH, UNDER MY MANAGEMENT... WITH MY TEAM CONCEPTUALIZING YOUR ROLL-OUT IN AMERICA, THE WHOLE COUNTRY IS GOING TO FALL IN LOVE WITH YOU, NO MATTER WHAT YOU'RE CALLED.
ALL THE TALENTS YOU HAVE--THE SINGING AND DANCING, THE ACTING...
...PLUS TAKING DOWN ALL THOSE GANGSTERS AND GIANT MONSTERS IN YOUR OWN COUNTRY. AMAZING!
WHY, THERE HASN'T BEEN THIS KIND OF HUMAN INTEREST POTENTIAL SINCE THE DAZZLER, AND THAT WAS A LOONNNG TIME AGO.
SHE HAD LIGHT POWERS TOO, DIDN'T SHE? THAT'S AN INTERESTING COINCIDENCE... ALTHOUGH I'M NOT A MUTANT.
HMM, PERHAPS I SHOULD PAY HER A VISIT WHILE I'M HERE IN THE STATES.
WELL, GOOD LUCK FINDING HER, FOR STARTERS.
'SIDES, HONESTLY, RYOKO, ANY ASSOCIATION WITH THE "M-WORD"--ESPECIALLY COMPARING YOURSELF TO ONE--WOULDN'T GO DOWN WELL IN THIS COUNTRY... ESPECIALLY NOT IN THE HEARTLAND.
NO, INSTEAD LET'S CONCENTRATE ON YOU!
YOUR HAVING DUAL AMERICAN/ JAPANESE CITIZENSHIP ISN'T GOING TO HURT.
"RYOKO SABUKI-- AMERICAN GIRL COMES HOME." THAT SORT OF THING.
AND YOU ALL SWEET SMILES AND BRIGHT LIGHTS, IT'LL BE A SLAM DUNK TO--

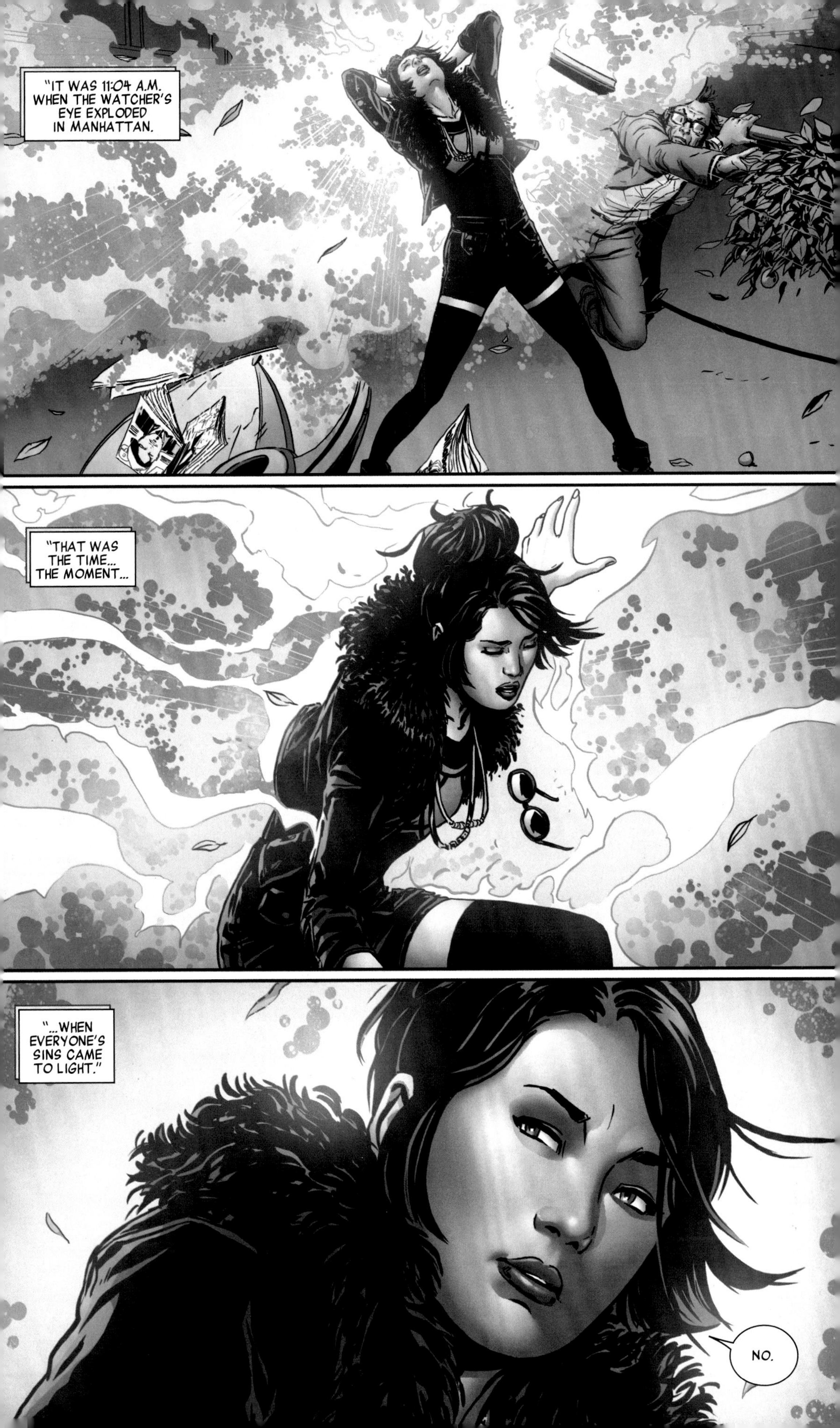
"IT WAS 11:04 A.M. WHEN THE WATCHER'S EYE EXPLODED IN MANHATTAN.
"THAT WAS THE TIME... THE MOMENT...
"...WHEN EVERYONE'S SINS CAME TO LIGHT."
NO.

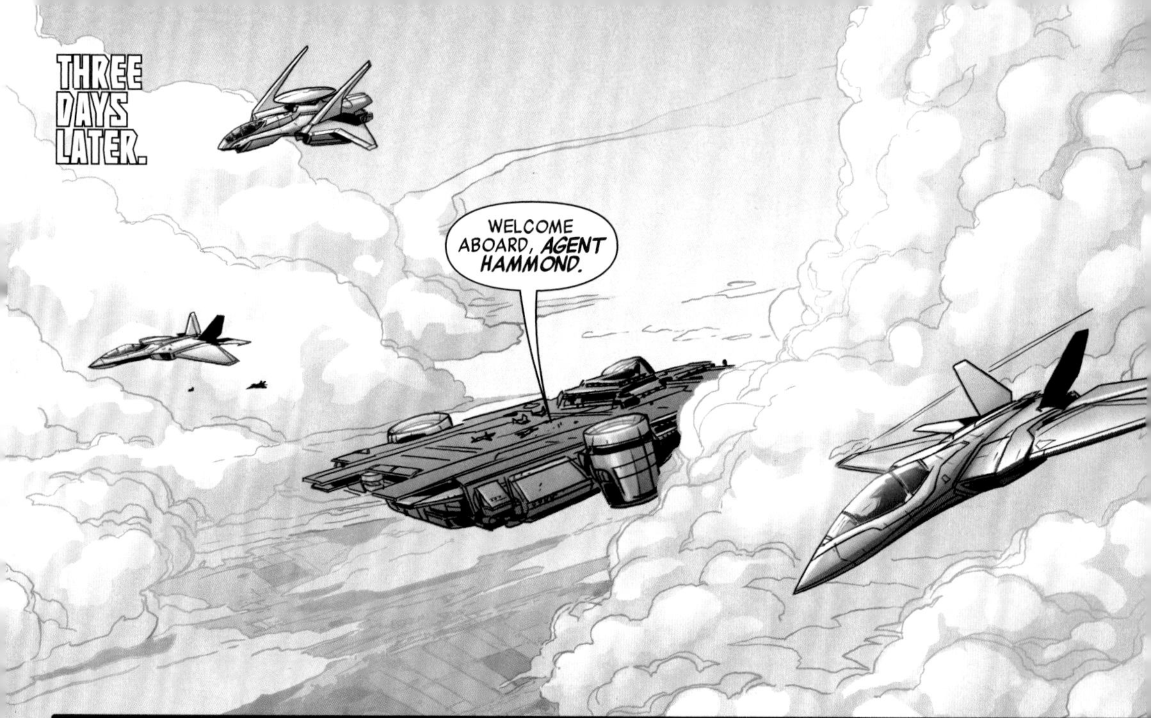
THREE DAYS LATER.
WELCOME ABOARD, AGENT HAMMOND.

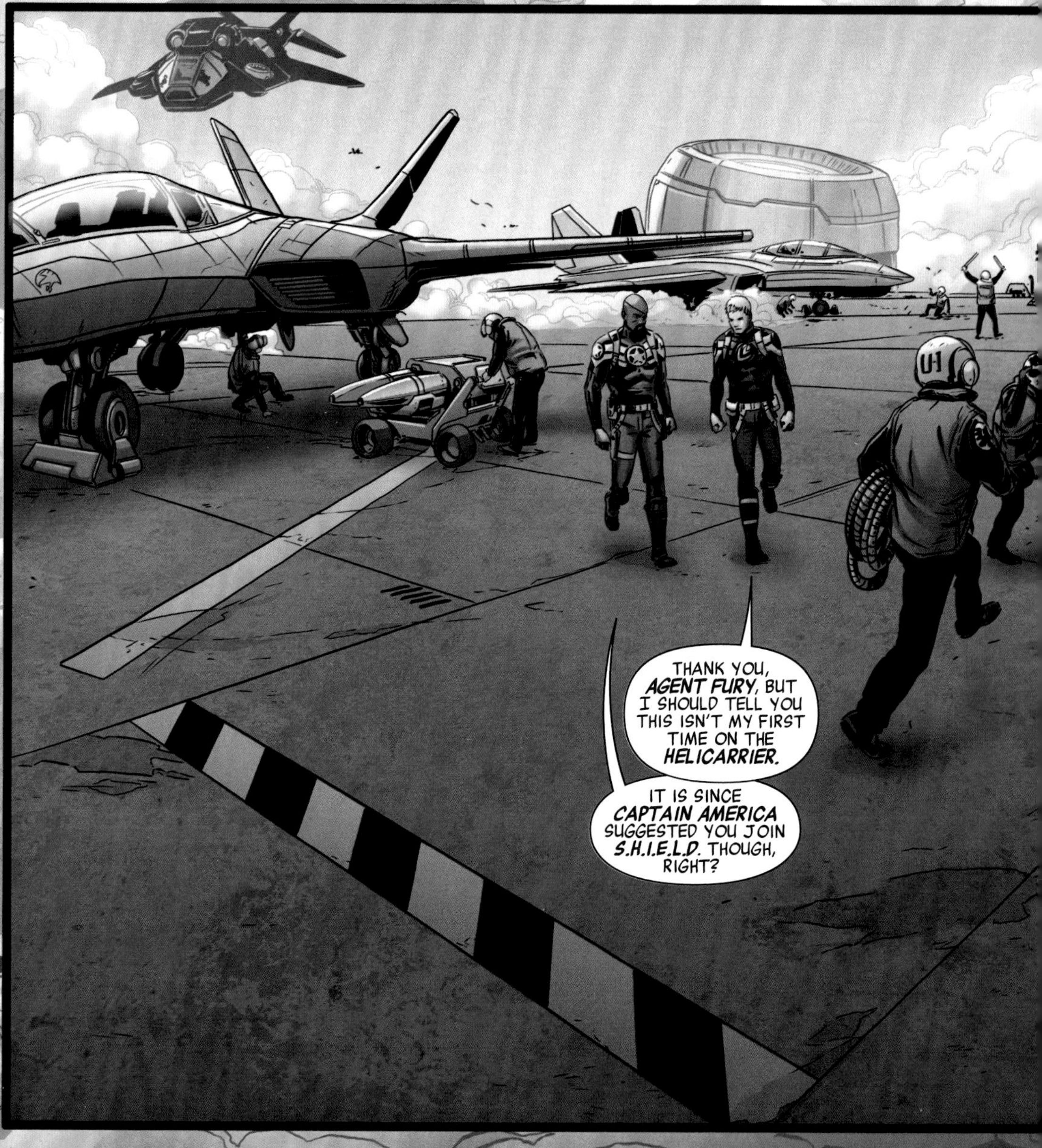
THANK YOU, AGENT FURY, BUT I SHOULD TELL YOU THIS ISN'T MY FIRST TIME ON THE HELICARRIER.
IT IS SINCE CAPTAIN AMERICA SUGGESTED YOU JOIN S.H.I.E.L.D. THOUGH, RIGHT?

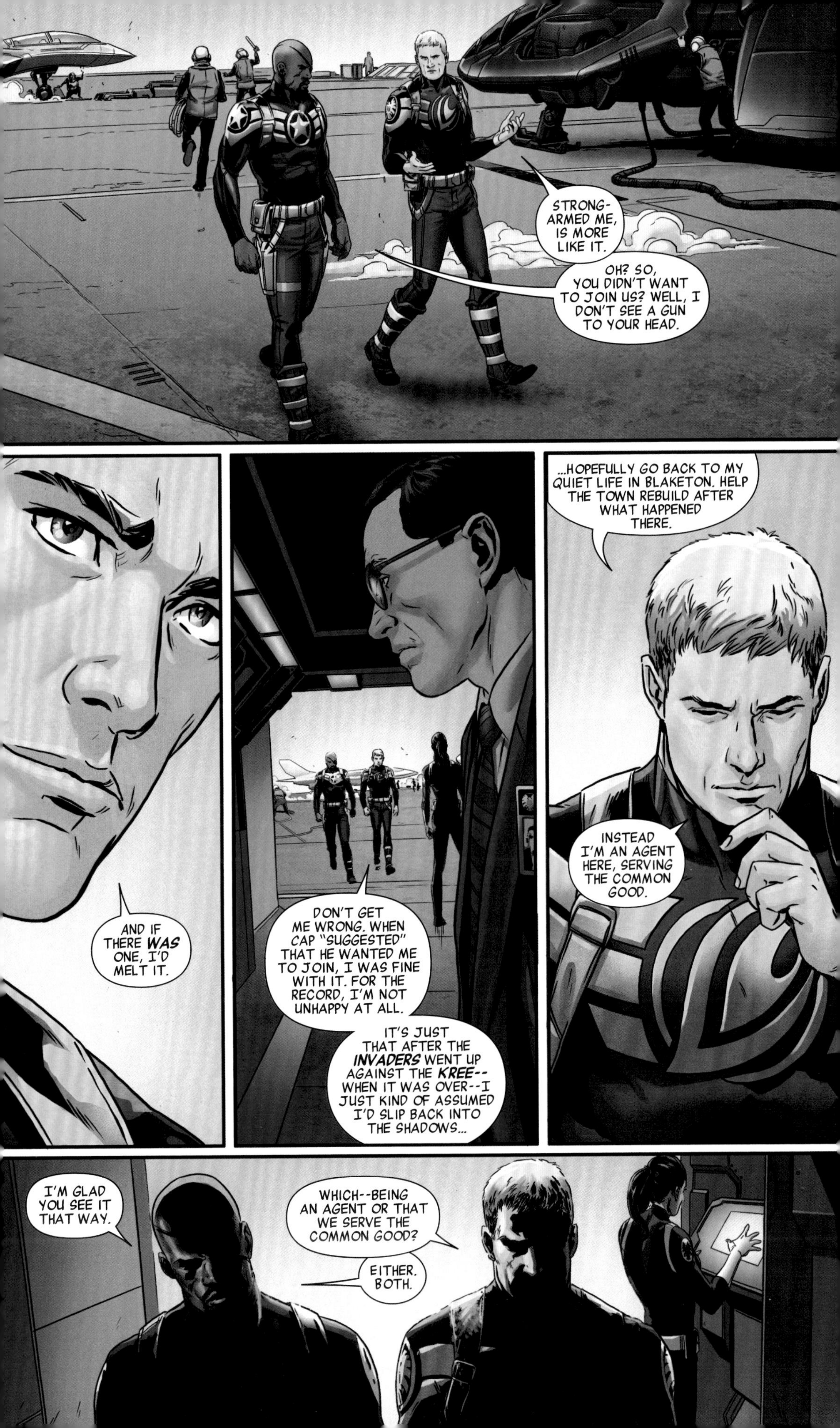
STRONG-ARMED ME, IS MORE LIKE IT.
OH? SO, YOU DIDN'T WANT TO JOIN US? WELL, I DON'T SEE A GUN TO YOUR HEAD.
AND IF THERE WAS ONE, I'D MELT IT.
DON'T GET ME WRONG. WHEN CAP "SUGGESTED" THAT HE WANTED ME TO JOIN, I WAS FINE WITH IT. FOR THE RECORD, I'M NOT UNHAPPY AT ALL.
IT'S JUST THAT AFTER THE INVADERS WENT UP AGAINST THE KREE--WHEN IT WAS OVER--I JUST KIND OF ASSUMED I'D SLIP BACK INTO THE SHADOWS...
...HOPEFULLY GO BACK TO MY QUIET LIFE IN BLAKETON. HELP THE TOWN REBUILD AFTER WHAT HAPPENED THERE.
INSTEAD I'M AN AGENT HERE, SERVING THE COMMON GOOD.
I'M GLAD YOU SEE IT THAT WAY.
WHICH--BEING AN AGENT OR THAT WE SERVE THE COMMON GOOD?
EITHER. BOTH.

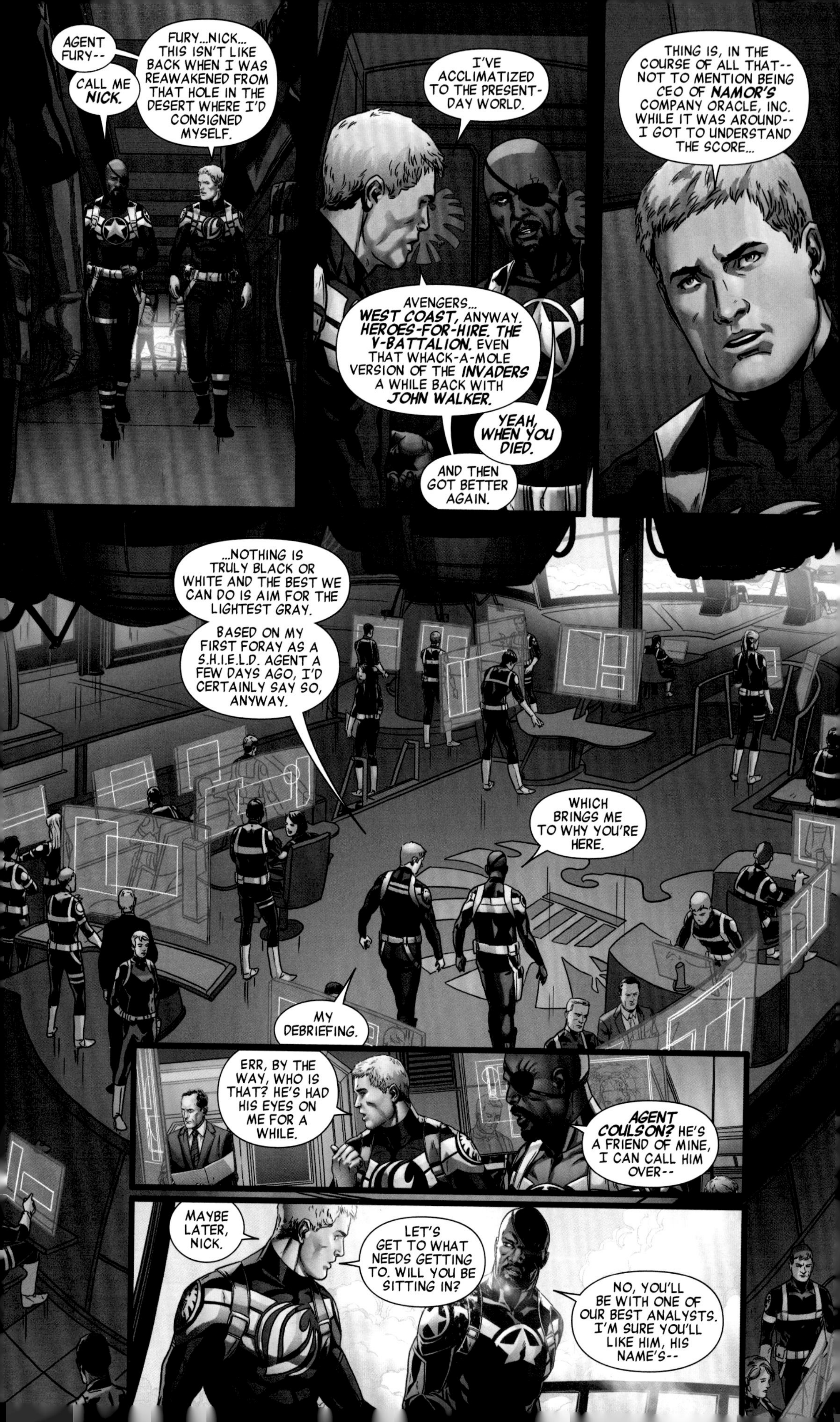
AGENT FURY--
CALL ME NICK.
FURY...NICK... THIS ISN'T LIKE BACK WHEN I WAS REAWAKENED FROM THAT HOLE IN THE DESERT WHERE I'D CONSIGNED MYSELF.
I'VE ACCLIMATIZED TO THE PRESENT-DAY WORLD.
AVENGERS... WEST COAST, ANYWAY. HEROES-FOR-HIRE. THE V-BATTALION. EVEN THAT WHACK-A-MOLE VERSION OF THE INVADERS A WHILE BACK WITH JOHN WALKER.
YEAH, WHEN YOU DIED.
AND THEN GOT BETTER AGAIN.
THING IS, IN THE COURSE OF ALL THAT-- NOT TO MENTION BEING CEO OF NAMOR'S COMPANY ORACLE, INC. WHILE IT WAS AROUND-- I GOT TO UNDERSTAND THE SCORE...
...NOTHING IS TRULY BLACK OR WHITE AND THE BEST WE CAN DO IS AIM FOR THE LIGHTEST GRAY.
BASED ON MY FIRST FORAY AS A S.H.I.E.L.D. AGENT A FEW DAYS AGO, I'D CERTAINLY SAY SO, ANYWAY.
WHICH BRINGS ME TO WHY YOU'RE HERE.
MY DEBRIEFING.
ERR, BY THE WAY, WHO IS THAT? HE'S HAD HIS EYES ON ME FOR A WHILE.
AGENT COULSON? HE'S A FRIEND OF MINE, I CAN CALL HIM OVER--
MAYBE LATER, NICK.
LET'S GET TO WHAT NEEDS GETTING TO. WILL YOU BE SITTING IN?
NO, YOU'LL BE WITH ONE OF OUR BEST ANALYSTS. I'M SURE YOU'LL LIKE HIM, HIS NAME'S--

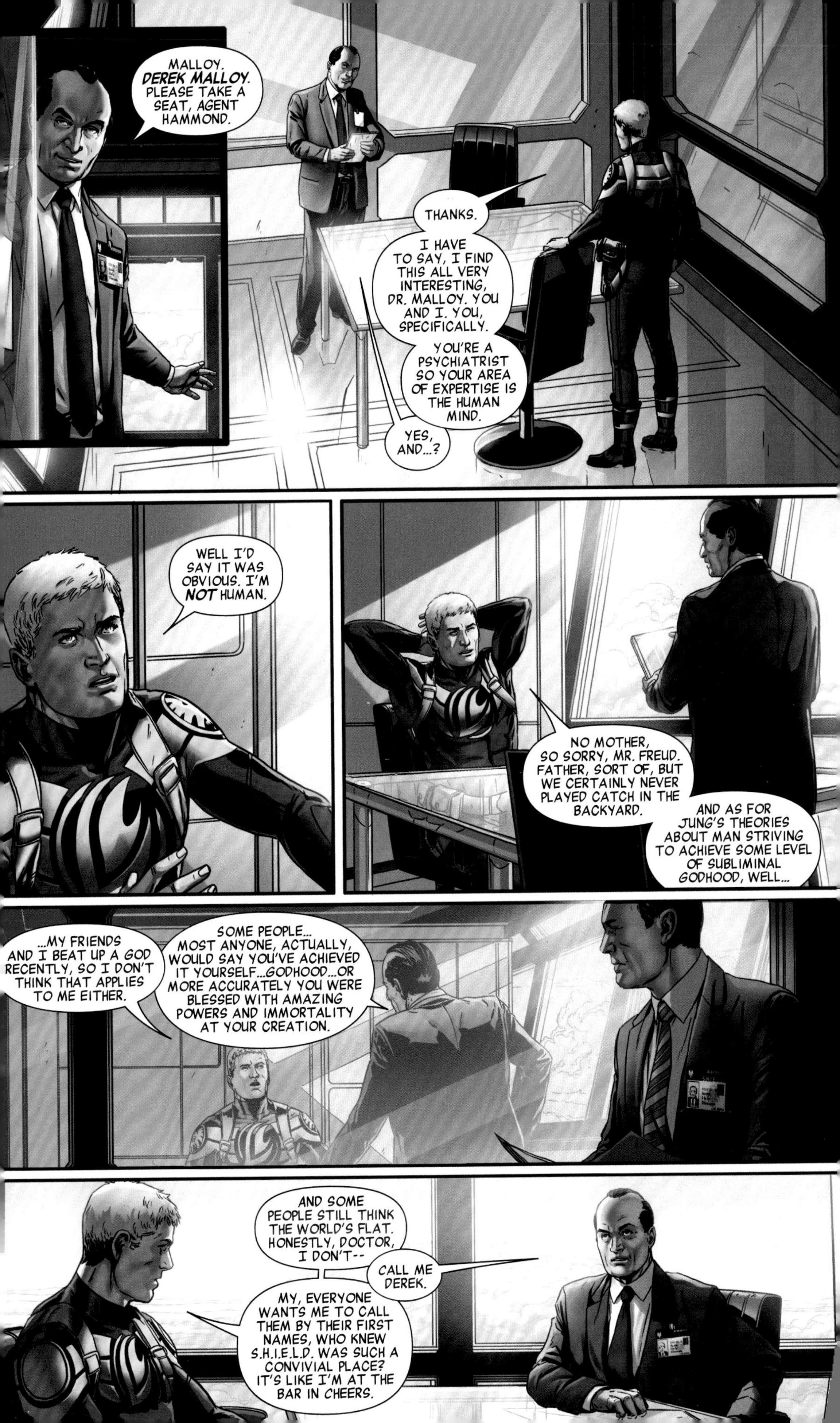

MALLOY. DEREK MALLOY. PLEASE TAKE A SEAT, AGENT HAMMOND.
THANKS.
I HAVE TO SAY, I FIND THIS ALL VERY INTERESTING, DR. MALLOY. YOU AND I. YOU, SPECIFICALLY.
YOU'RE A PSYCHIATRIST SO YOUR AREA OF EXPERTISE IS THE HUMAN MIND.
YES, AND...?
WELL I'D SAY IT WAS OBVIOUS. I'M **NOT** HUMAN.
NO MOTHER, SO SORRY, MR. FREUD. FATHER, SORT OF, BUT WE CERTAINLY NEVER PLAYED CATCH IN THE BACKYARD.
AND AS FOR JUNG'S THEORIES ABOUT MAN STRIVING TO ACHIEVE SOME LEVEL OF SUBLIMINAL GODHOOD, WELL...
...MY FRIENDS AND I BEAT UP A GOD RECENTLY, SO I DON'T THINK THAT APPLIES TO ME EITHER.
SOME PEOPLE... MOST ANYONE, ACTUALLY, WOULD SAY YOU'VE ACHIEVED IT YOURSELF...GODHOOD...OR MORE ACCURATELY YOU WERE BLESSED WITH AMAZING POWERS AND IMMORTALITY AT YOUR CREATION.
AND SOME PEOPLE STILL THINK THE WORLD'S FLAT. HONESTLY, DOCTOR, I DON'T--
CALL ME DEREK.
MY, EVERYONE WANTS ME TO CALL THEM BY THEIR FIRST NAMES, WHO KNEW S.H.I.E.L.D. WAS SUCH A CONVIVIAL PLACE? IT'S LIKE I'M AT THE BAR IN CHEERS.

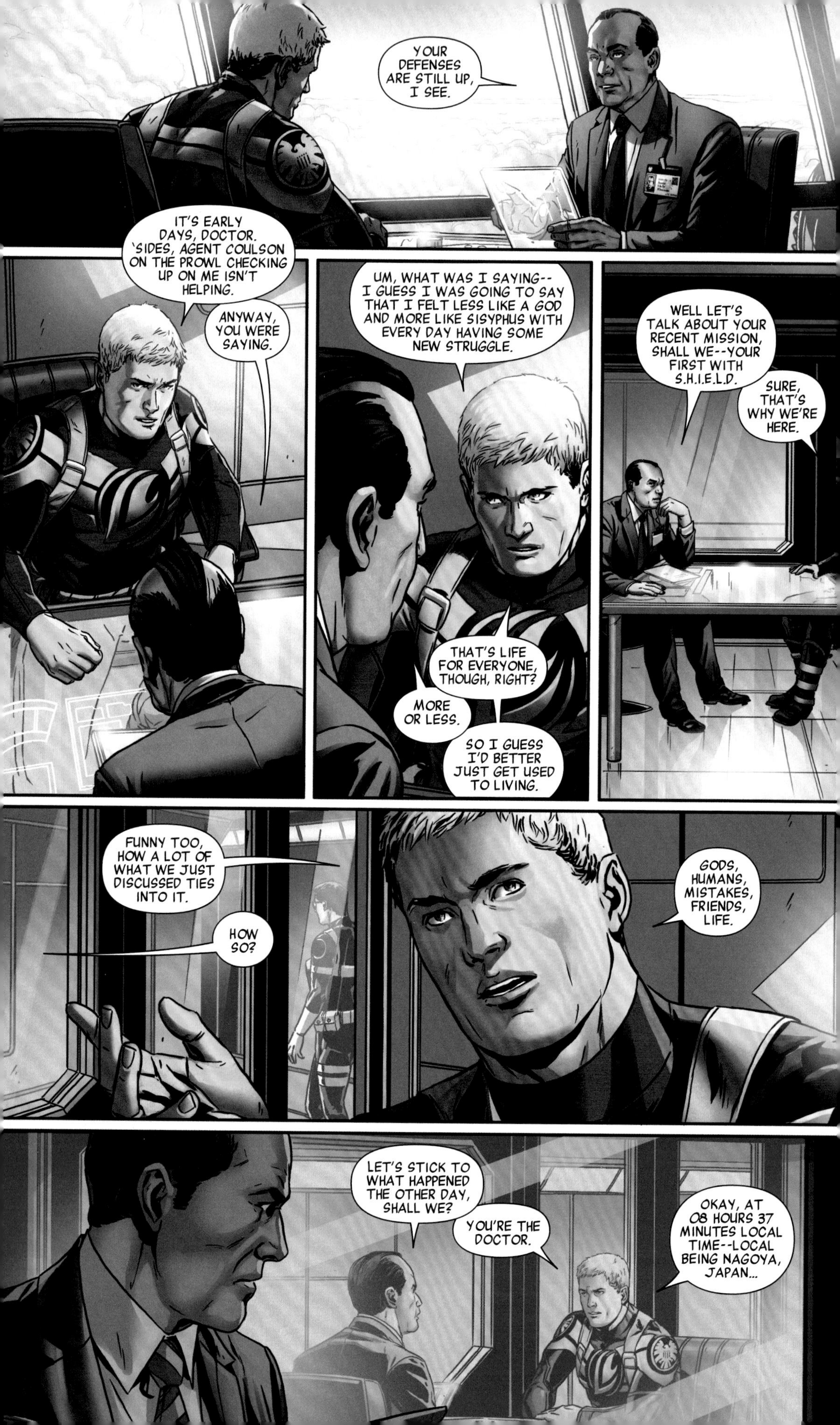

YOUR DEFENSES ARE STILL UP, I SEE.
IT'S EARLY DAYS, DOCTOR. 'SIDES, AGENT COULSON ON THE PROWL CHECKING UP ON ME ISN'T HELPING.
ANYWAY, YOU WERE SAYING.
UM, WHAT WAS I SAYING-- I GUESS I WAS GOING TO SAY THAT I FELT LESS LIKE A GOD AND MORE LIKE SISYPHUS WITH EVERY DAY HAVING SOME NEW STRUGGLE.
THAT'S LIFE FOR EVERYONE, THOUGH, RIGHT?
MORE OR LESS.
SO I GUESS I'D BETTER JUST GET USED TO LIVING.
WELL LET'S TALK ABOUT YOUR RECENT MISSION, SHALL WE--YOUR FIRST WITH S.H.I.E.L.D.
SURE, THAT'S WHY WE'RE HERE.
FUNNY TOO, HOW A LOT OF WHAT WE JUST DISCUSSED TIES INTO IT.
HOW SO?
GODS, HUMANS, MISTAKES, FRIENDS, LIFE.
LET'S STICK TO WHAT HAPPENED THE OTHER DAY, SHALL WE?
YOU'RE THE DOCTOR.
OKAY, AT 08 HOURS 37 MINUTES LOCAL TIME--LOCAL BEING NAGOYA, JAPAN...

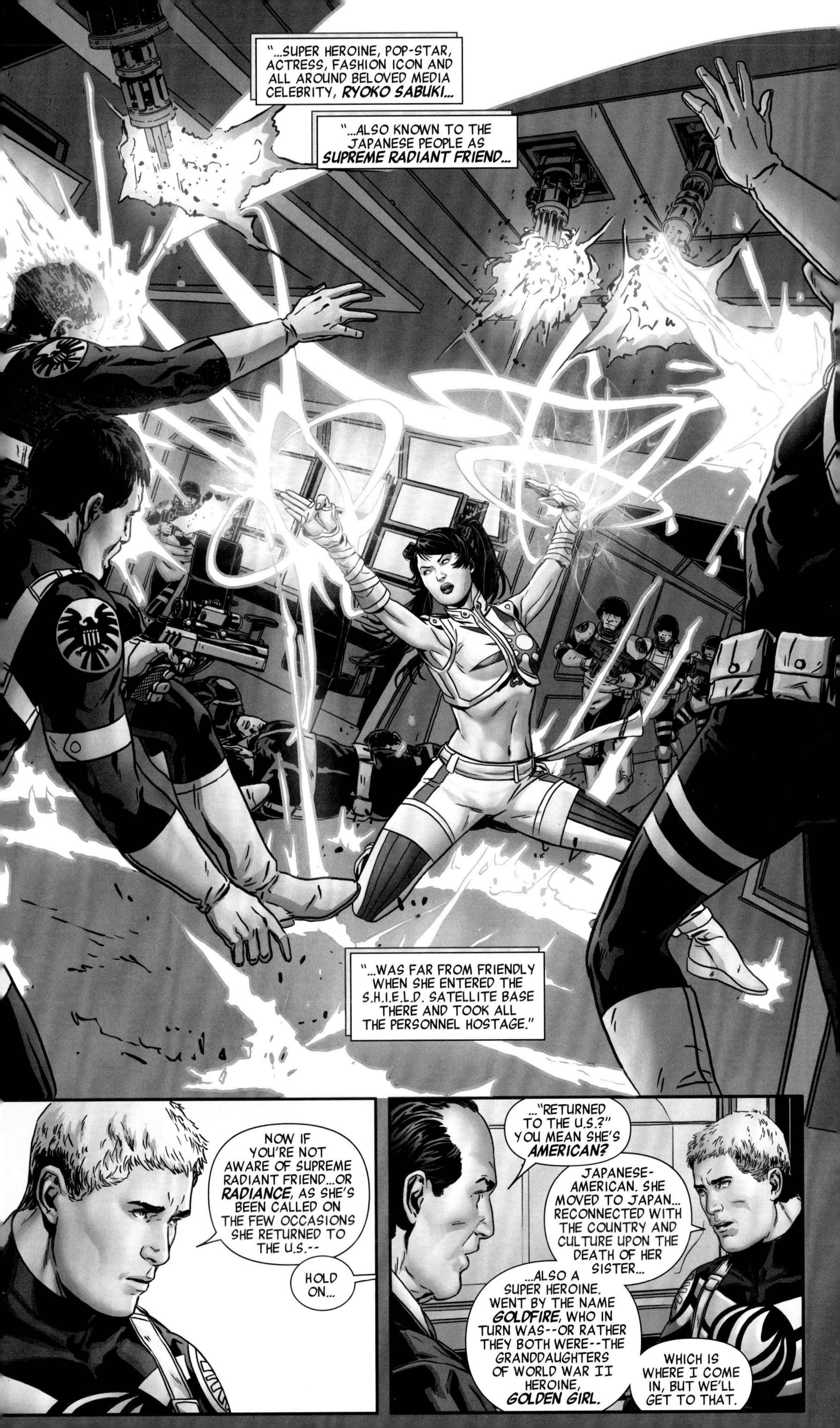
"...SUPER HEROINE, POP-STAR, ACTRESS, FASHION ICON AND ALL AROUND BELOVED MEDIA CELEBRITY, RYOKO SABUKI...
"...ALSO KNOWN TO THE JAPANESE PEOPLE AS SUPREME RADIANT FRIEND...
"...WAS FAR FROM FRIENDLY WHEN SHE ENTERED THE S.H.I.E.L.D. SATELLITE BASE THERE AND TOOK ALL THE PERSONNEL HOSTAGE."
NOW IF YOU'RE NOT AWARE OF SUPREME RADIANT FRIEND...OR RADIANCE, AS SHE'S BEEN CALLED ON THE FEW OCCASIONS SHE RETURNED TO THE U.S.--
HOLD ON...
..."RETURNED TO THE U.S.?" YOU MEAN SHE'S AMERICAN?
JAPANESE-AMERICAN. SHE MOVED TO JAPAN... RECONNECTED WITH THE COUNTRY AND CULTURE UPON THE DEATH OF HER SISTER...
...ALSO A SUPER HEROINE. WENT BY THE NAME GOLDFIRE, WHO IN TURN WAS--OR RATHER THEY BOTH WERE--THE GRANDDAUGHTERS OF WORLD WAR II HEROINE, GOLDEN GIRL.
WHICH IS WHERE I COME IN, BUT WE'LL GET TO THAT.

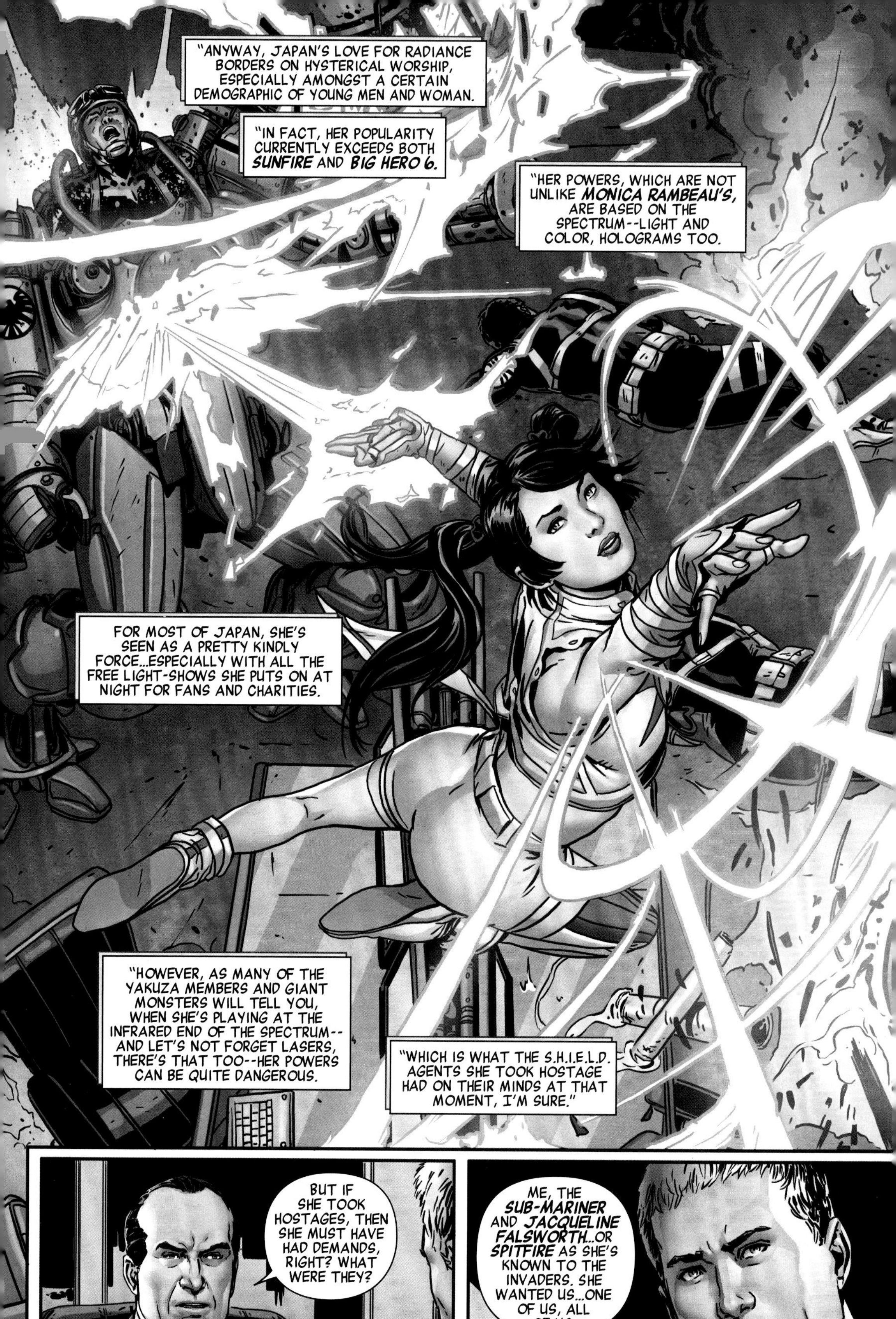
"ANYWAY, JAPAN'S LOVE FOR RADIANCE BORDERS ON HYSTERICAL WORSHIP, ESPECIALLY AMONGST A CERTAIN DEMOGRAPHIC OF YOUNG MEN AND WOMAN.
"IN FACT, HER POPULARITY CURRENTLY EXCEEDS BOTH SUNFIRE AND BIG HERO 6.
"HER POWERS, WHICH ARE NOT UNLIKE MONICA RAMBEAU'S, ARE BASED ON THE SPECTRUM--LIGHT AND COLOR, HOLOGRAMS TOO.
FOR MOST OF JAPAN, SHE'S SEEN AS A PRETTY KINDLY FORCE...ESPECIALLY WITH ALL THE FREE LIGHT-SHOWS SHE PUTS ON AT NIGHT FOR FANS AND CHARITIES.
"HOWEVER, AS MANY OF THE YAKUZA MEMBERS AND GIANT MONSTERS WILL TELL YOU, WHEN SHE'S PLAYING AT THE INFRARED END OF THE SPECTRUM--AND LET'S NOT FORGET LASERS, THERE'S THAT TOO--HER POWERS CAN BE QUITE DANGEROUS.
"WHICH IS WHAT THE S.H.I.E.L.D. AGENTS SHE TOOK HOSTAGE HAD ON THEIR MINDS AT THAT MOMENT, I'M SURE."

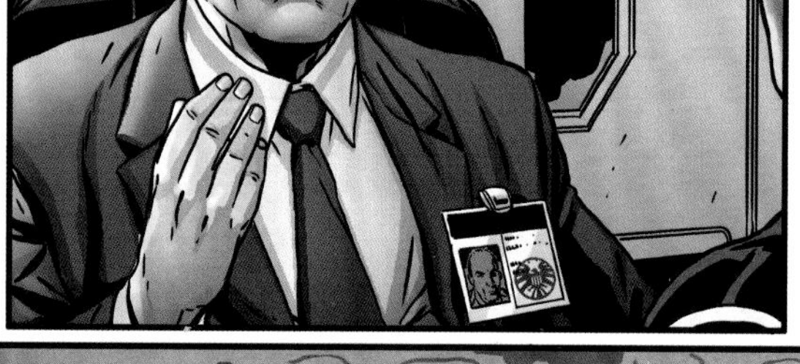
BUT IF SHE TOOK HOSTAGES, THEN SHE MUST HAVE HAD DEMANDS, RIGHT? WHAT WERE THEY?

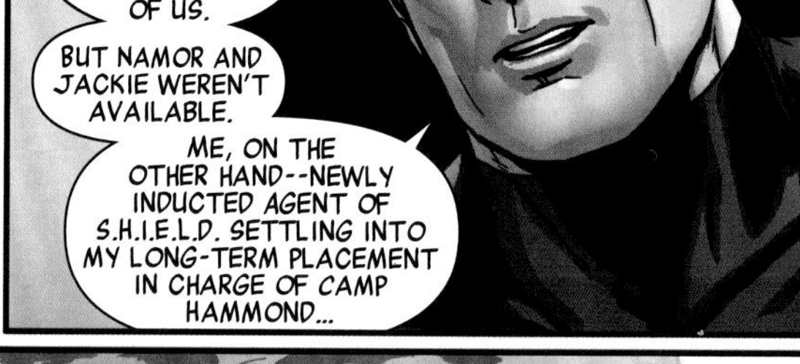
ME, THE SUB-MARINER AND JACQUELINE FALSWORTH...OR SPITFIRE AS SHE'S KNOWN TO THE INVADERS. SHE WANTED US...ONE OF US, ALL OF US.
BUT NAMOR AND JACKIE WEREN'T AVAILABLE.
ME, ON THE OTHER HAND--NEWLY INDUCTED AGENT OF S.H.I.E.L.D. SETTLING INTO MY LONG-TERM PLACEMENT IN CHARGE OF CAMP HAMMOND...

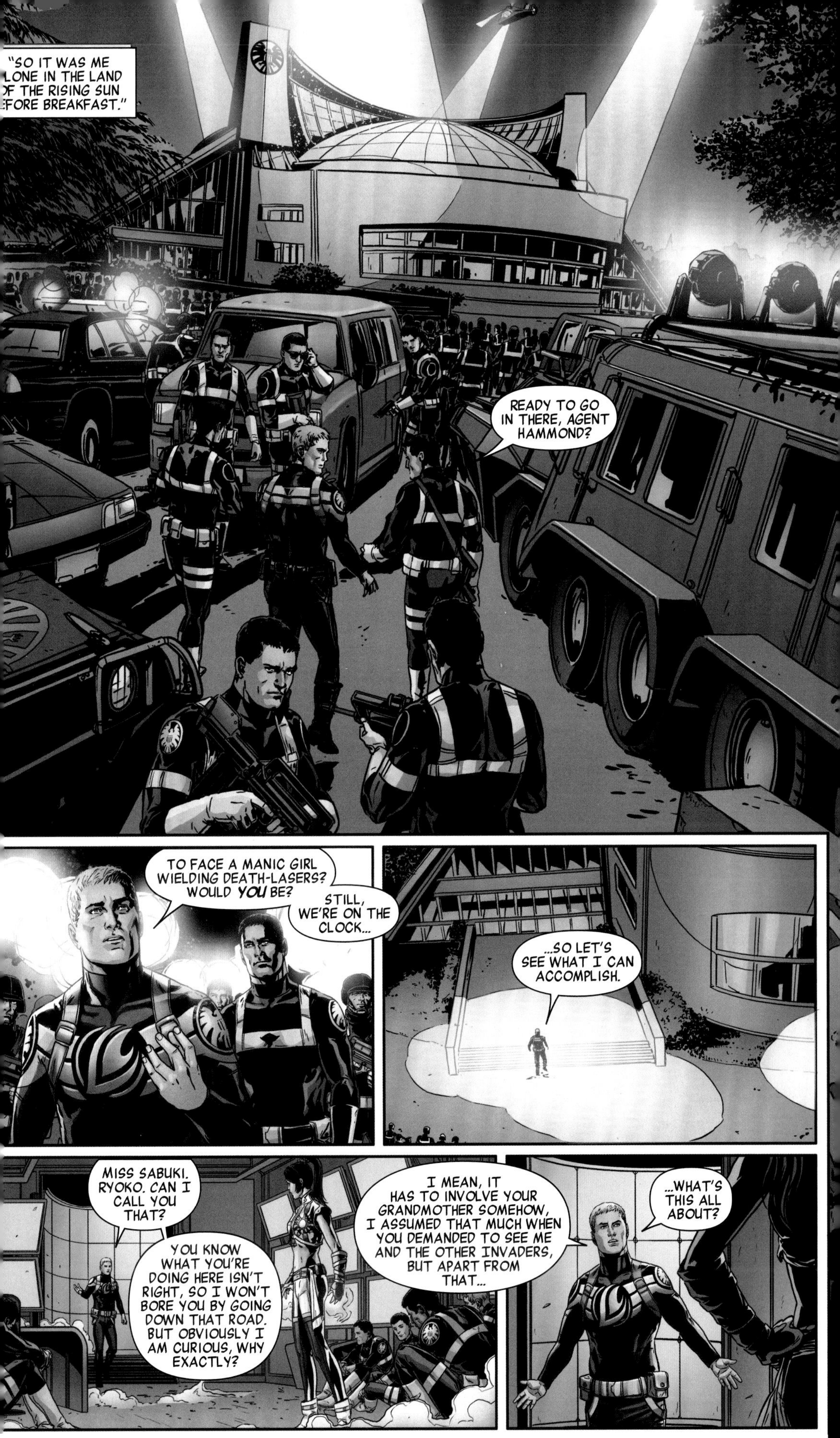
"SO IT WAS ME
LONE IN THE LAND
OF THE RISING SUN
EFORE BREAKFAST."
READY TO GO IN THERE, AGENT HAMMOND?
TO FACE A MANIC GIRL WIELDING DEATH-LASERS? WOULD YOU BE?
STILL, WE'RE ON THE CLOCK...
...SO LET'S SEE WHAT I CAN ACCOMPLISH.
MISS SABUKI. RYOKO. CAN I CALL YOU THAT?
YOU KNOW WHAT YOU'RE DOING HERE ISN'T RIGHT, SO I WON'T BORE YOU BY GOING DOWN THAT ROAD. BUT OBVIOUSLY I AM CURIOUS, WHY EXACTLY?
I MEAN, IT HAS TO INVOLVE YOUR GRANDMOTHER SOMEHOW, I ASSUMED THAT MUCH WHEN YOU DEMANDED TO SEE ME AND THE OTHER INVADERS, BUT APART FROM THAT...
...WHAT'S THIS ALL ABOUT?

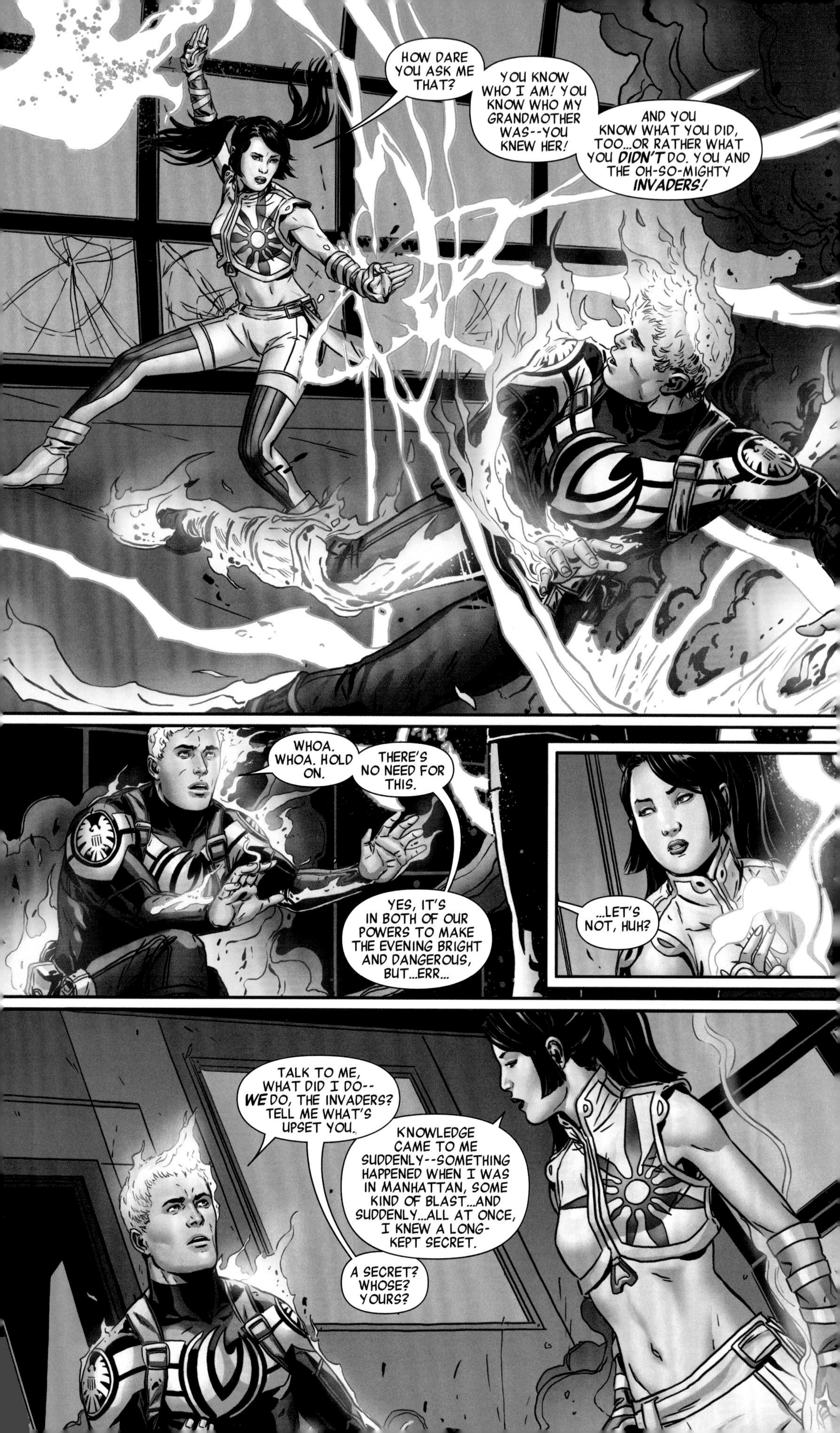
HOW DARE YOU ASK ME THAT?
YOU KNOW WHO I AM! YOU KNOW WHO MY GRANDMOTHER WAS--YOU KNEW HER!
AND YOU KNOW WHAT YOU DID, TOO...OR RATHER WHAT YOU DIDN'T DO. YOU AND THE OH-SO-MIGHTY INVADERS!
WHOA. WHOA. HOLD ON.
THERE'S NO NEED FOR THIS.
YES, IT'S IN BOTH OF OUR POWERS TO MAKE THE EVENING BRIGHT AND DANGEROUS, BUT...ERR...
...LET'S NOT, HUH?
TALK TO ME, WHAT DID I DO-- WE DO, THE INVADERS? TELL ME WHAT'S UPSET YOU.
KNOWLEDGE CAME TO ME SUDDENLY--SOMETHING HAPPENED WHEN I WAS IN MANHATTAN, SOME KIND OF BLAST...AND SUDDENLY...ALL AT ONCE, I KNEW A LONG-KEPT SECRET.
A SECRET? WHOSE? YOURS?

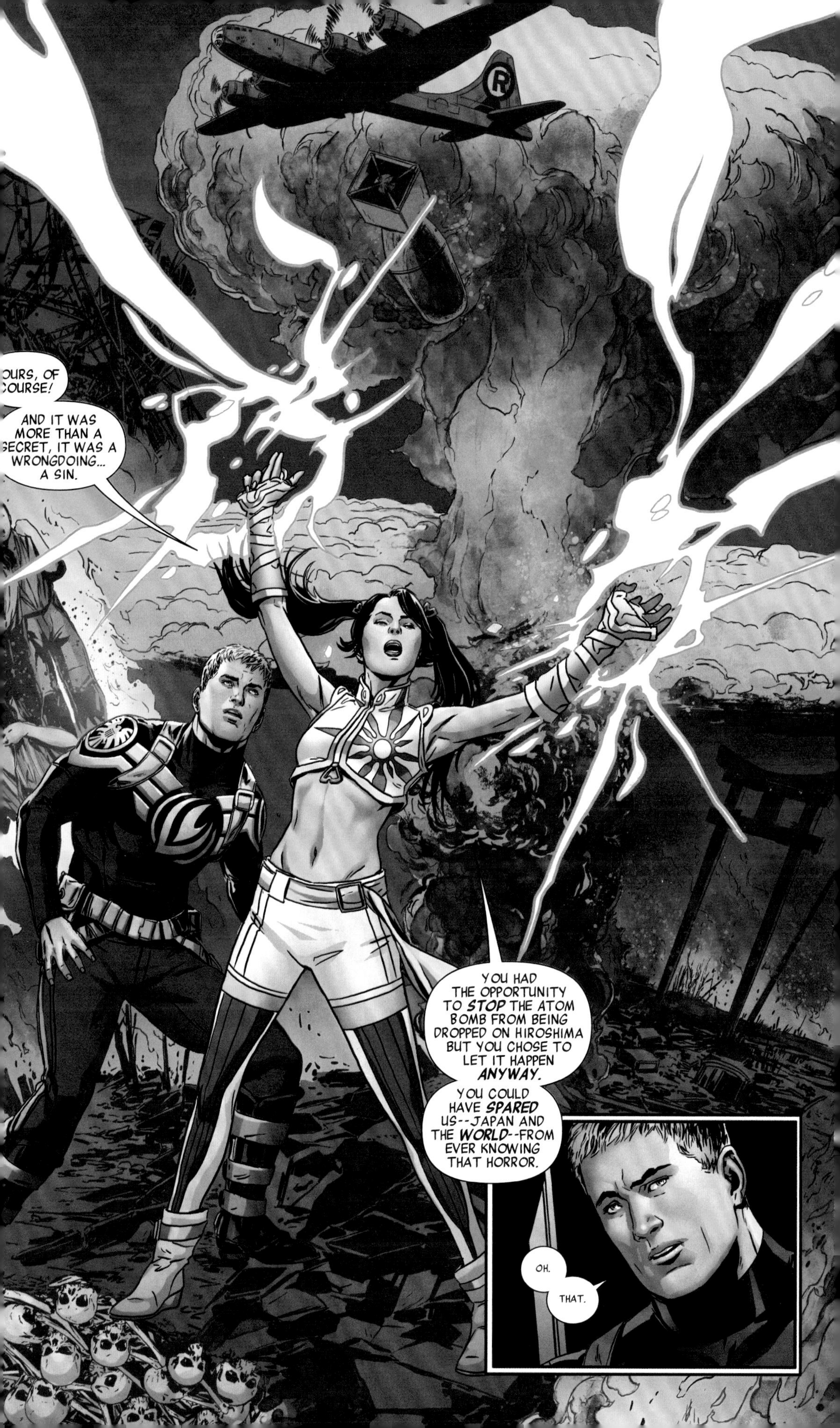
OURS, OF COURSE!
AND IT WAS MORE THAN A SECRET, IT WAS A WRONGDOING... A SIN.
YOU HAD THE OPPORTUNITY TO STOP THE ATOM BOMB FROM BEING DROPPED ON HIROSHIMA BUT YOU CHOSE TO LET IT HAPPEN ANYWAY.
YOU COULD HAVE SPARED US--JAPAN AND THE WORLD--FROM EVER KNOWING THAT HORROR.
OH.
THAT.

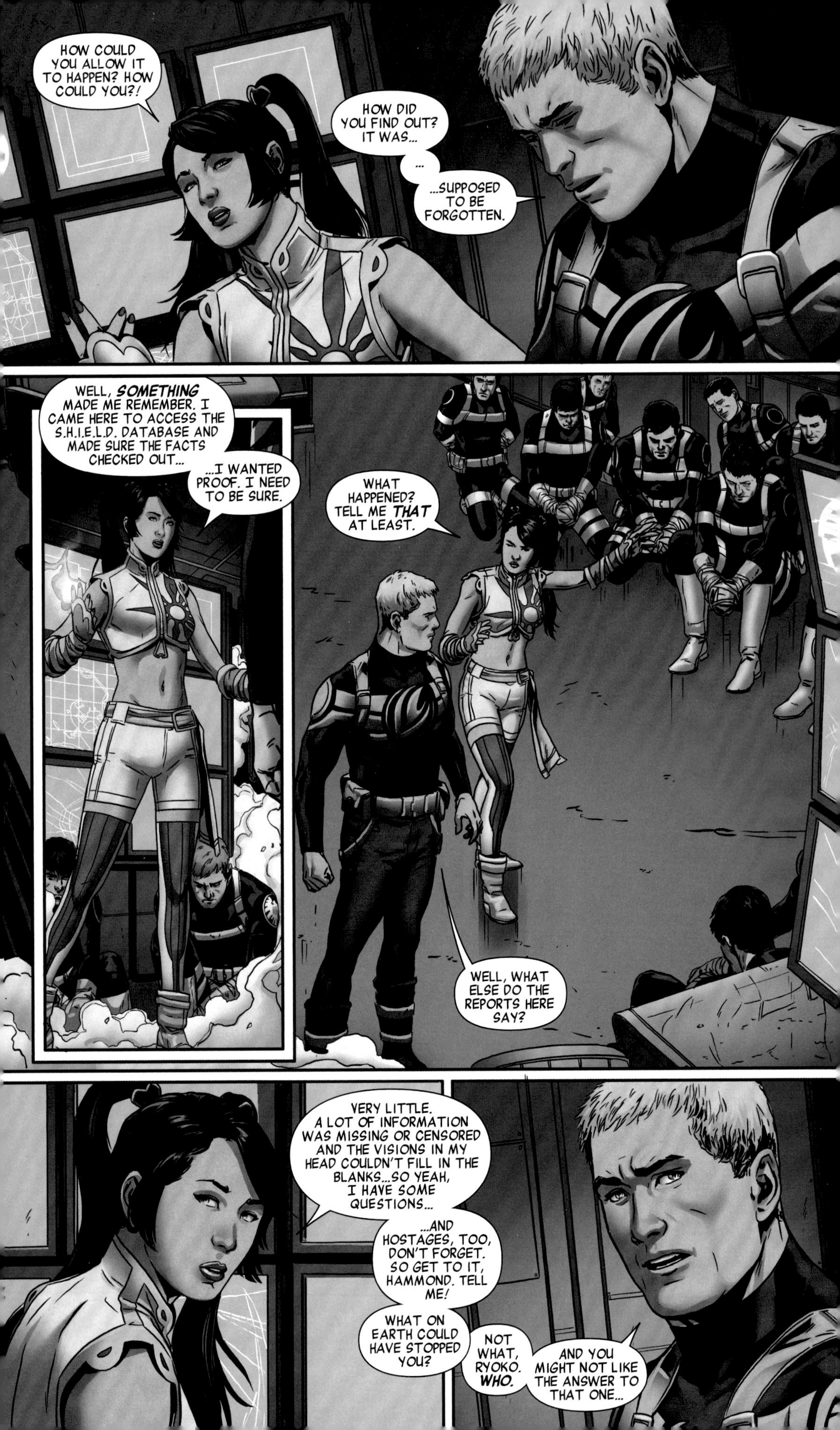
HOW COULD YOU ALLOW IT TO HAPPEN? HOW COULD YOU?!
HOW DID YOU FIND OUT? IT WAS...
...
...SUPPOSED TO BE FORGOTTEN.
WELL, SOMETHING MADE ME REMEMBER. I CAME HERE TO ACCESS THE S.H.I.E.L.D. DATABASE AND MADE SURE THE FACTS CHECKED OUT...
...I WANTED PROOF. I NEED TO BE SURE.
WHAT HAPPENED? TELL ME THAT AT LEAST.
WELL, WHAT ELSE DO THE REPORTS HERE SAY?
VERY LITTLE. A LOT OF INFORMATION WAS MISSING OR CENSORED AND THE VISIONS IN MY HEAD COULDN'T FILL IN THE BLANKS...SO YEAH, I HAVE SOME QUESTIONS...
...AND HOSTAGES, TOO, DON'T FORGET. SO GET TO IT, HAMMOND. TELL ME!
WHAT ON EARTH COULD HAVE STOPPED YOU?
NOT WHAT, RYOKO. WHO.
AND YOU MIGHT NOT LIKE THE ANSWER TO THAT ONE...

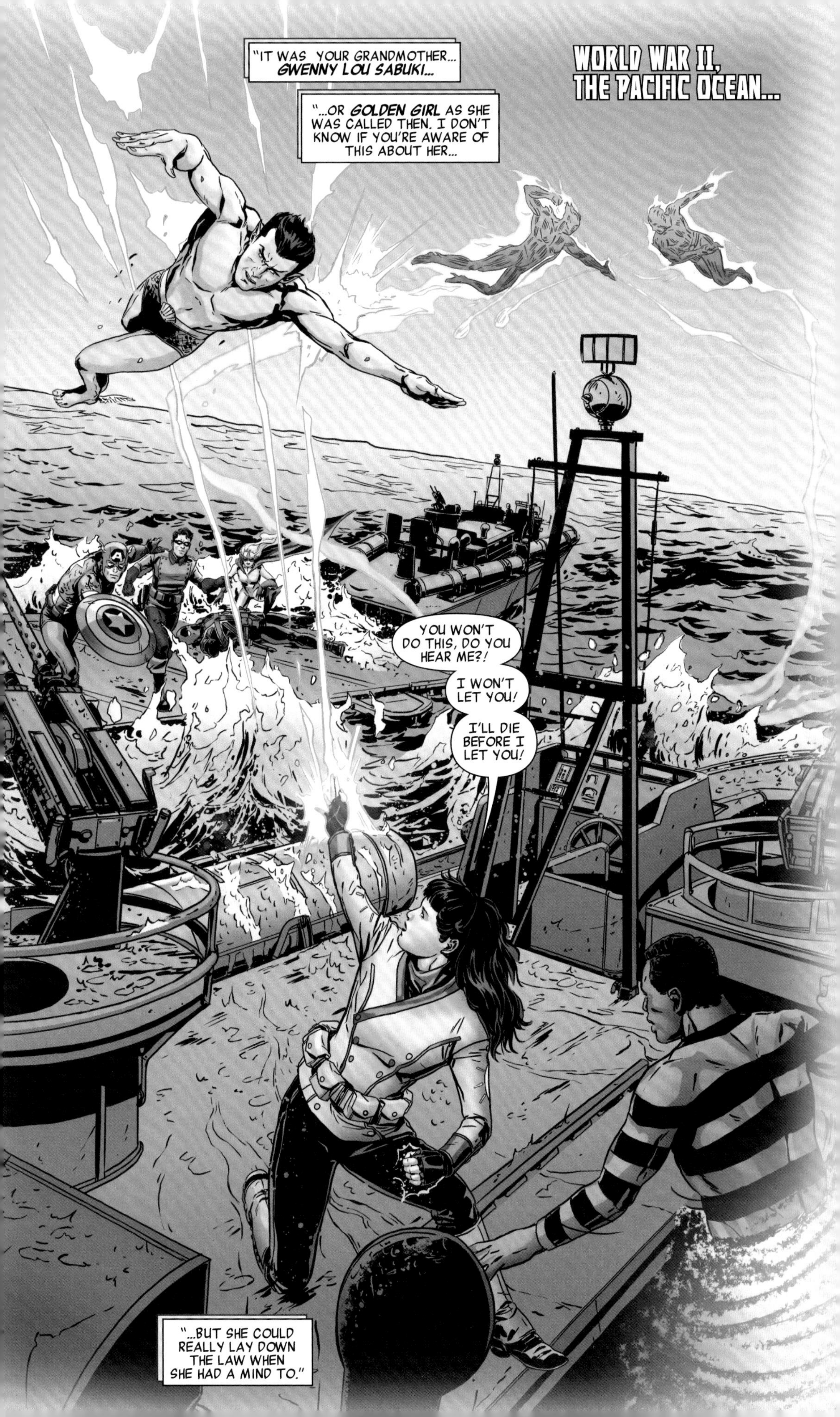
WORLD WAR II, THE PACIFIC OCEAN...
"IT WAS YOUR GRANDMOTHER... GWENNY LOU SABUKI...
"...OR GOLDEN GIRL AS SHE WAS CALLED THEN. I DON'T KNOW IF YOU'RE AWARE OF THIS ABOUT HER...
YOU WON'T DO THIS, DO YOU HEAR ME?!
I WON'T LET YOU!
I'LL DIE BEFORE I LET YOU!
"...BUT SHE COULD REALLY LAY DOWN THE LAW WHEN SHE HAD A MIND TO."

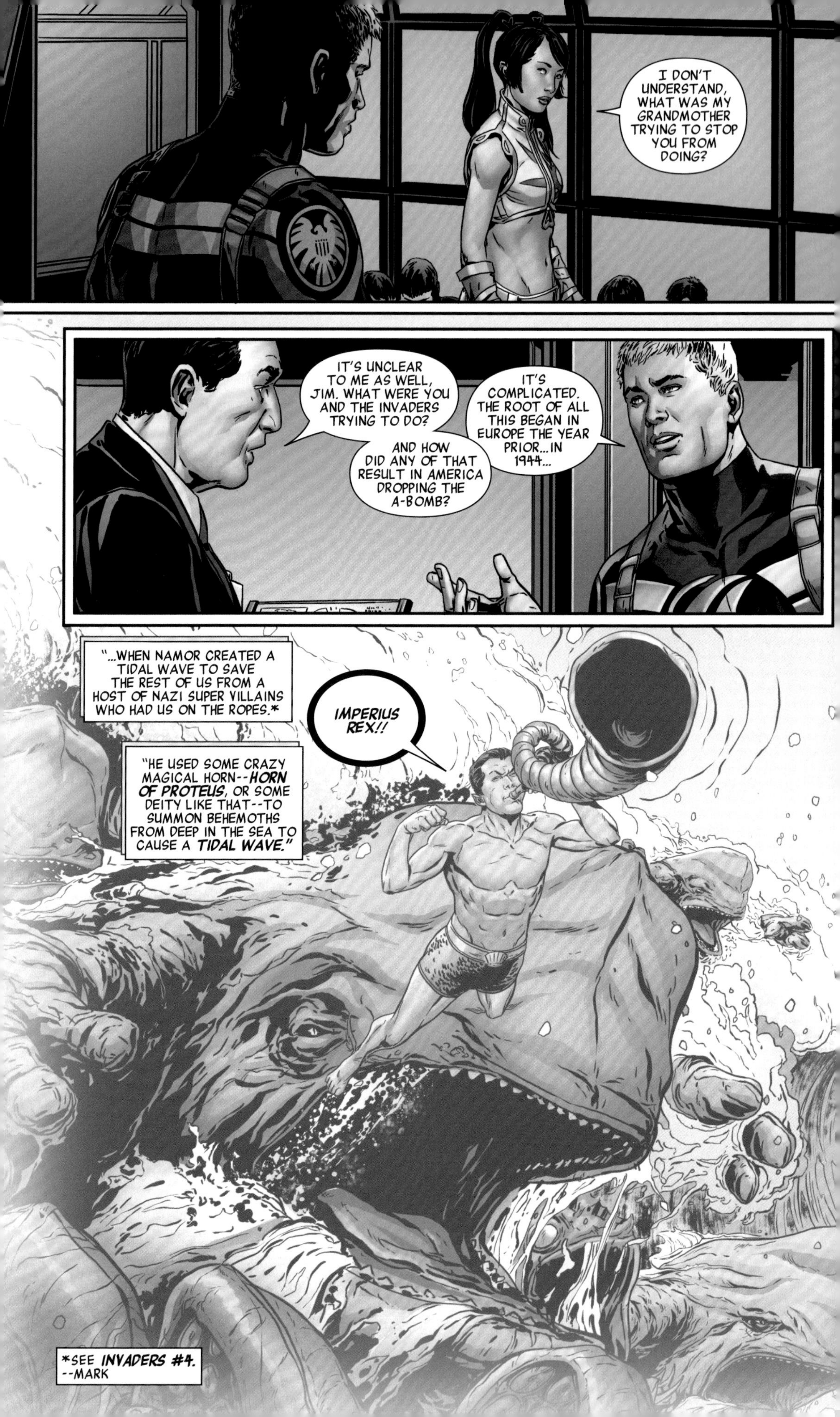
I DON'T UNDERSTAND, WHAT WAS MY GRANDMOTHER TRYING TO STOP YOU FROM DOING?
IT'S UNCLEAR TO ME AS WELL, JIM. WHAT WERE YOU AND THE INVADERS TRYING TO DO?
AND HOW DID ANY OF THAT RESULT IN AMERICA DROPPING THE A-BOMB?
IT'S COMPLICATED. THE ROOT OF ALL THIS BEGAN IN EUROPE THE YEAR PRIOR...IN 1944...
"...WHEN NAMOR CREATED A TIDAL WAVE TO SAVE THE REST OF US FROM A HOST OF NAZI SUPER VILLAINS WHO HAD US ON THE ROPES.*
IMPERIUS REX!!
"HE USED SOME CRAZY MAGICAL HORN--HORN OF PROTEUS, OR SOME DEITY LIKE THAT--TO SUMMON BEHEMOTHS FROM DEEP IN THE SEA TO CAUSE A TIDAL WAVE."
*SEE INVADERS #4. --MARK

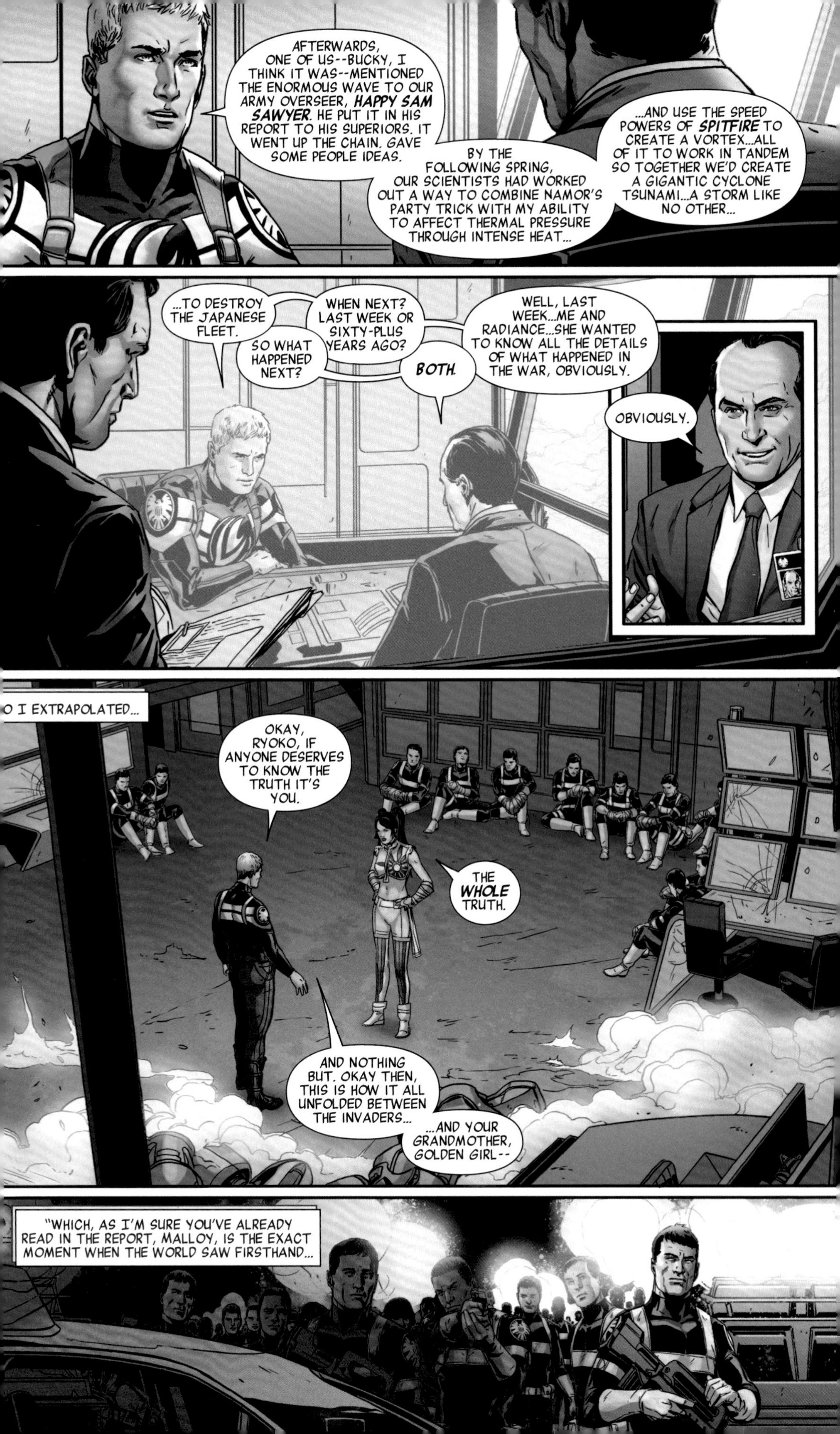
AFTERWARDS, ONE OF US--BUCKY, I THINK IT WAS--MENTIONED THE ENORMOUS WAVE TO OUR ARMY OVERSEER, HAPPY SAM SAWYER. HE PUT IT IN HIS REPORT TO HIS SUPERIORS. IT WENT UP THE CHAIN. GAVE SOME PEOPLE IDEAS.
BY THE FOLLOWING SPRING, OUR SCIENTISTS HAD WORKED OUT A WAY TO COMBINE NAMOR'S PARTY TRICK WITH MY ABILITY TO AFFECT THERMAL PRESSURE THROUGH INTENSE HEAT...
...AND USE THE SPEED POWERS OF SPITFIRE TO CREATE A VORTEX...ALL OF IT TO WORK IN TANDEM SO TOGETHER WE'D CREATE A GIGANTIC CYCLONE TSUNAMI...A STORM LIKE NO OTHER...
...TO DESTROY THE JAPANESE FLEET.
SO WHAT HAPPENED NEXT?
WHEN NEXT? LAST WEEK OR SIXTY-PLUS YEARS AGO?
BOTH.
WELL, LAST WEEK...ME AND RADIANCE...SHE WANTED TO KNOW ALL THE DETAILS OF WHAT HAPPENED IN THE WAR, OBVIOUSLY.
OBVIOUSLY.
O I EXTRAPOLATED...
OKAY, RYOKO, IF ANYONE DESERVES TO KNOW THE TRUTH IT'S YOU.
THE WHOLE TRUTH.
AND NOTHING BUT. OKAY THEN, THIS IS HOW IT ALL UNFOLDED BETWEEN THE INVADERS...
...AND YOUR GRANDMOTHER, GOLDEN GIRL--
"WHICH, AS I'M SURE YOU'VE ALREADY READ IN THE REPORT, MALLOY, IS THE EXACT MOMENT WHEN THE WORLD SAW FIRSTHAND...

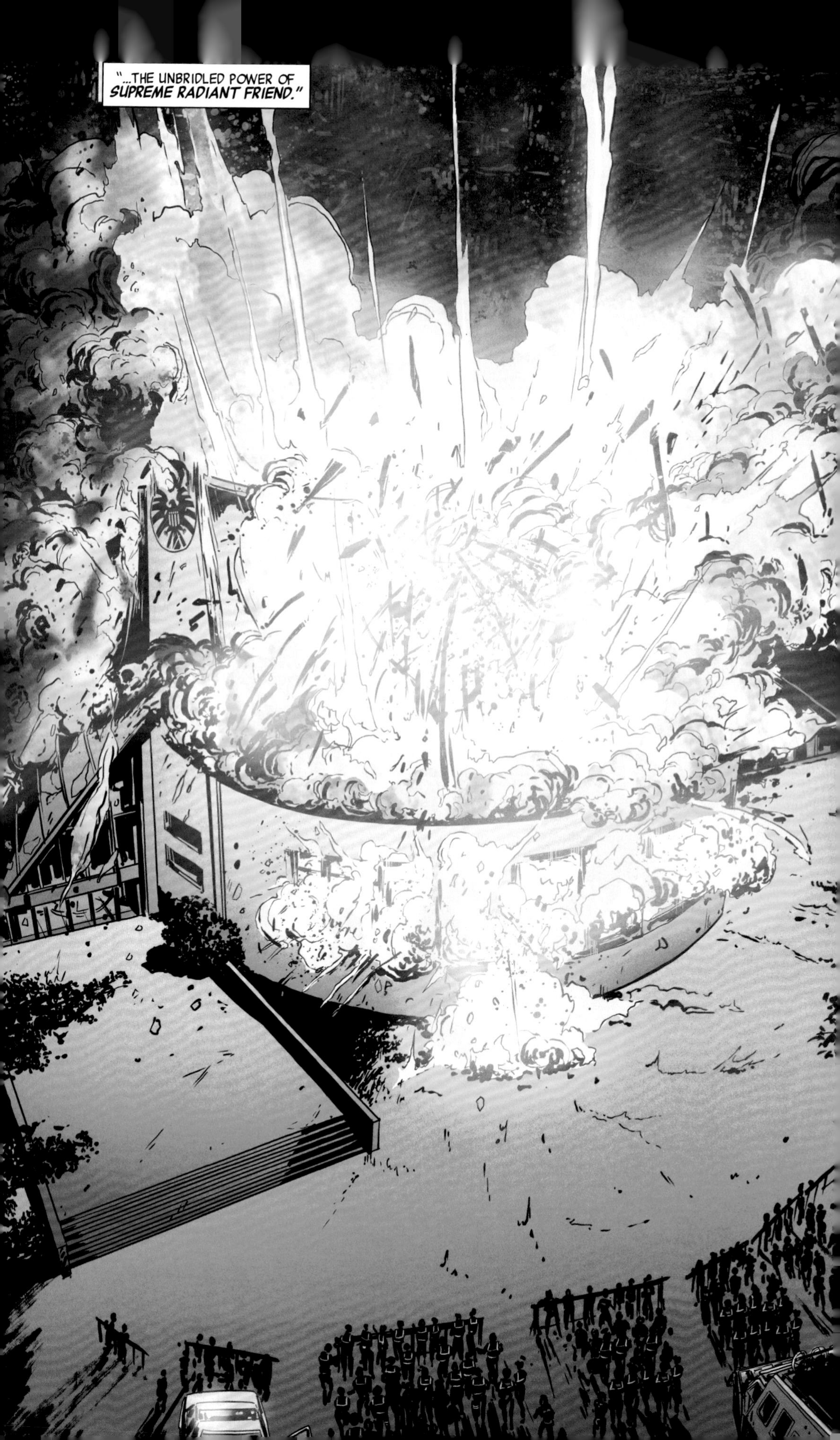
"...THE UNBRIDLED POWER OF *SUPREME RADIANT FRIEND.*"

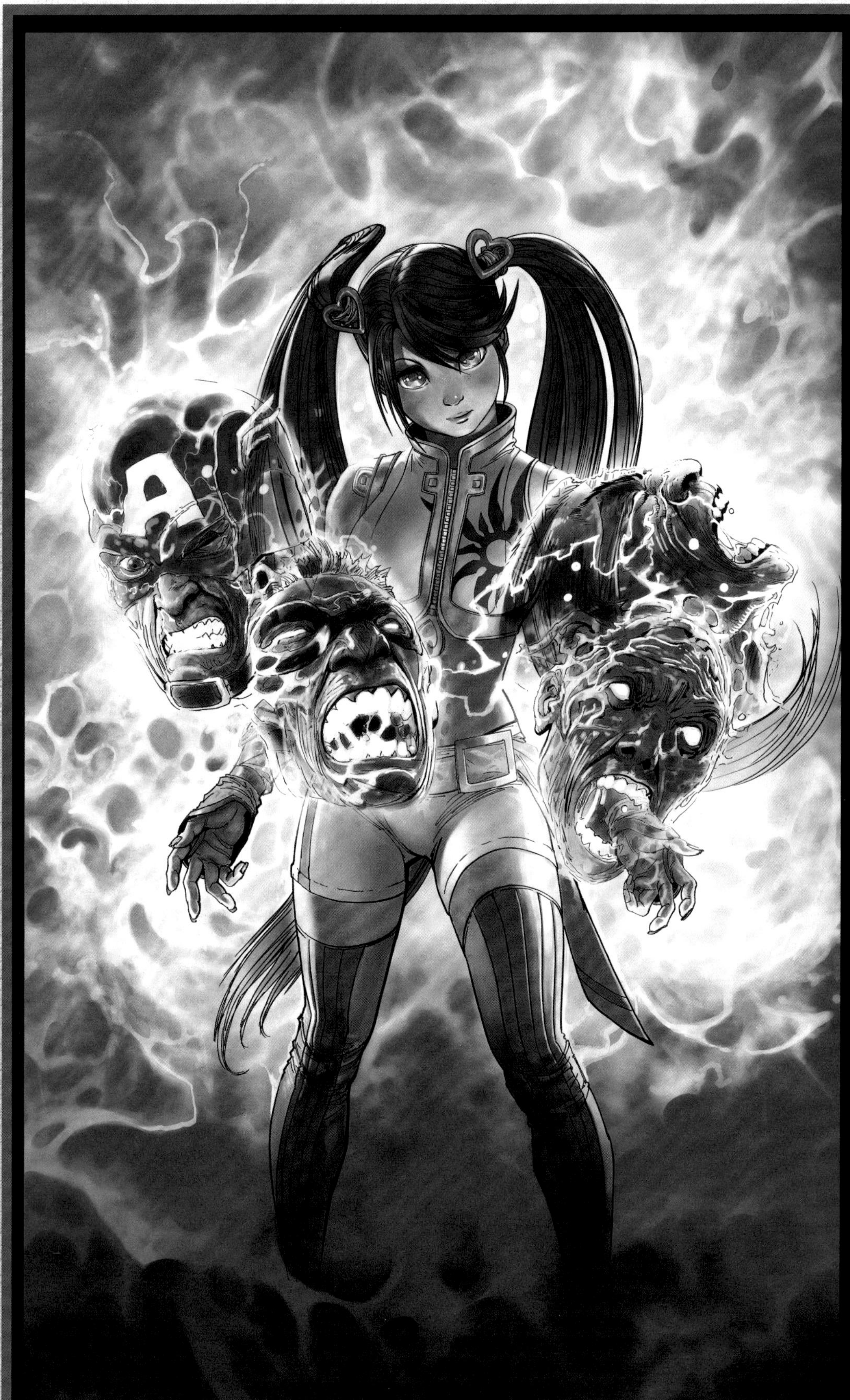

#7

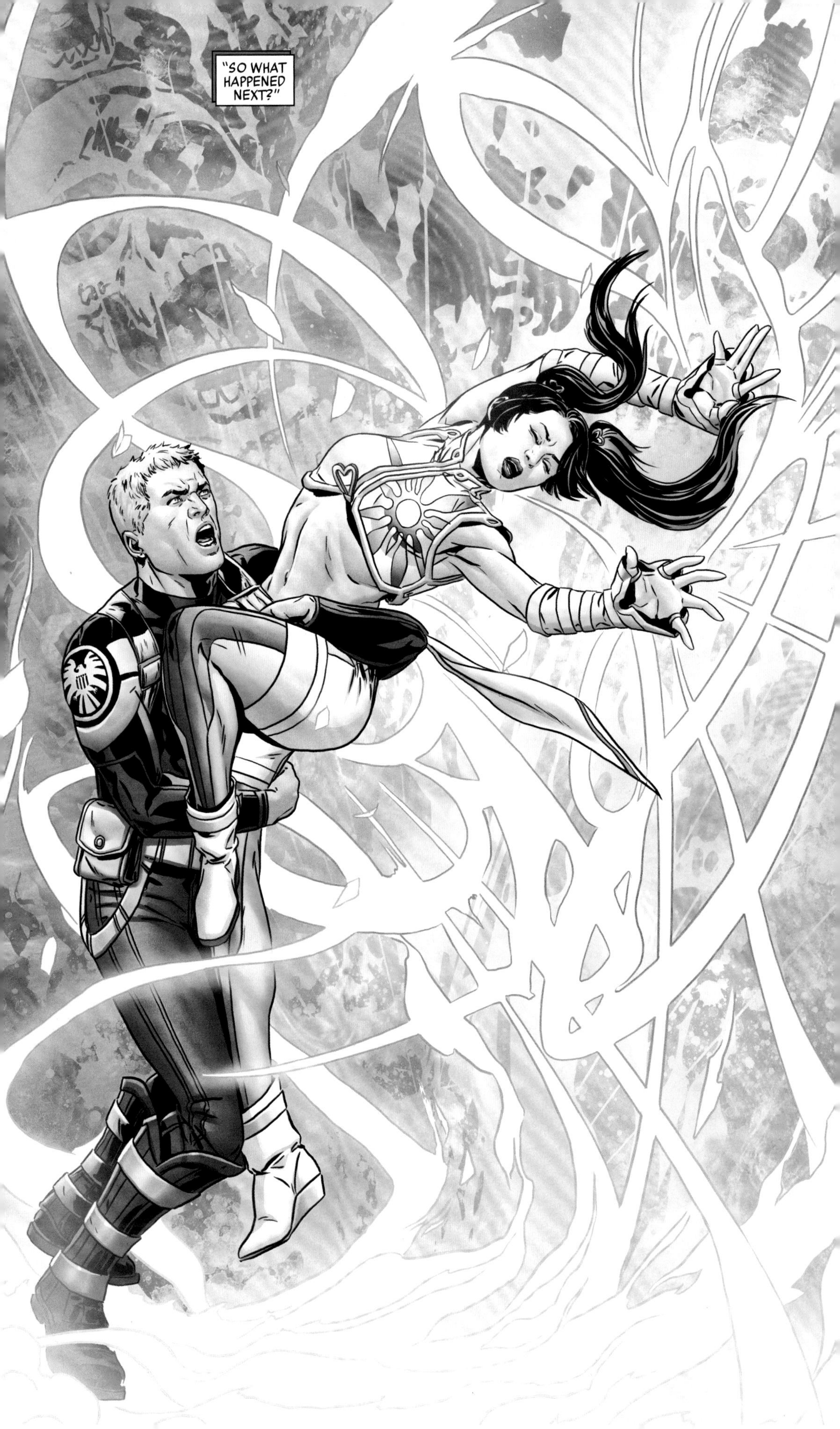
"SO WHAT HAPPENED NEXT?"

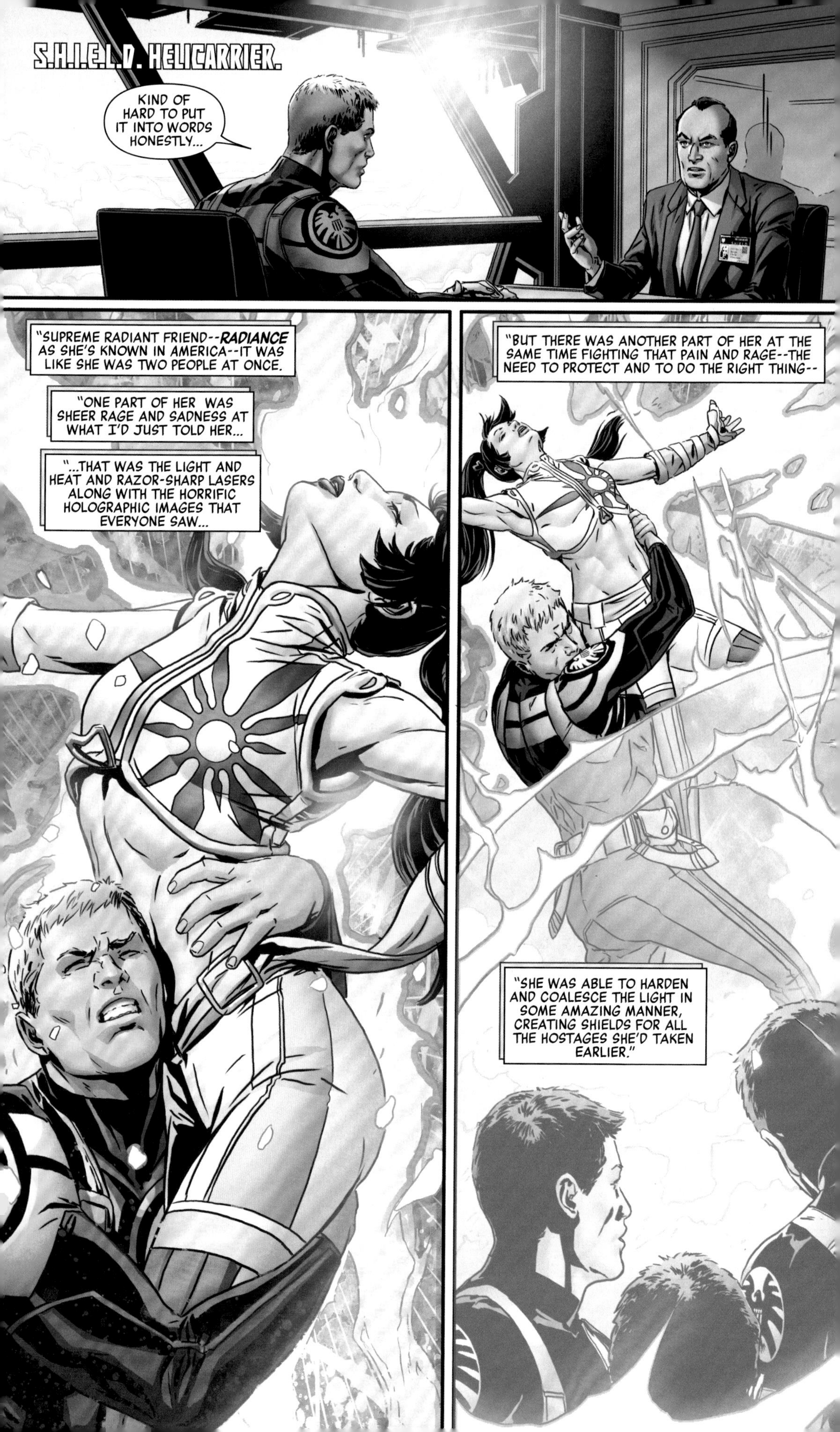
S.H.I.E.L.D. HELICARRIER.
KIND OF HARD TO PUT IT INTO WORDS HONESTLY...
"SUPREME RADIANT FRIEND--RADIANCE AS SHE'S KNOWN IN AMERICA--IT WAS LIKE SHE WAS TWO PEOPLE AT ONCE.
"ONE PART OF HER WAS SHEER RAGE AND SADNESS AT WHAT I'D JUST TOLD HER...
"...THAT WAS THE LIGHT AND HEAT AND RAZOR-SHARP LASERS ALONG WITH THE HORRIFIC HOLOGRAPHIC IMAGES THAT EVERYONE SAW...
"BUT THERE WAS ANOTHER PART OF HER AT THE SAME TIME FIGHTING THAT PAIN AND RAGE--THE NEED TO PROTECT AND TO DO THE RIGHT THING--
"SHE WAS ABLE TO HARDEN AND COALESCE THE LIGHT IN SOME AMAZING MANNER, CREATING SHIELDS FOR ALL THE HOSTAGES SHE'D TAKEN EARLIER."

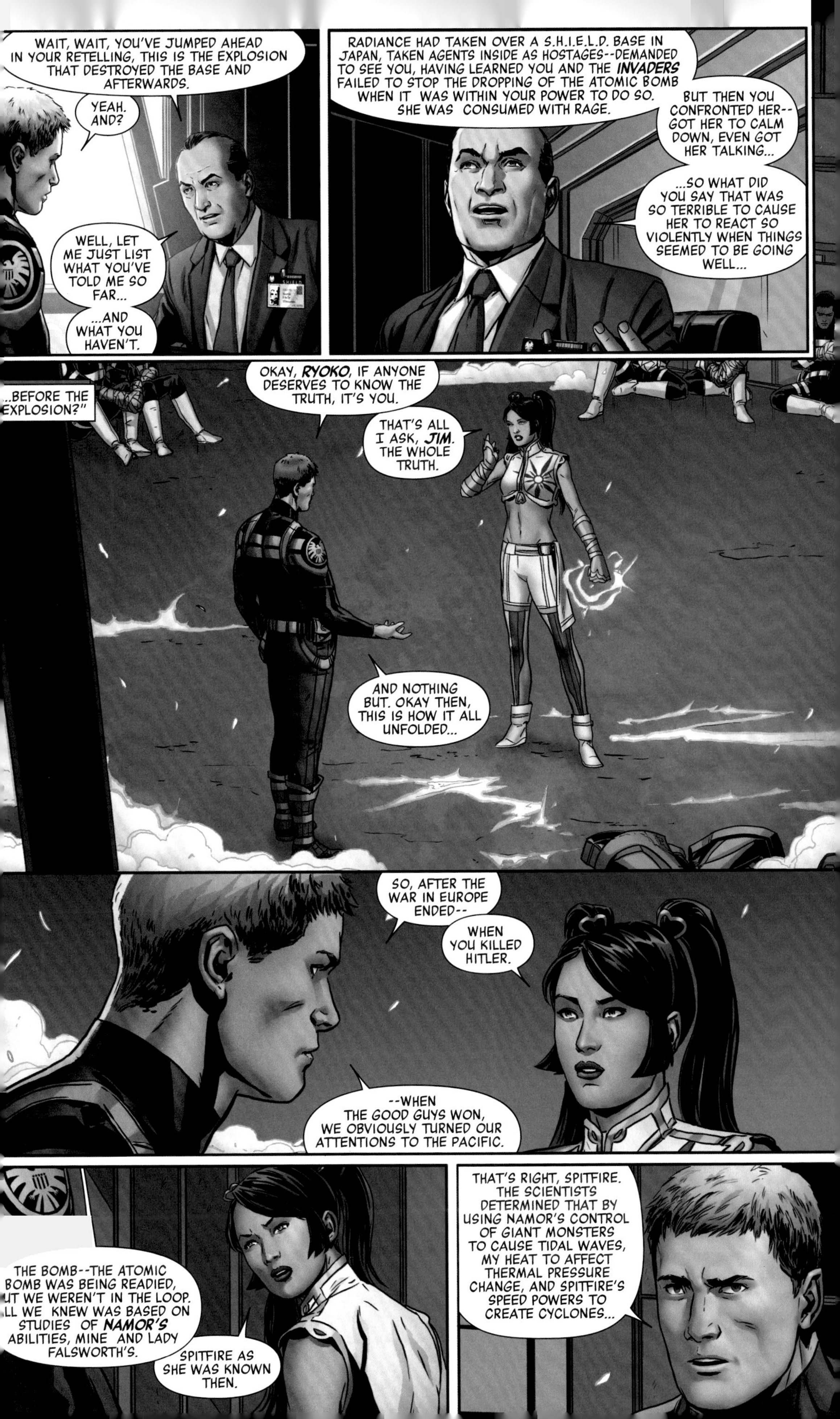
WAIT, WAIT, YOU'VE JUMPED AHEAD IN YOUR RETELLING, THIS IS THE EXPLOSION THAT DESTROYED THE BASE AND AFTERWARDS.
YEAH. AND?
WELL, LET ME JUST LIST WHAT YOU'VE TOLD ME SO FAR...
...AND WHAT YOU HAVEN'T.
RADIANCE HAD TAKEN OVER A S.H.I.E.L.D. BASE IN JAPAN, TAKEN AGENTS INSIDE AS HOSTAGES--DEMANDED TO SEE YOU, HAVING LEARNED YOU AND THE INVADERS FAILED TO STOP THE DROPPING OF THE ATOMIC BOMB WHEN IT WAS WITHIN YOUR POWER TO DO SO. SHE WAS CONSUMED WITH RAGE.
BUT THEN YOU CONFRONTED HER--GOT HER TO CALM DOWN, EVEN GOT HER TALKING...
...SO WHAT DID YOU SAY THAT WAS SO TERRIBLE TO CAUSE HER TO REACT SO VIOLENTLY WHEN THINGS SEEMED TO BE GOING WELL...
..BEFORE THE EXPLOSION?"
OKAY, RYOKO, IF ANYONE DESERVES TO KNOW THE TRUTH, IT'S YOU.
THAT'S ALL I ASK, JIM. THE WHOLE TRUTH.
AND NOTHING BUT. OKAY THEN, THIS IS HOW IT ALL UNFOLDED...
SO, AFTER THE WAR IN EUROPE ENDED--
WHEN YOU KILLED HITLER.
--WHEN THE GOOD GUYS WON, WE OBVIOUSLY TURNED OUR ATTENTIONS TO THE PACIFIC.
THE BOMB--THE ATOMIC BOMB WAS BEING READIED, UT WE WEREN'T IN THE LOOP. LL WE KNEW WAS BASED ON STUDIES OF NAMOR'S ABILITIES, MINE AND LADY FALSWORTH'S.
SPITFIRE AS SHE WAS KNOWN THEN.
THAT'S RIGHT, SPITFIRE. THE SCIENTISTS DETERMINED THAT BY USING NAMOR'S CONTROL OF GIANT MONSTERS TO CAUSE TIDAL WAVES, MY HEAT TO AFFECT THERMAL PRESSURE CHANGE, AND SPITFIRE'S SPEED POWERS TO CREATE CYCLONES...

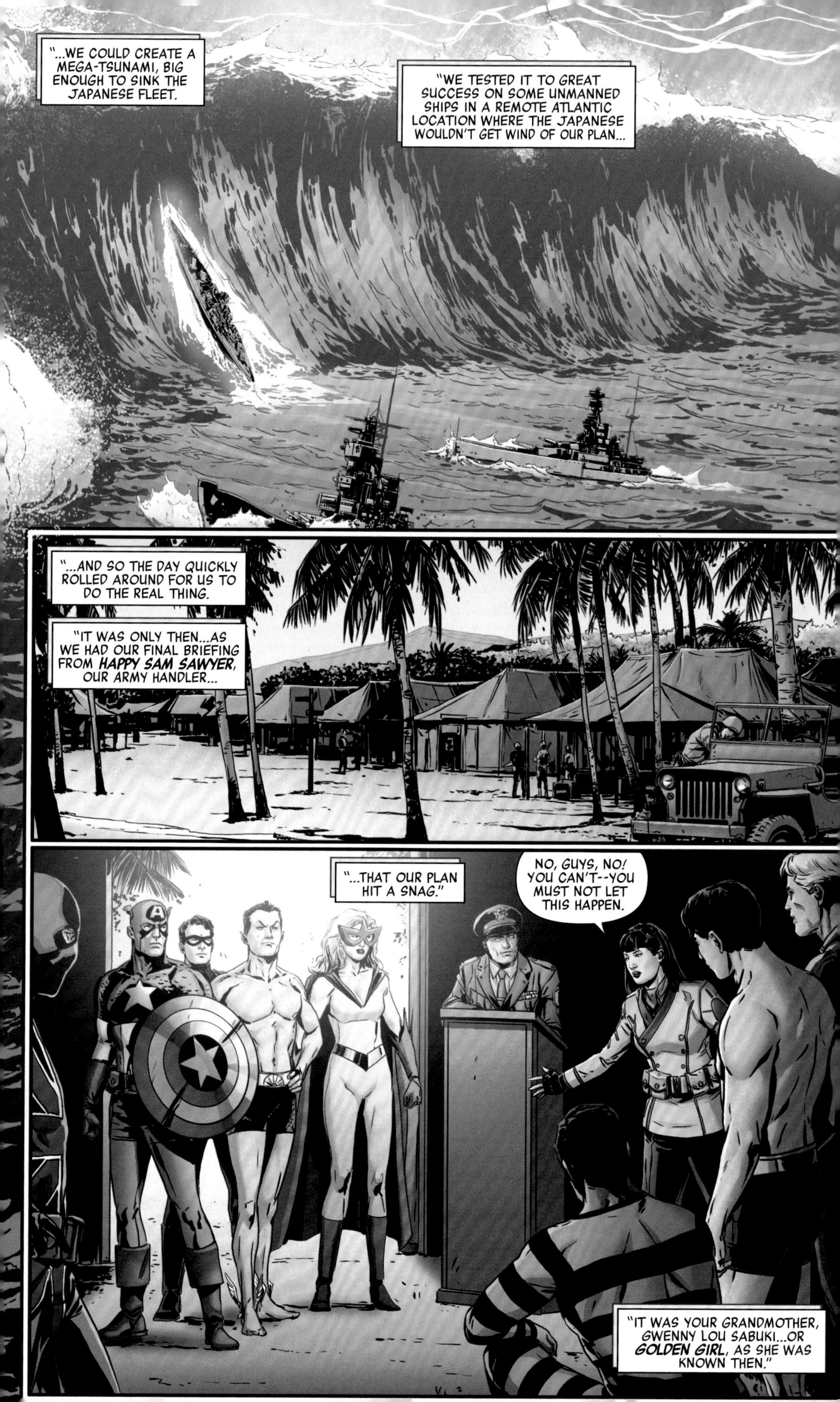
"...WE COULD CREATE A MEGA-TSUNAMI, BIG ENOUGH TO SINK THE JAPANESE FLEET.
"WE TESTED IT TO GREAT SUCCESS ON SOME UNMANNED SHIPS IN A REMOTE ATLANTIC LOCATION WHERE THE JAPANESE WOULDN'T GET WIND OF OUR PLAN...
"...AND SO THE DAY QUICKLY ROLLED AROUND FOR US TO DO THE REAL THING.
"IT WAS ONLY THEN...AS WE HAD OUR FINAL BRIEFING FROM HAPPY SAM SAWYER, OUR ARMY HANDLER...
"...THAT OUR PLAN HIT A SNAG."
NO, GUYS, NO! YOU CAN'T--YOU MUST NOT LET THIS HAPPEN.
"IT WAS YOUR GRANDMOTHER, GWENNY LOU SABUKI...OR GOLDEN GIRL, AS SHE WAS KNOWN THEN."

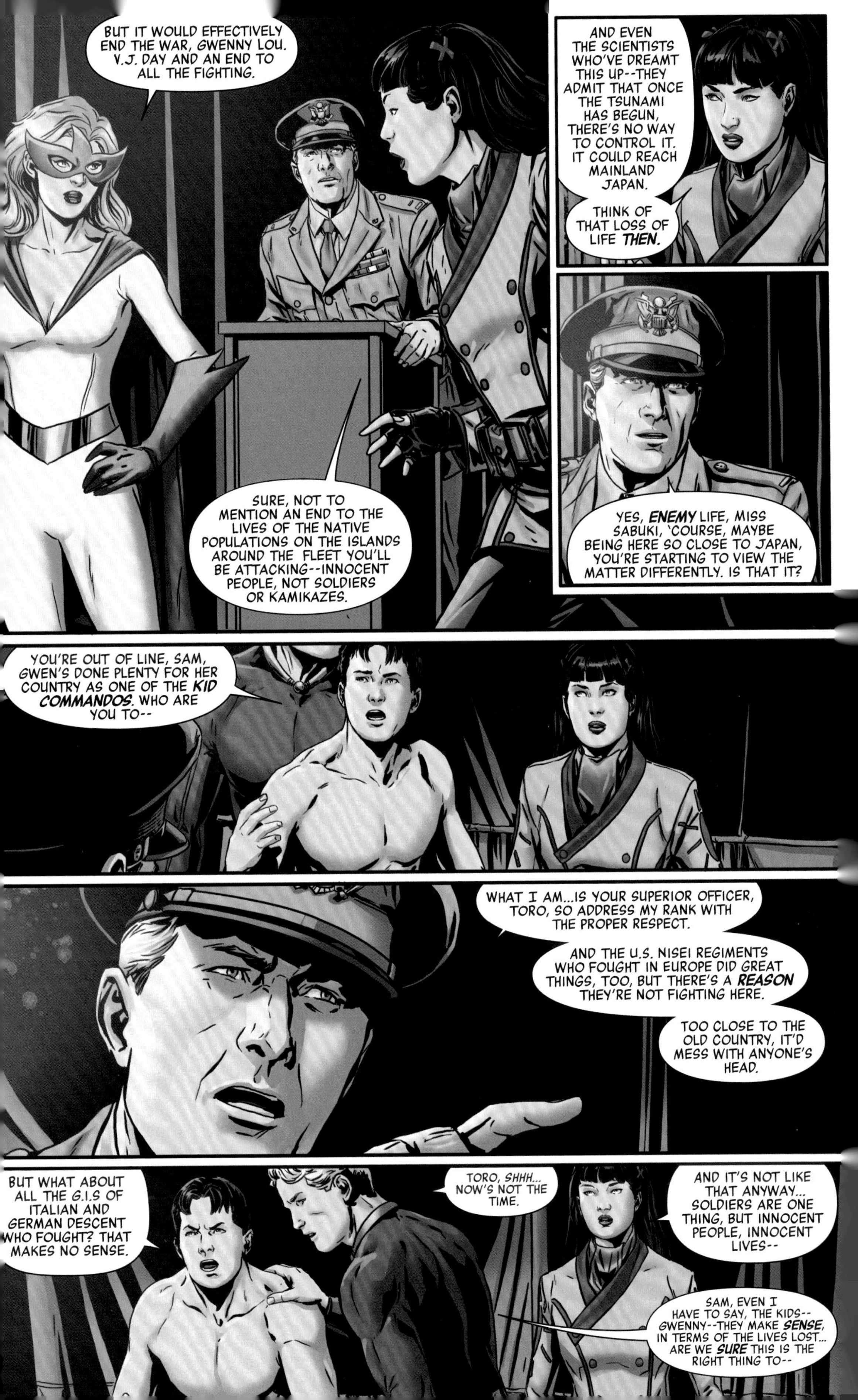

BUT IT WOULD EFFECTIVELY END THE WAR, GWENNY LOU. V.J. DAY AND AN END TO ALL THE FIGHTING.
SURE, NOT TO MENTION AN END TO THE LIVES OF THE NATIVE POPULATIONS ON THE ISLANDS AROUND THE FLEET YOU'LL BE ATTACKING--INNOCENT PEOPLE, NOT SOLDIERS OR KAMIKAZES.
AND EVEN THE SCIENTISTS WHO'VE DREAMT THIS UP--THEY ADMIT THAT ONCE THE TSUNAMI HAS BEGUN, THERE'S NO WAY TO CONTROL IT. IT COULD REACH MAINLAND JAPAN.
THINK OF THAT LOSS OF LIFE THEN.
YES, ENEMY LIFE, MISS SABUKI, 'COURSE, MAYBE BEING HERE SO CLOSE TO JAPAN, YOU'RE STARTING TO VIEW THE MATTER DIFFERENTLY. IS THAT IT?
YOU'RE OUT OF LINE, SAM, GWEN'S DONE PLENTY FOR HER COUNTRY AS ONE OF THE KID COMMANDOS. WHO ARE YOU TO--
WHAT I AM...IS YOUR SUPERIOR OFFICER, TORO, SO ADDRESS MY RANK WITH THE PROPER RESPECT.
AND THE U.S. NISEI REGIMENTS WHO FOUGHT IN EUROPE DID GREAT THINGS, TOO, BUT THERE'S A REASON THEY'RE NOT FIGHTING HERE.
TOO CLOSE TO THE OLD COUNTRY, IT'D MESS WITH ANYONE'S HEAD.
BUT WHAT ABOUT ALL THE G.I.S OF ITALIAN AND GERMAN DESCENT WHO FOUGHT? THAT MAKES NO SENSE.
TORO, SHHH... NOW'S NOT THE TIME.
AND IT'S NOT LIKE THAT ANYWAY... SOLDIERS ARE ONE THING, BUT INNOCENT PEOPLE, INNOCENT LIVES--
SAM, EVEN I HAVE TO SAY, THE KIDS-- GWENNY--THEY MAKE SENSE, IN TERMS OF THE LIVES LOST... ARE WE SURE THIS IS THE RIGHT THING TO--

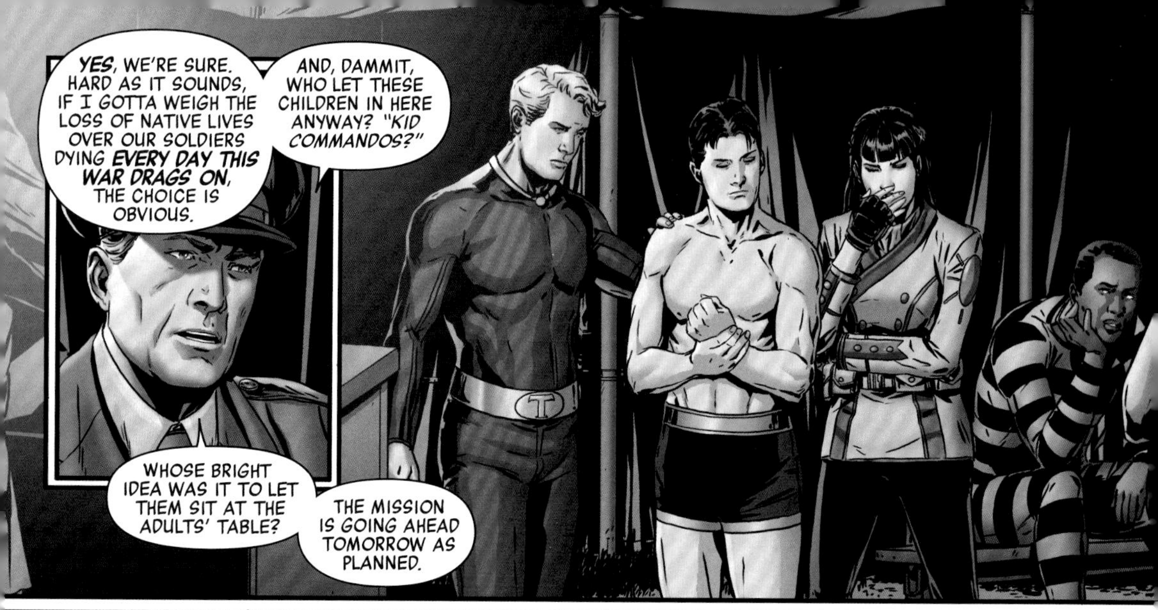
YES, WE'RE SURE. HARD AS IT SOUNDS, IF I GOTTA WEIGH THE LOSS OF NATIVE LIVES OVER OUR SOLDIERS DYING EVERY DAY THIS WAR DRAGS ON, THE CHOICE IS OBVIOUS.
AND, DAMMIT, WHO LET THESE CHILDREN IN HERE ANYWAY? "KID COMMANDOS?"
WHOSE BRIGHT IDEA WAS IT TO LET THEM SIT AT THE ADULTS' TABLE?
THE MISSION IS GOING AHEAD TOMORROW AS PLANNED.

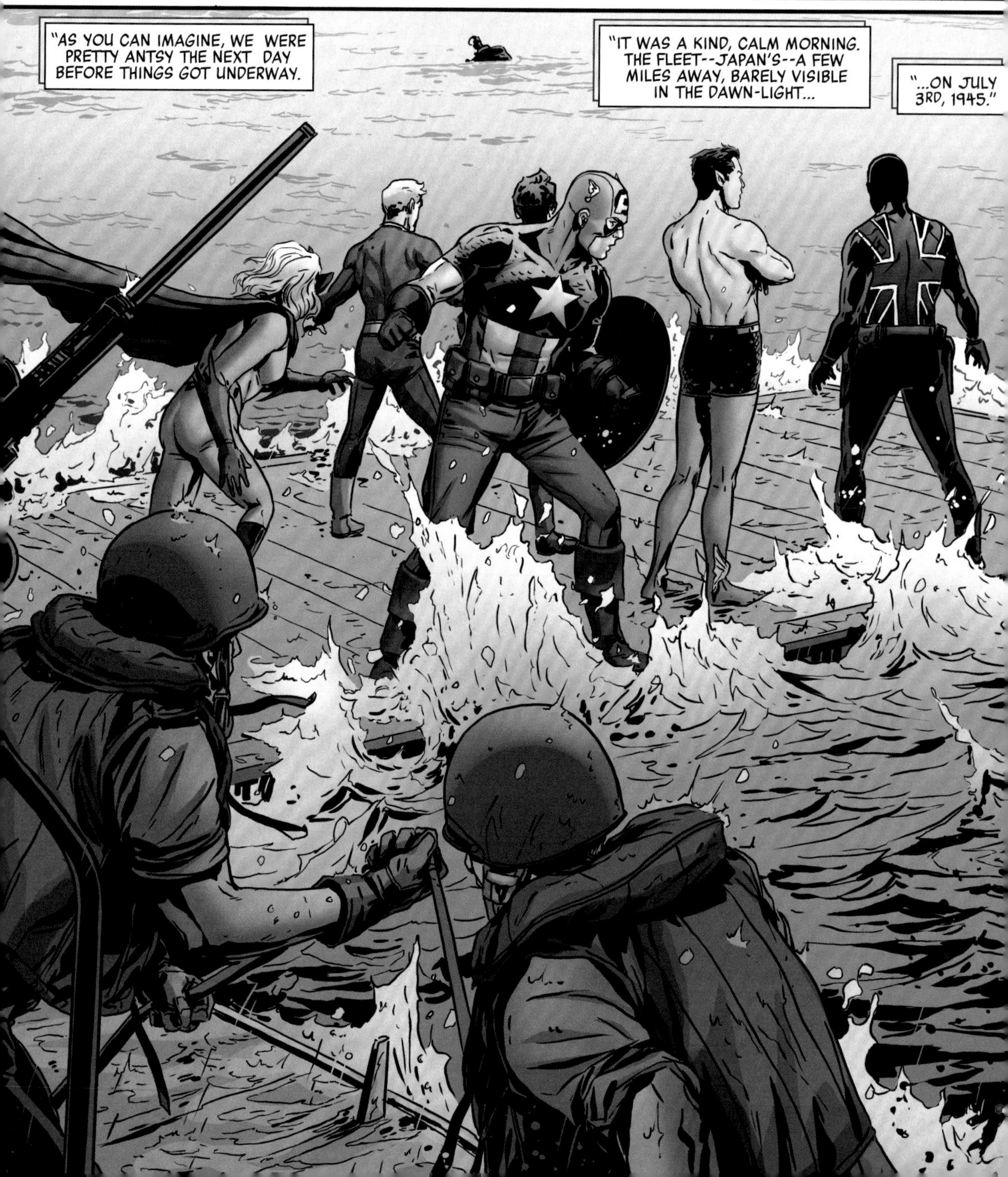
"AS YOU CAN IMAGINE, WE WERE PRETTY ANTSY THE NEXT DAY BEFORE THINGS GOT UNDERWAY.
"IT WAS A KIND, CALM MORNING. THE FLEET--JAPAN'S--A FEW MILES AWAY, BARELY VISIBLE IN THE DAWN-LIGHT...
"...ON JULY 3RD, 1945."

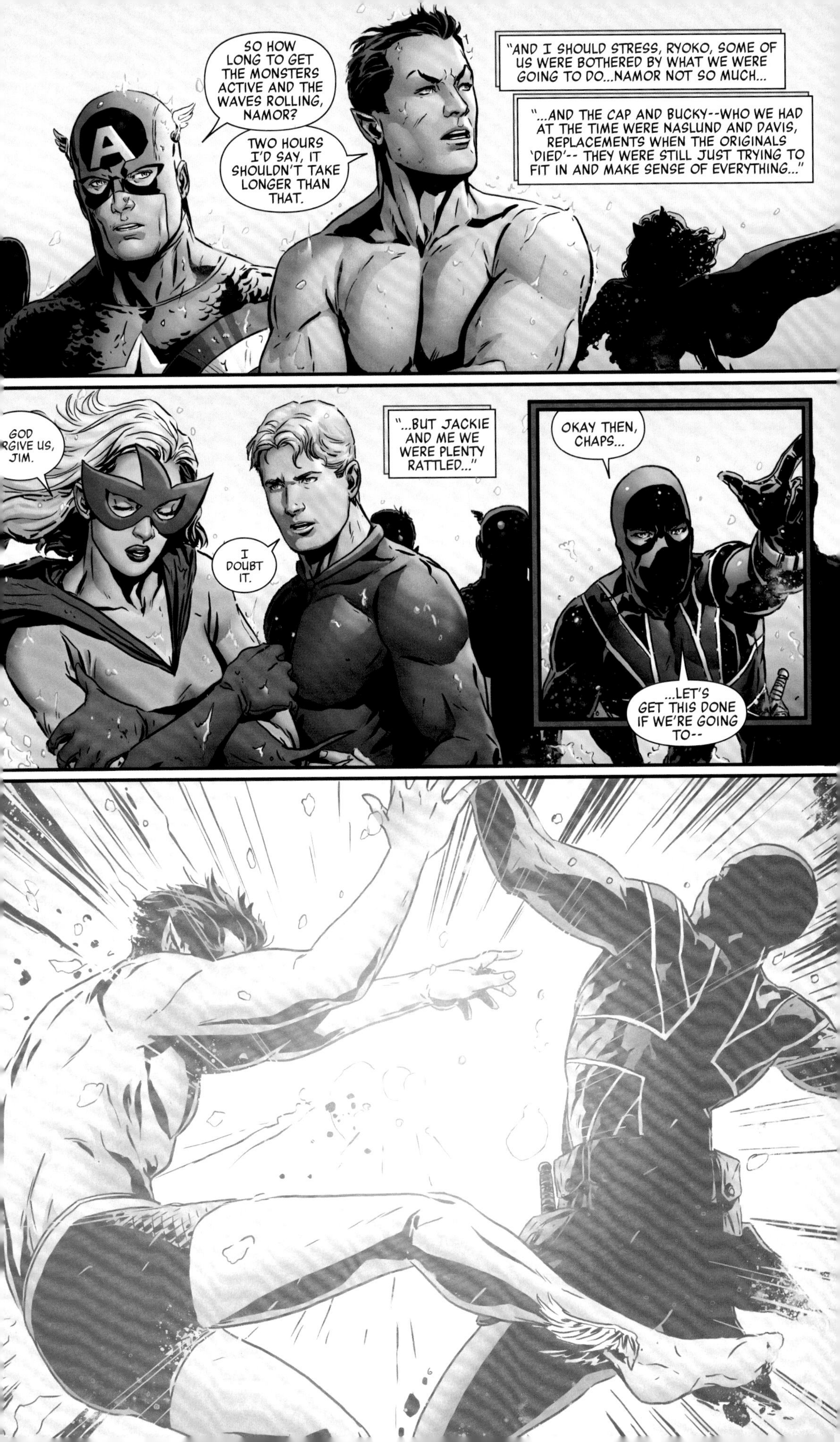
SO HOW LONG TO GET THE MONSTERS ACTIVE AND THE WAVES ROLLING, NAMOR?
TWO HOURS I'D SAY, IT SHOULDN'T TAKE LONGER THAN THAT.
"AND I SHOULD STRESS, RYOKO, SOME OF US WERE BOTHERED BY WHAT WE WERE GOING TO DO...NAMOR NOT SO MUCH...
"...AND THE CAP AND BUCKY--WHO WE HAD AT THE TIME WERE NASLUND AND DAVIS, REPLACEMENTS WHEN THE ORIGINALS 'DIED'-- THEY WERE STILL JUST TRYING TO FIT IN AND MAKE SENSE OF EVERYTHING..."
GOD RGIVE US, JIM.
I DOUBT IT.
"...BUT JACKIE AND ME WE WERE PLENTY RATTLED..."
OKAY THEN, CHAPS...
...LET'S GET THIS DONE IF WE'RE GOING TO--

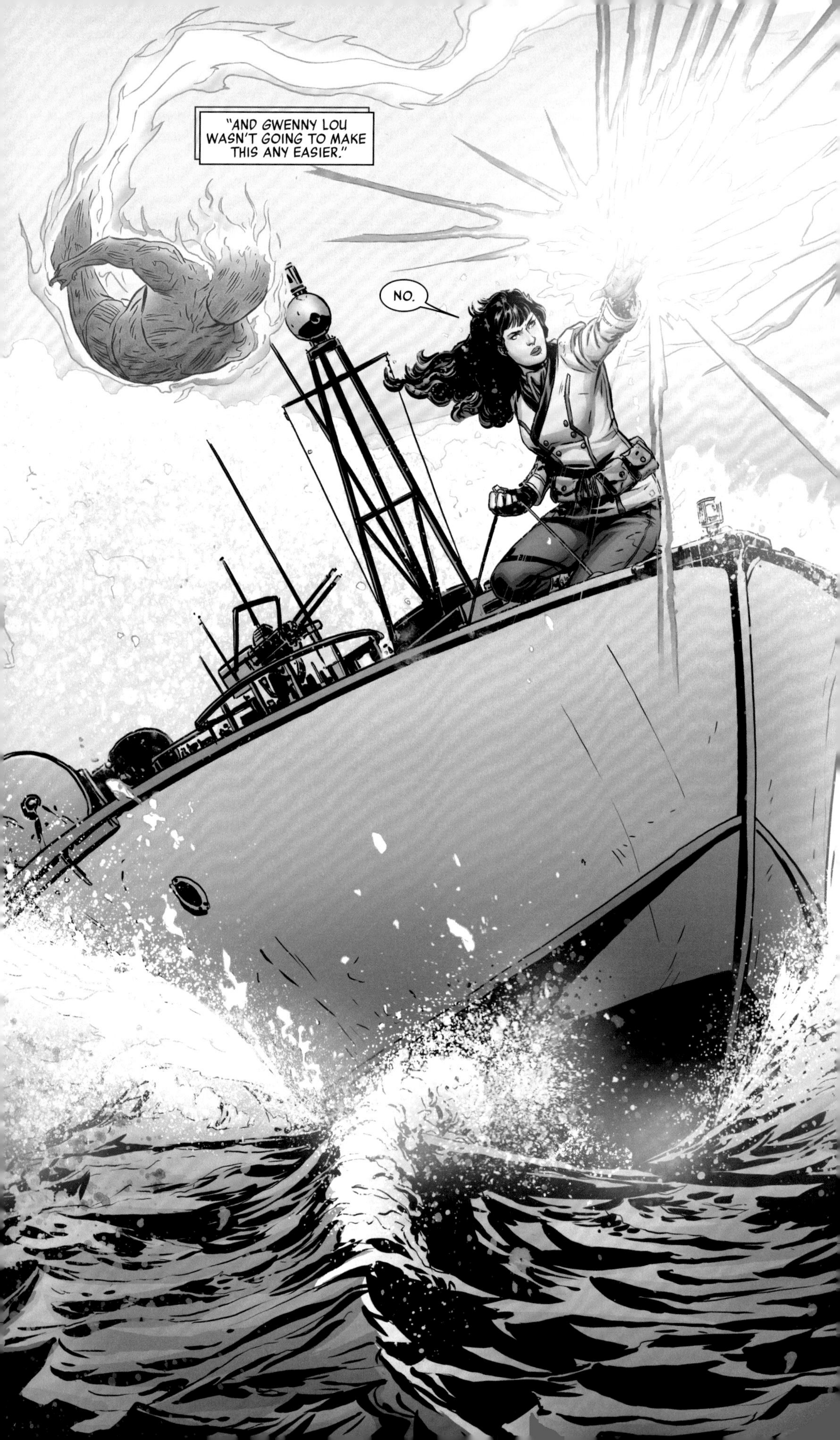
"AND GWENNY LOU WASN'T GOING TO MAKE THIS ANY EASIER."
NO.

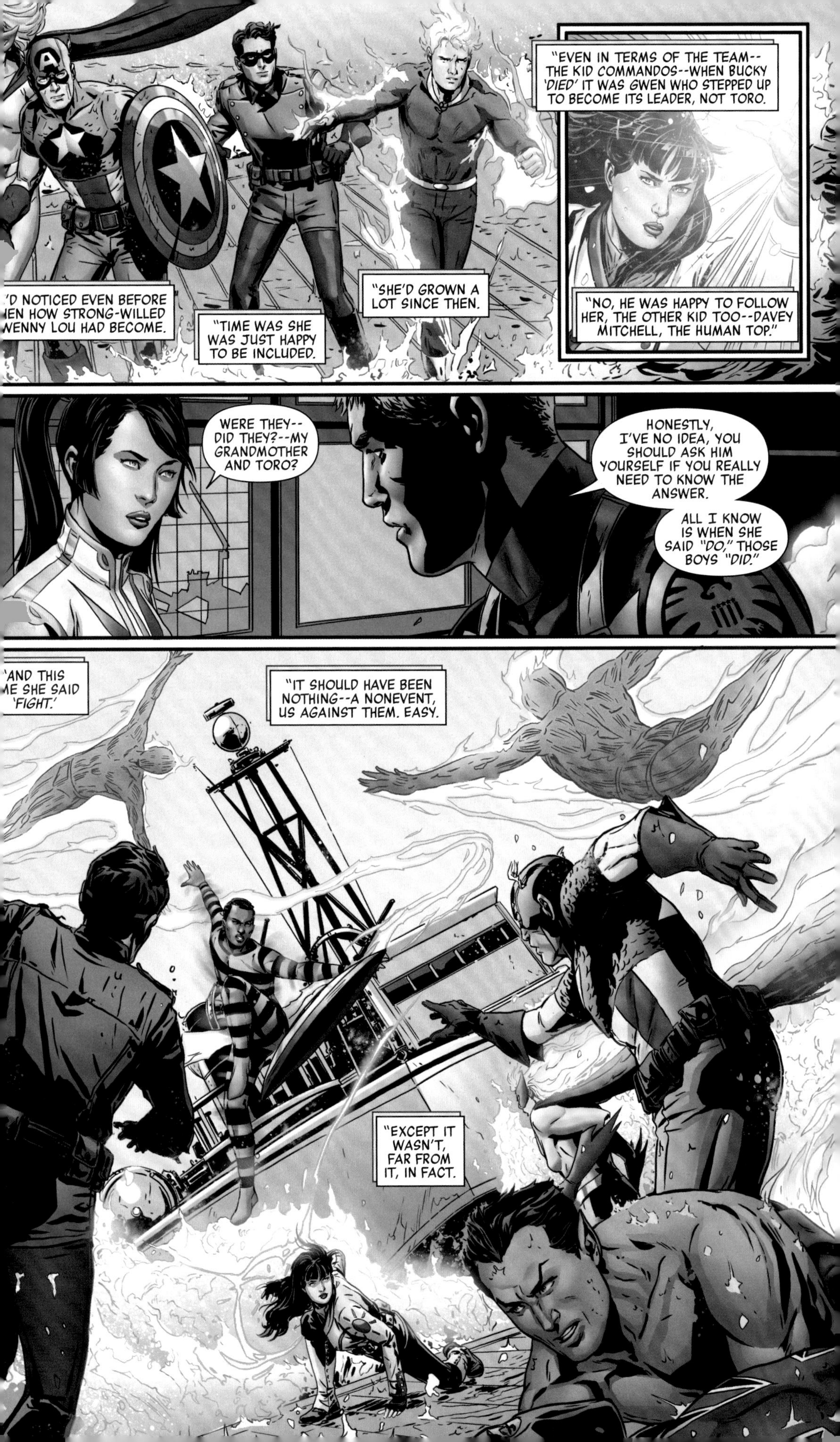

"EVEN IN TERMS OF THE TEAM-- THE KID COMMANDOS--WHEN BUCKY 'DIED' IT WAS GWEN WHO STEPPED UP TO BECOME ITS LEADER, NOT TORO.
'D NOTICED EVEN BEFORE IEN HOW STRONG-WILLED WENNY LOU HAD BECOME.
"TIME WAS SHE WAS JUST HAPPY TO BE INCLUDED.
"SHE'D GROWN A LOT SINCE THEN.
"NO, HE WAS HAPPY TO FOLLOW HER, THE OTHER KID TOO--DAVEY MITCHELL, THE HUMAN TOP."
WERE THEY-- DID THEY?--MY GRANDMOTHER AND TORO?
HONESTLY, I'VE NO IDEA, YOU SHOULD ASK HIM YOURSELF IF YOU REALLY NEED TO KNOW THE ANSWER.
ALL I KNOW IS WHEN SHE SAID "DO," THOSE BOYS "DID."
'AND THIS ME SHE SAID 'FIGHT.'
"IT SHOULD HAVE BEEN NOTHING--A NONEVENT, US AGAINST THEM. EASY.
"EXCEPT IT WASN'T, FAR FROM IT, IN FACT.

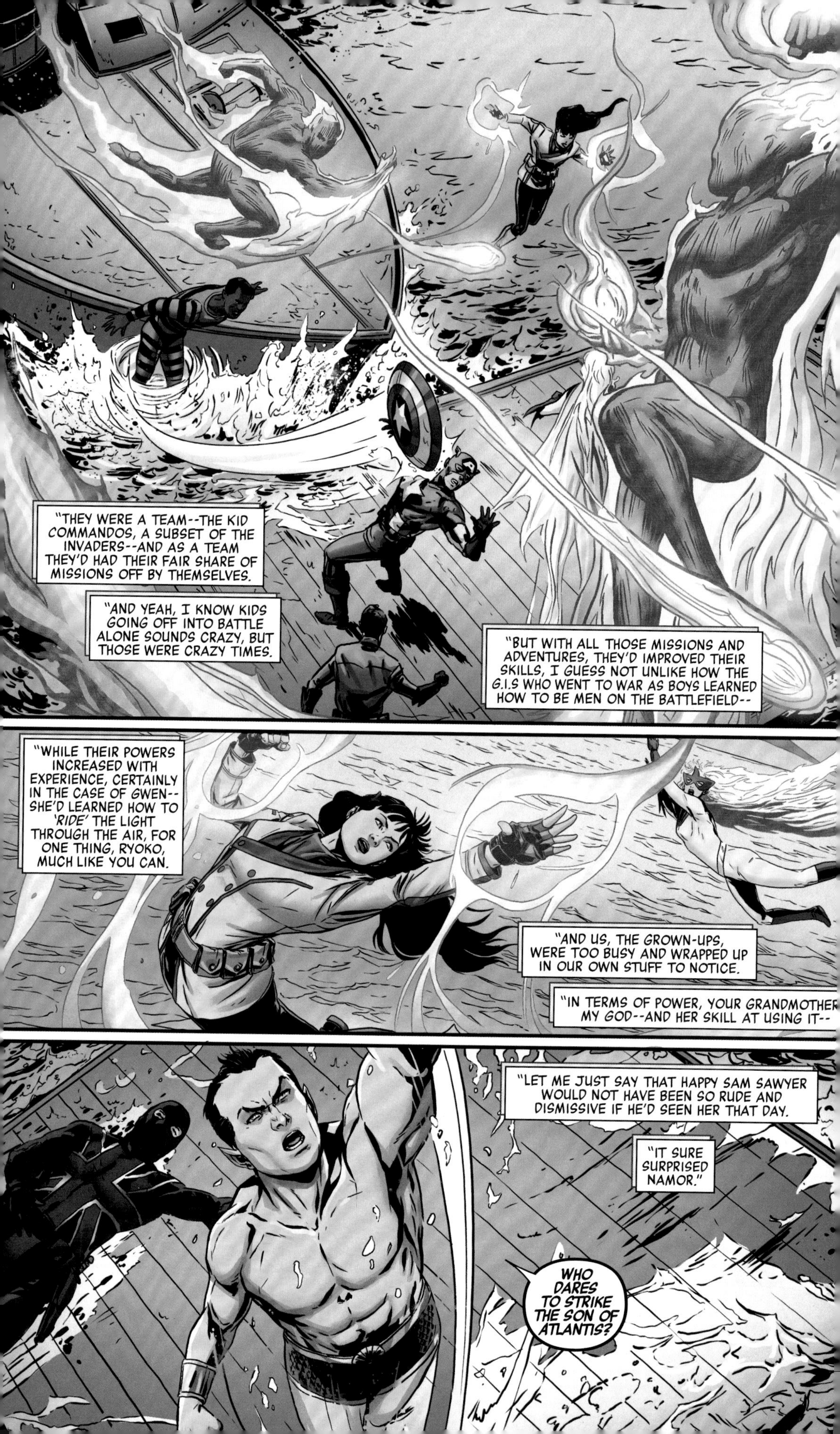

"THEY WERE A TEAM--THE KID COMMANDOS, A SUBSET OF THE INVADERS--AND AS A TEAM THEY'D HAD THEIR FAIR SHARE OF MISSIONS OFF BY THEMSELVES.
"AND YEAH, I KNOW KIDS GOING OFF INTO BATTLE ALONE SOUNDS CRAZY, BUT THOSE WERE CRAZY TIMES.
"BUT WITH ALL THOSE MISSIONS AND ADVENTURES, THEY'D IMPROVED THEIR SKILLS, I GUESS NOT UNLIKE HOW THE G.I.S WHO WENT TO WAR AS BOYS LEARNED HOW TO BE MEN ON THE BATTLEFIELD--
"WHILE THEIR POWERS INCREASED WITH EXPERIENCE, CERTAINLY IN THE CASE OF GWEN--SHE'D LEARNED HOW TO *'RIDE'* THE LIGHT THROUGH THE AIR, FOR ONE THING, RYOKO, MUCH LIKE YOU CAN.
"AND US, THE GROWN-UPS, WERE TOO BUSY AND WRAPPED UP IN OUR OWN STUFF TO NOTICE.
"IN TERMS OF POWER, YOUR GRANDMOTHER MY GOD--AND HER SKILL AT USING IT--
"LET ME JUST SAY THAT HAPPY SAM SAWYER WOULD NOT HAVE BEEN SO RUDE AND DISMISSIVE IF HE'D SEEN HER THAT DAY.
"IT SURE SURPRISED NAMOR."
WHO DARES TO STRIKE THE SON OF ATLANTIS?

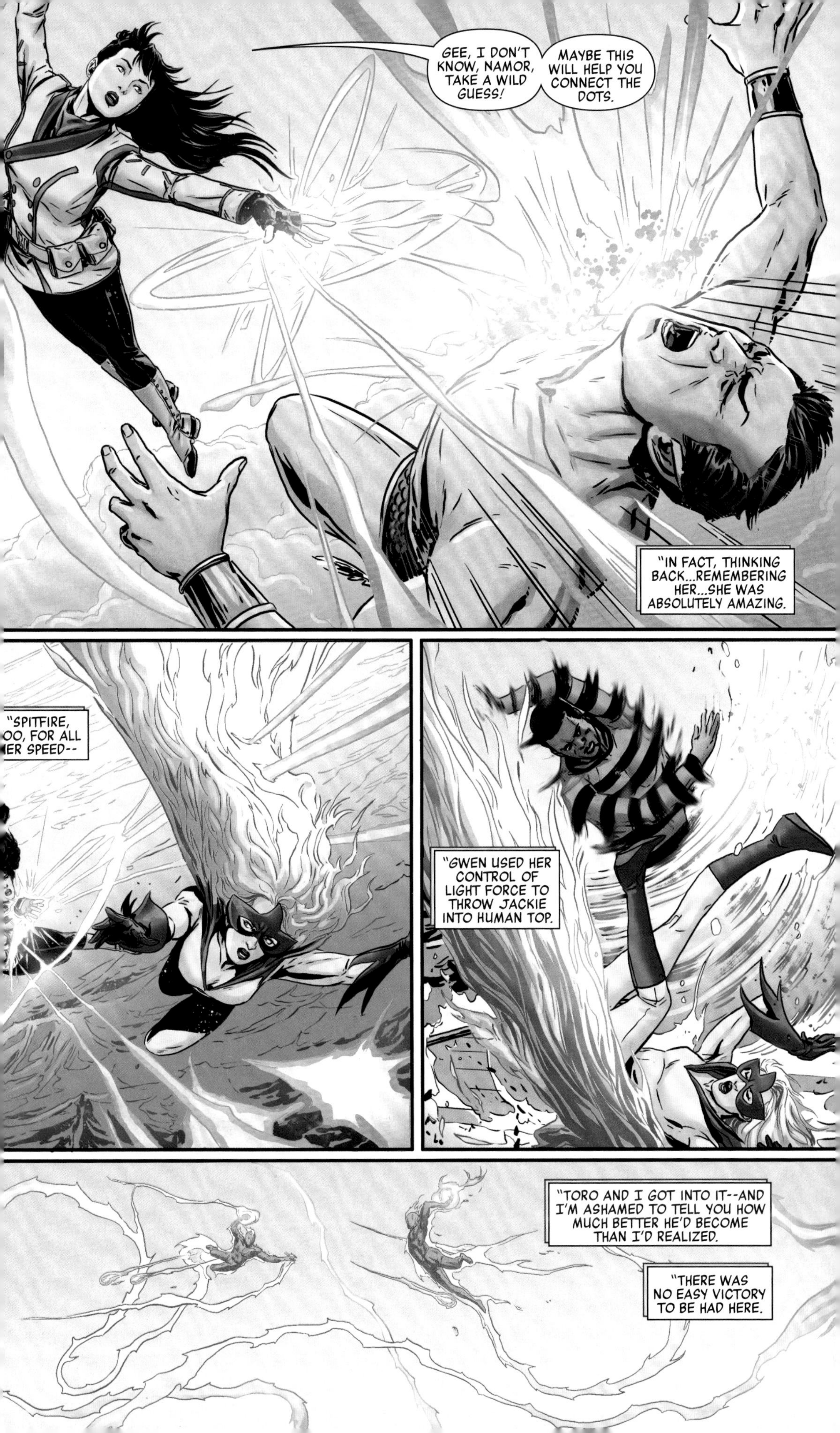
GEE, I DON'T KNOW, NAMOR, TAKE A WILD GUESS!
MAYBE THIS WILL HELP YOU CONNECT THE DOTS.
"IN FACT, THINKING BACK...REMEMBERING HER...SHE WAS ABSOLUTELY AMAZING.
"SPITFIRE, OO, FOR ALL ER SPEED--
"GWEN USED HER CONTROL OF LIGHT FORCE TO THROW JACKIE INTO HUMAN TOP.
"TORO AND I GOT INTO IT--AND I'M ASHAMED TO TELL YOU HOW MUCH BETTER HE'D BECOME THAN I'D REALIZED.
"THERE WAS NO EASY VICTORY TO BE HAD HERE.

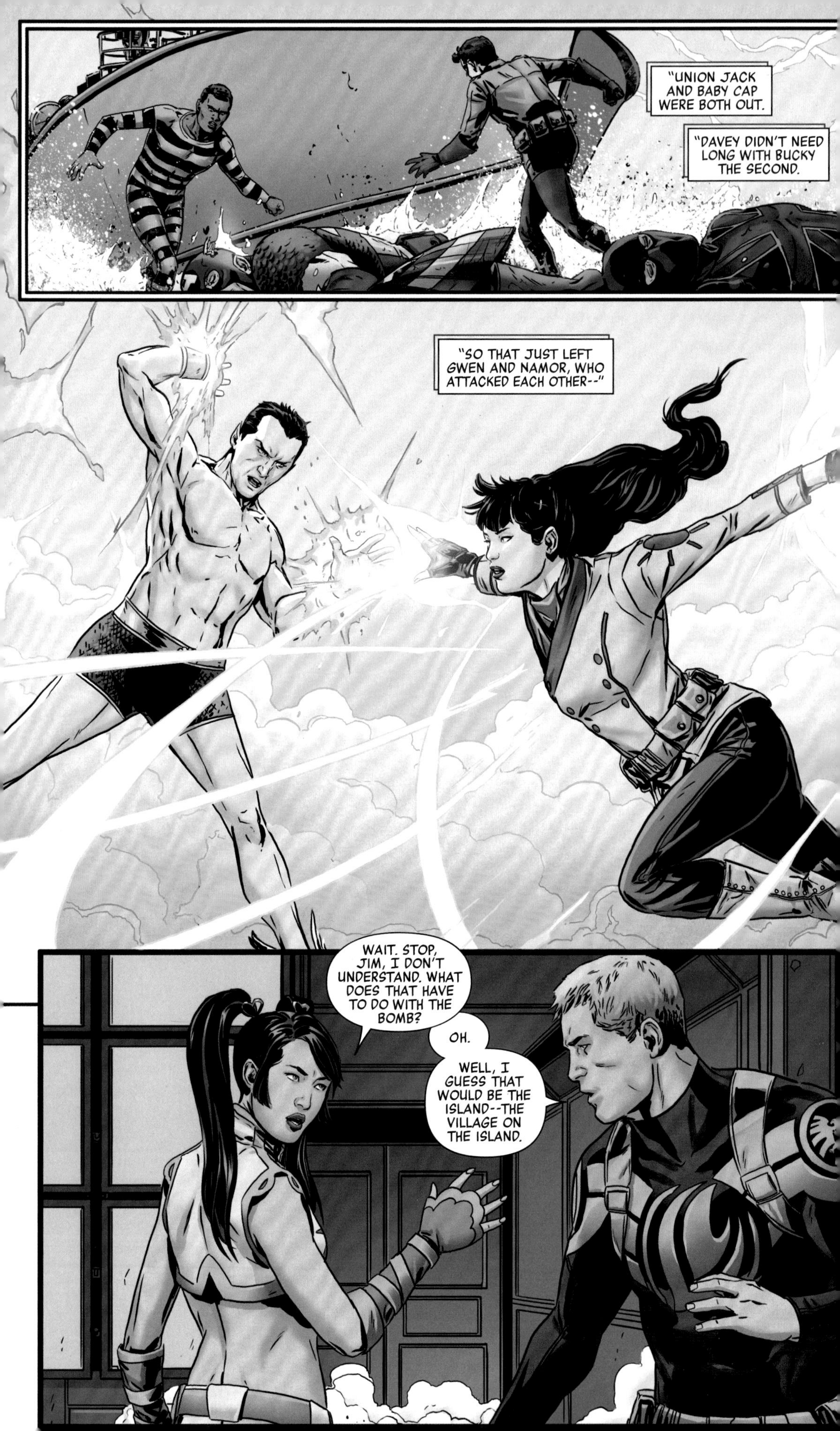
"UNION JACK AND BABY CAP WERE BOTH OUT.
"DAVEY DIDN'T NEED LONG WITH BUCKY THE SECOND.
"SO THAT JUST LEFT GWEN AND NAMOR, WHO ATTACKED EACH OTHER--"
WAIT. STOP, JIM, I DON'T UNDERSTAND. WHAT DOES THAT HAVE TO DO WITH THE BOMB?
OH.
WELL, I GUESS THAT WOULD BE THE ISLAND--THE VILLAGE ON THE ISLAND.

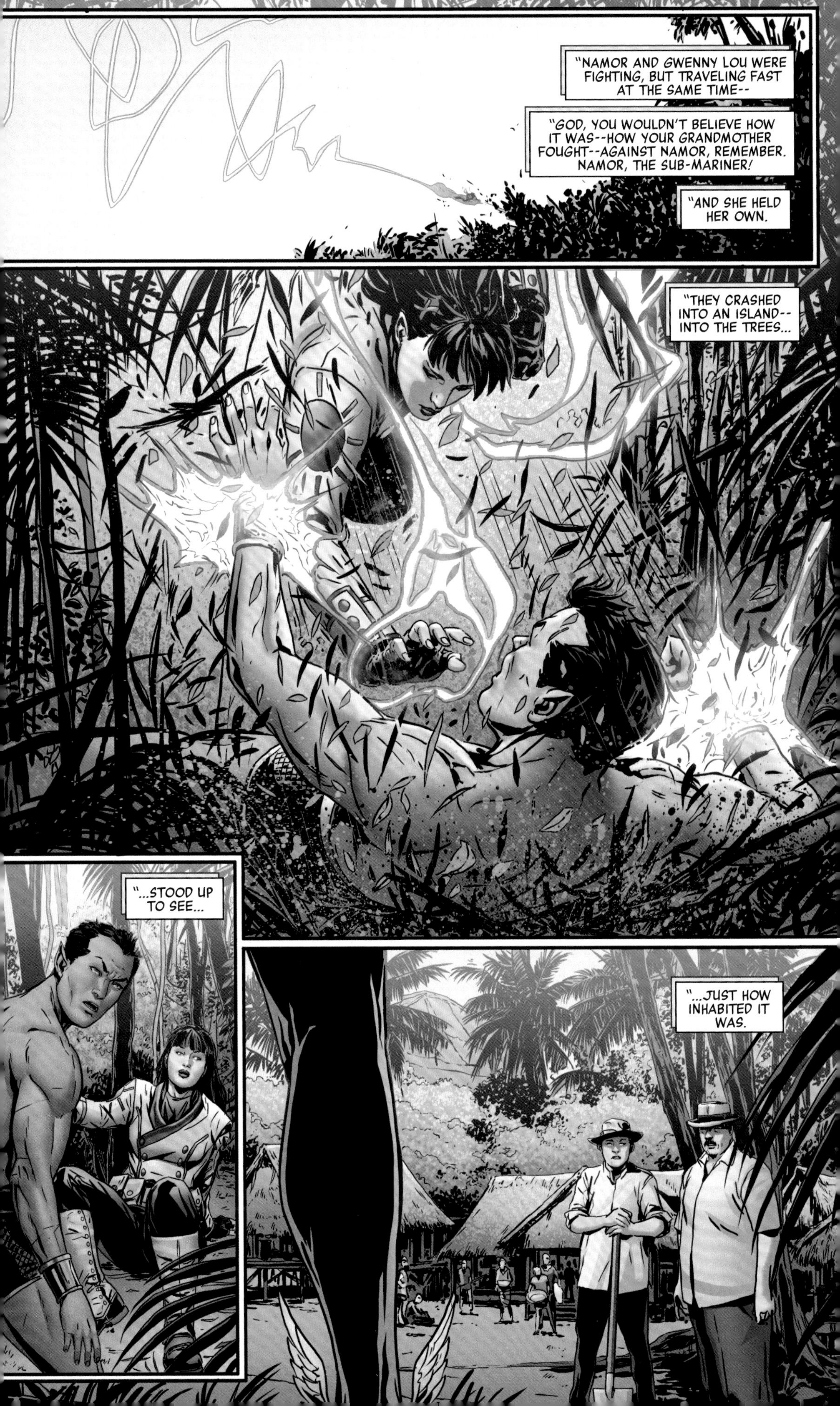
"NAMOR AND GWENNY LOU WERE FIGHTING, BUT TRAVELING FAST AT THE SAME TIME--
"GOD, YOU WOULDN'T BELIEVE HOW IT WAS--HOW YOUR GRANDMOTHER FOUGHT--AGAINST NAMOR, REMEMBER. NAMOR, THE SUB-MARINER!
"AND SHE HELD HER OWN.
"THEY CRASHED INTO AN ISLAND--INTO THE TREES...
"...STOOD UP TO SEE...
"...JUST HOW INHABITED IT WAS.

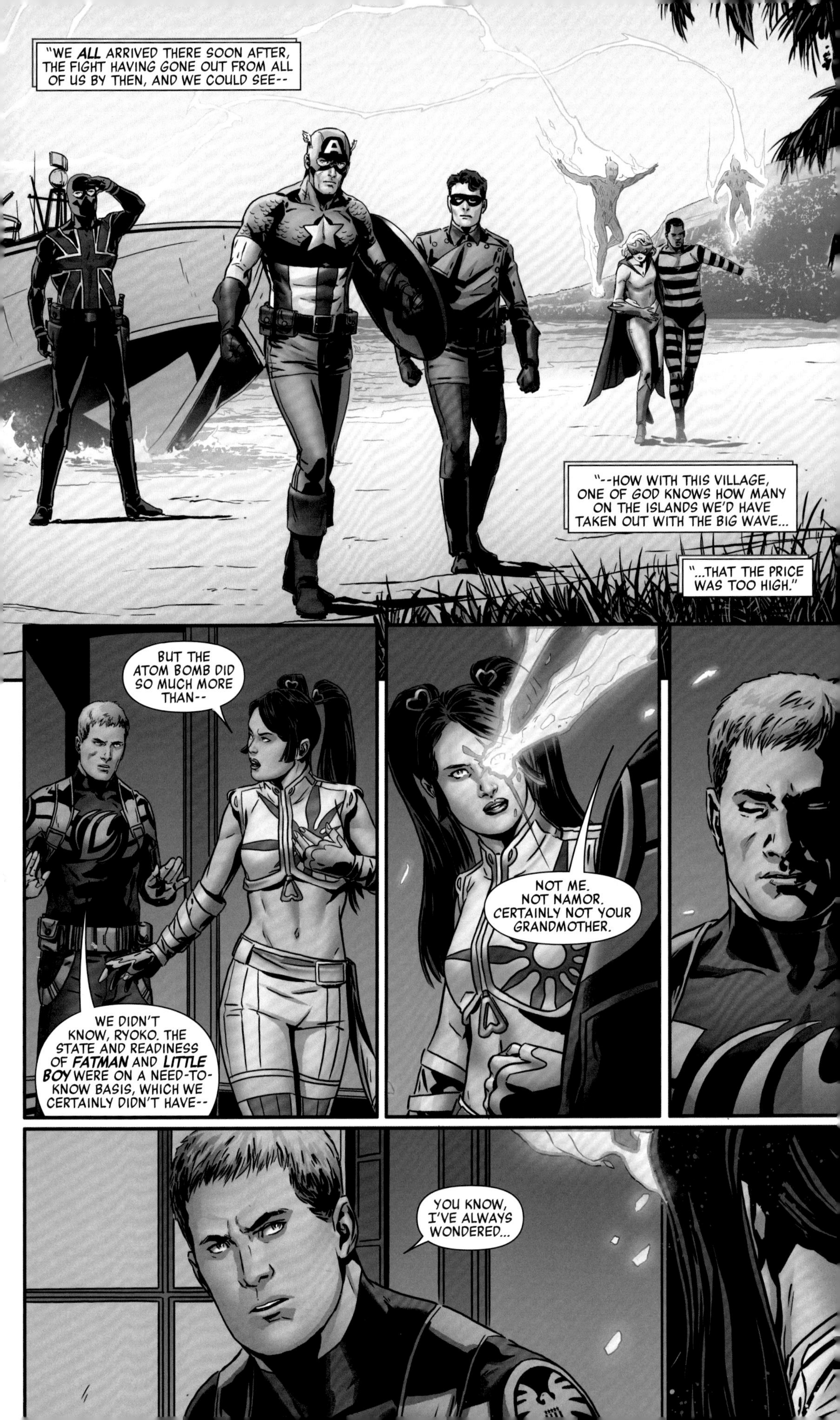
"WE ALL ARRIVED THERE SOON AFTER, THE FIGHT HAVING GONE OUT FROM ALL OF US BY THEN, AND WE COULD SEE--
"--HOW WITH THIS VILLAGE, ONE OF GOD KNOWS HOW MANY ON THE ISLANDS WE'D HAVE TAKEN OUT WITH THE BIG WAVE...
"...THAT THE PRICE WAS TOO HIGH."
BUT THE ATOM BOMB DID SO MUCH MORE THAN--
WE DIDN'T KNOW, RYOKO. THE STATE AND READINESS OF FATMAN AND LITTLE BOY WERE ON A NEED-TO-KNOW BASIS, WHICH WE CERTAINLY DIDN'T HAVE--
NOT ME. NOT NAMOR. CERTAINLY NOT YOUR GRANDMOTHER.
YOU KNOW, I'VE ALWAYS WONDERED...

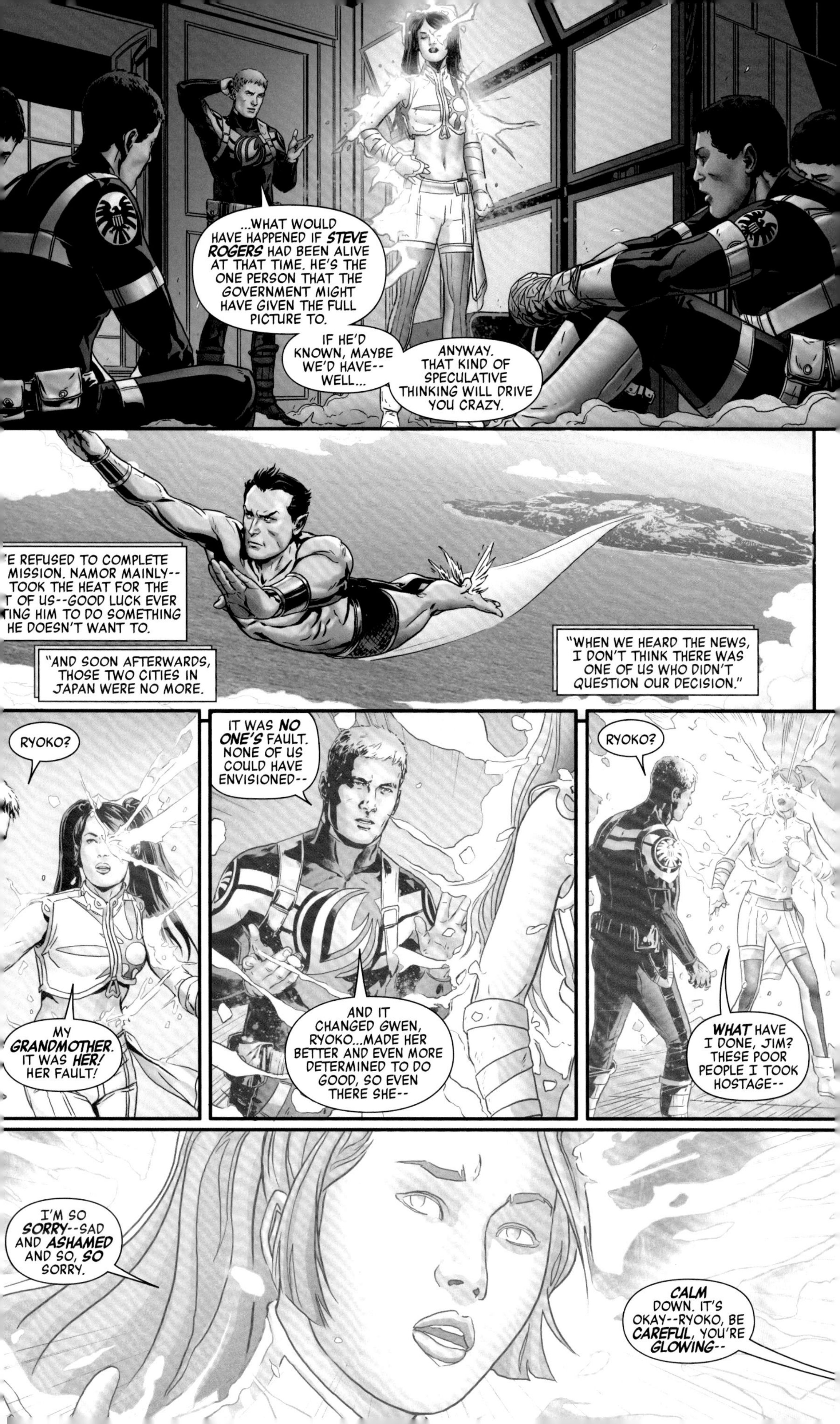
...WHAT WOULD HAVE HAPPENED IF STEVE ROGERS HAD BEEN ALIVE AT THAT TIME. HE'S THE ONE PERSON THAT THE GOVERNMENT MIGHT HAVE GIVEN THE FULL PICTURE TO.
IF HE'D KNOWN, MAYBE WE'D HAVE-- WELL...
ANYWAY. THAT KIND OF SPECULATIVE THINKING WILL DRIVE YOU CRAZY.
'E REFUSED TO COMPLETE MISSION. NAMOR MAINLY-- TOOK THE HEAT FOR THE OF US--GOOD LUCK EVER TING HIM TO DO SOMETHING HE DOESN'T WANT TO.
"AND SOON AFTERWARDS, THOSE TWO CITIES IN JAPAN WERE NO MORE.
"WHEN WE HEARD THE NEWS, I DON'T THINK THERE WAS ONE OF US WHO DIDN'T QUESTION OUR DECISION."
RYOKO?
MY GRANDMOTHER. IT WAS HER! HER FAULT!
IT WAS NO ONE'S FAULT. NONE OF US COULD HAVE ENVISIONED--
AND IT CHANGED GWEN, RYOKO...MADE HER BETTER AND EVEN MORE DETERMINED TO DO GOOD, SO EVEN THERE SHE--
RYOKO?
WHAT HAVE I DONE, JIM? THESE POOR PEOPLE I TOOK HOSTAGE--
I'M SO SORRY--SAD AND ASHAMED AND SO, SO SORRY.
CALM DOWN. IT'S OKAY--RYOKO, BE CAREFUL, YOU'RE GLOWING--

SO SHE DESTROYED THE BASE BUT SAVED EVERYONE'S LIVES.

THAT'S THE UPSHOT, YEAH, AND THEN THE NICE YOUNG MEN AND WOMEN OF S.H.I.E.L.D. MOVED IN WITH THEIR SHINY GUNS AND BODY ARMOR.

WHICH IS WHAT I'M REALLY CURIOUS ABOUT-- WHY YOU DID WHAT YOU DID THEN.

DO NOT MOVE, RADIANCE! DO NOT %^$*E*^ MOVE, OR WE'LL BE FORCED TO--

DO WHAT, SON? LEARN SOME MANNERS? QUITE THE MOUTH ON YOU.

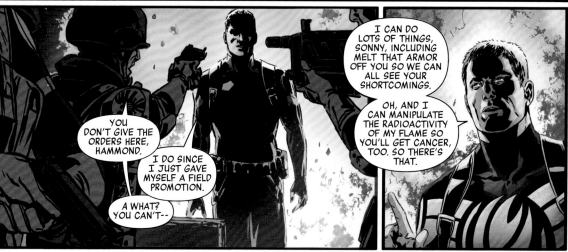

YOU DON'T GIVE THE ORDERS HERE, HAMMOND.

I DO SINCE I JUST GAVE MYSELF A FIELD PROMOTION.

A WHAT? YOU CAN'T--

I CAN DO LOTS OF THINGS, SONNY, INCLUDING MELT THAT ARMOR OFF YOU SO WE CAN ALL SEE YOUR SHORTCOMINGS.

OH, AND I CAN MANIPULATE THE RADIOACTIVITY OF MY FLAME SO YOU'LL GET CANCER, TOO. SO THERE'S THAT.

ALL RADIANCE HERE DID WAS SAVE THE AGENTS IN THE BUILDING.

CAN THEY CORROBORATE THAT?

AT PRESENT THEY'RE ALL UNCONSCIOUS.

CONVENIENT.

WHAT CAN I TELL YOU?

JIM, YOU DIDN'T HAVE TO DO THIS. I WAS MORE THAN PREPARED TO FACE THE MUSIC.

YEAH, THING IS, FROM WHAT I CAN TELL, MOST PEOPLE WOULD PREFER YOU SIMPLY MADE MUSIC INSTEAD.

OH, AND DEFEND YOUR ISLAND NATION FROM GIANT MONSTERS AND CYBORG YAKUZA.

SO GO GET.

I'M SORRY FOR WHAT YOU FOUND OUT. AND THE WAY YOU FOUND OUT FOR THAT MATTER.

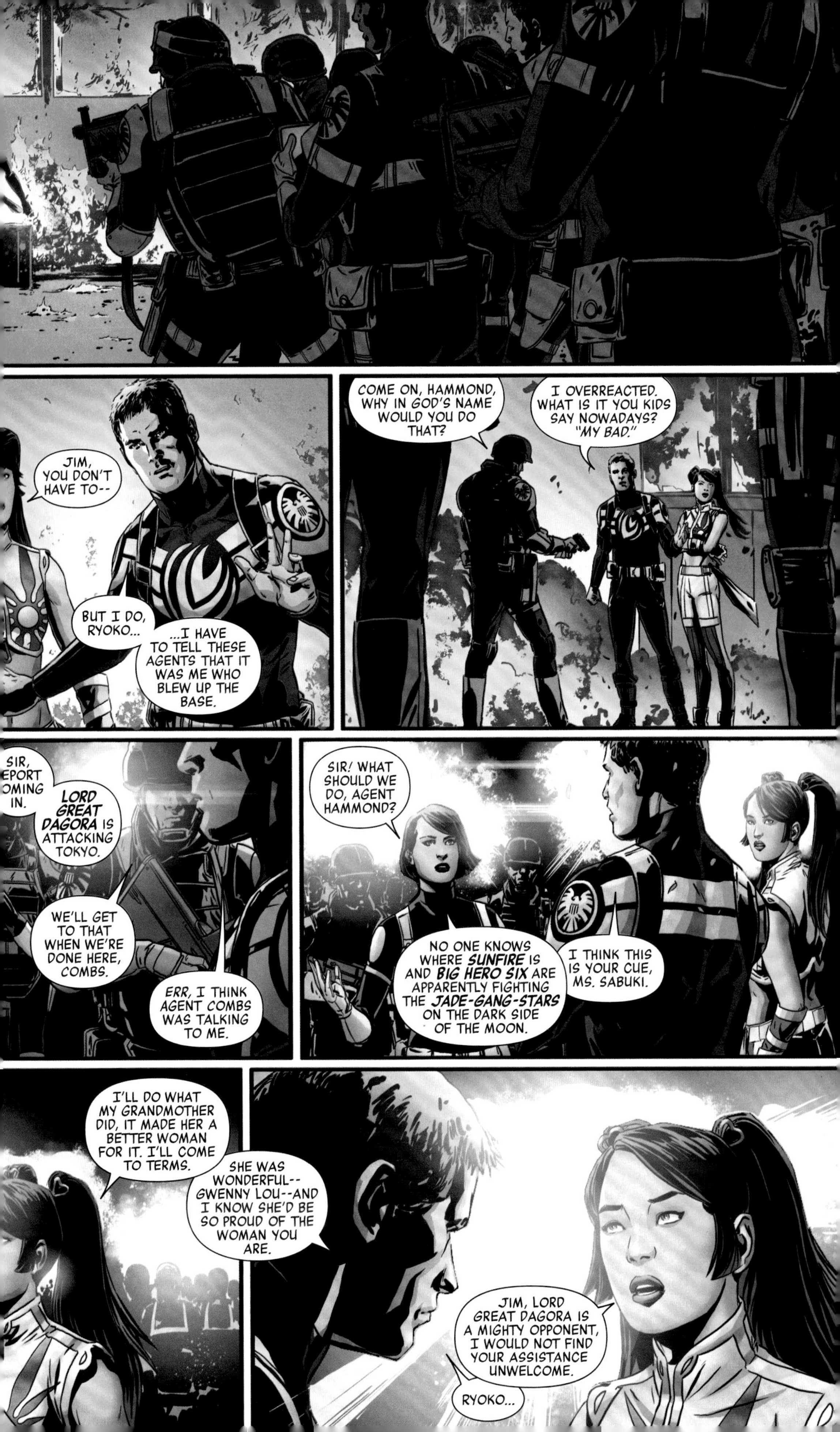
JIM, YOU DON'T HAVE TO--
BUT I DO, RYOKO...
...I HAVE TO TELL THESE AGENTS THAT IT WAS ME WHO BLEW UP THE BASE.
COME ON, HAMMOND, WHY IN GOD'S NAME WOULD YOU DO THAT?
I OVERREACTED. WHAT IS IT YOU KIDS SAY NOWADAYS? "MY BAD."
SIR, EPORT OMING IN. LORD GREAT DAGORA IS ATTACKING TOKYO.
WE'LL GET TO THAT WHEN WE'RE DONE HERE, COMBS.
ERR, I THINK AGENT COMBS WAS TALKING TO ME.
SIR! WHAT SHOULD WE DO, AGENT HAMMOND?
NO ONE KNOWS WHERE SUNFIRE IS AND BIG HERO SIX ARE APPARENTLY FIGHTING THE JADE-GANG-STARS ON THE DARK SIDE OF THE MOON.
I THINK THIS IS YOUR CUE, MS. SABUKI.
I'LL DO WHAT MY GRANDMOTHER DID, IT MADE HER A BETTER WOMAN FOR IT. I'LL COME TO TERMS.
SHE WAS WONDERFUL-- GWENNY LOU--AND I KNOW SHE'D BE SO PROUD OF THE WOMAN YOU ARE.
JIM, LORD GREAT DAGORA IS A MIGHTY OPPONENT, I WOULD NOT FIND YOUR ASSISTANCE UNWELCOME.
RYOKO...

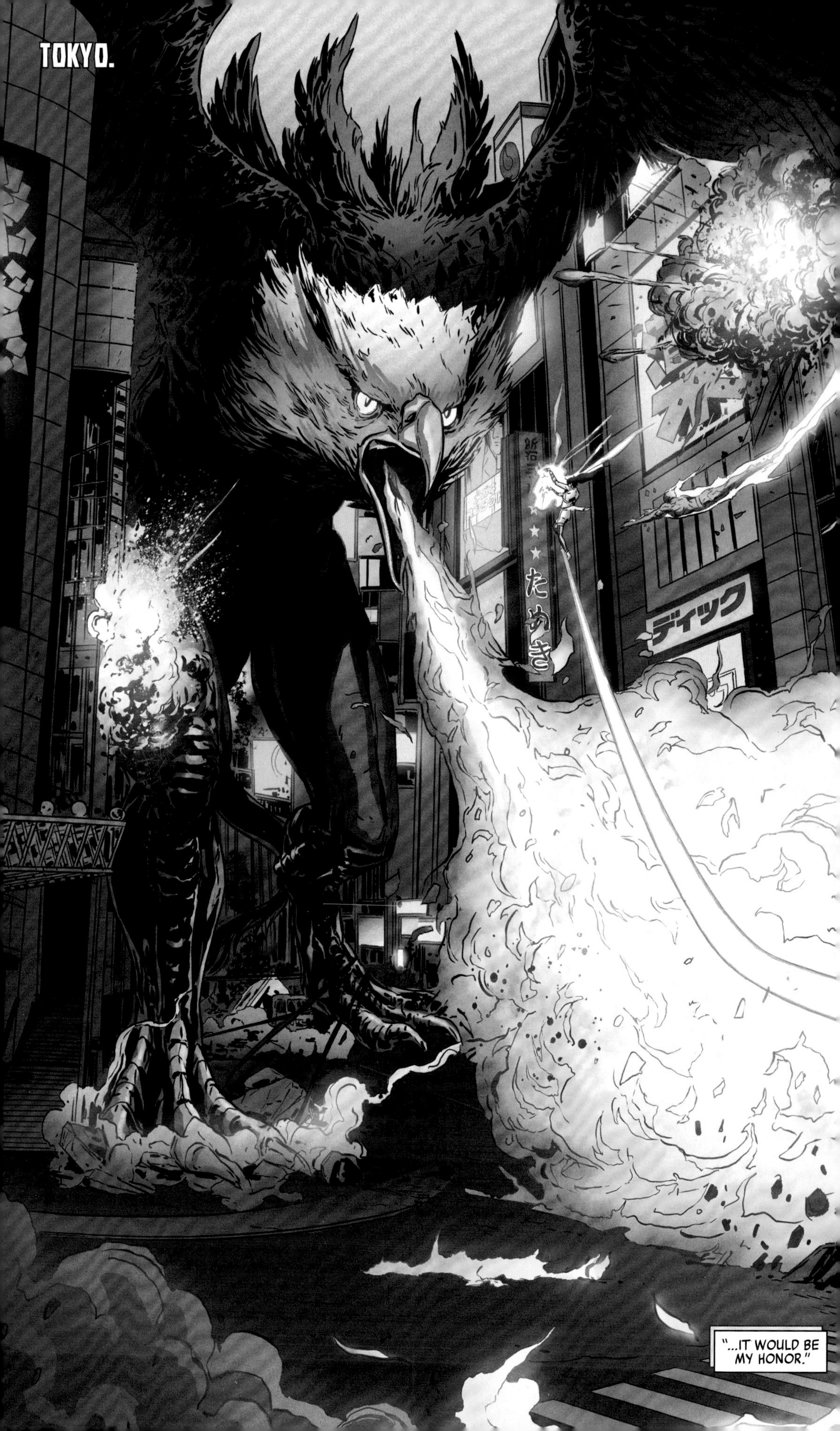
TOKYO.
たぬき
ディック
"...IT WOULD BE MY HONOR."

SO WHY *DID* YOU DO IT, AGENT HAMMOND? WHY DID YOU TAKE THE BLAME?

BECAUSE I COULD. AND MAYBE BECAUSE SHE DESERVED IT. OR MAYBE BECAUSE THAT BOSSY, RUDE S.H.I.E.L.D. AGENT BUGGED THE HELL OUT OF ME.

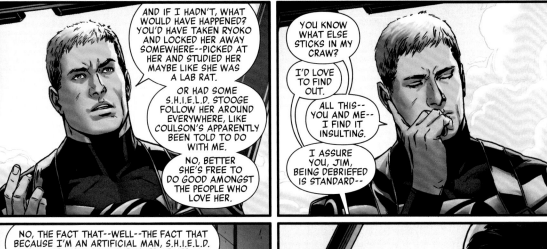

AND IF I HADN'T, WHAT WOULD HAVE HAPPENED? YOU'D HAVE TAKEN RYOKO AND LOCKED HER AWAY SOMEWHERE--PICKED AT HER AND STUDIED HER MAYBE LIKE SHE WAS A LAB RAT.

OR HAD SOME S.H.I.E.L.D. STOOGE FOLLOW HER AROUND EVERYWHERE, LIKE COULSON'S APPARENTLY BEEN TOLD TO DO WITH ME.

NO, BETTER SHE'S FREE TO DO GOOD AMONGST THE PEOPLE WHO LOVE HER.

YOU KNOW WHAT ELSE STICKS IN MY CRAW?

I'D LOVE TO FIND OUT.

ALL THIS-- YOU AND ME-- I FIND IT INSULTING.

I ASSURE YOU, JIM, BEING DEBRIEFED IS STANDARD--

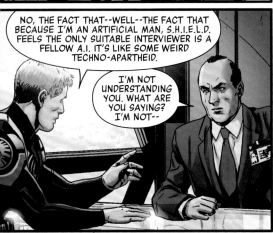

NO, THE FACT THAT--WELL--THE FACT THAT BECAUSE I'M AN ARTIFICIAL MAN, S.H.I.E.L.D. FEELS THE ONLY SUITABLE INTERVIEWER IS A FELLOW A.I. IT'S LIKE SOME WEIRD TECHNO-APARTHEID.

I'M NOT UNDERSTANDING YOU. WHAT ARE YOU SAYING? I'M NOT--

OH COME ON, "MALLOY," I'VE KNOWN FROM THE MOMENT I SAT DOWN. I CAN ALWAYS TELL, NO MATTER HOW SOPHISTICATED--

AGENT HAMMOND, I ASSURE YOU THAT-- THAT--

OH, TO HELL WITH IT...

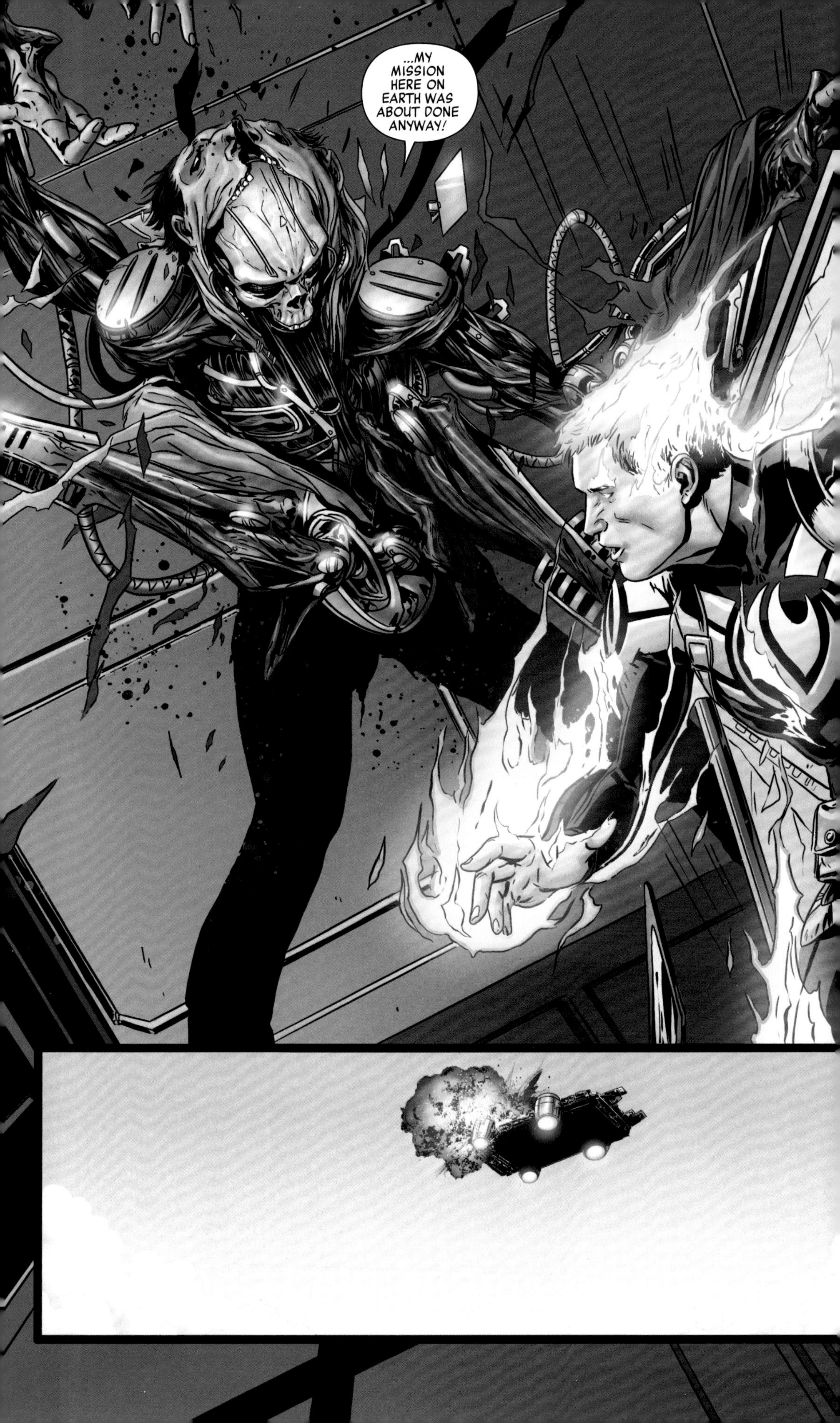
...MY MISSION HERE ON EARTH WAS ABOUT DONE ANYWAY!

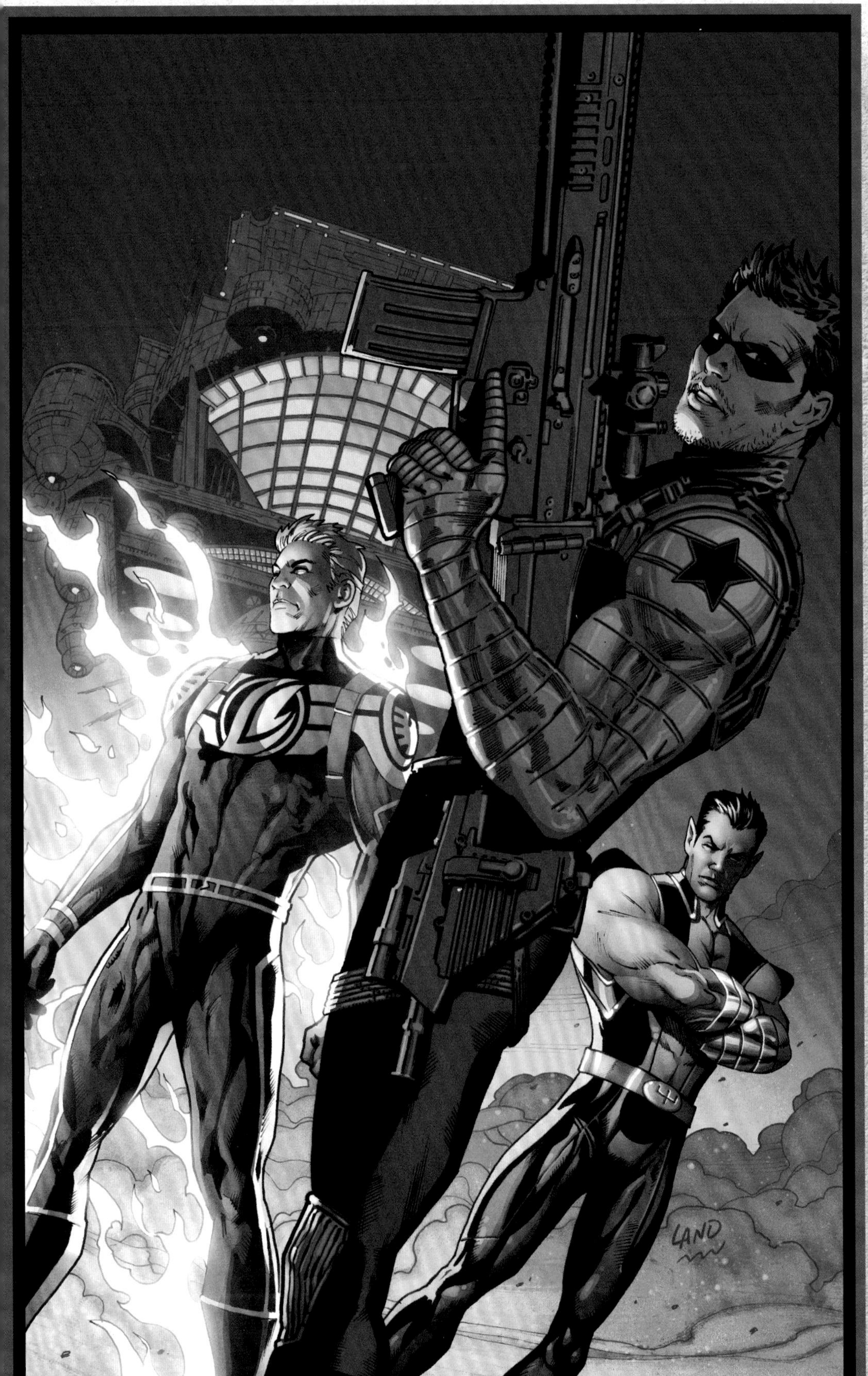
LAND

#8

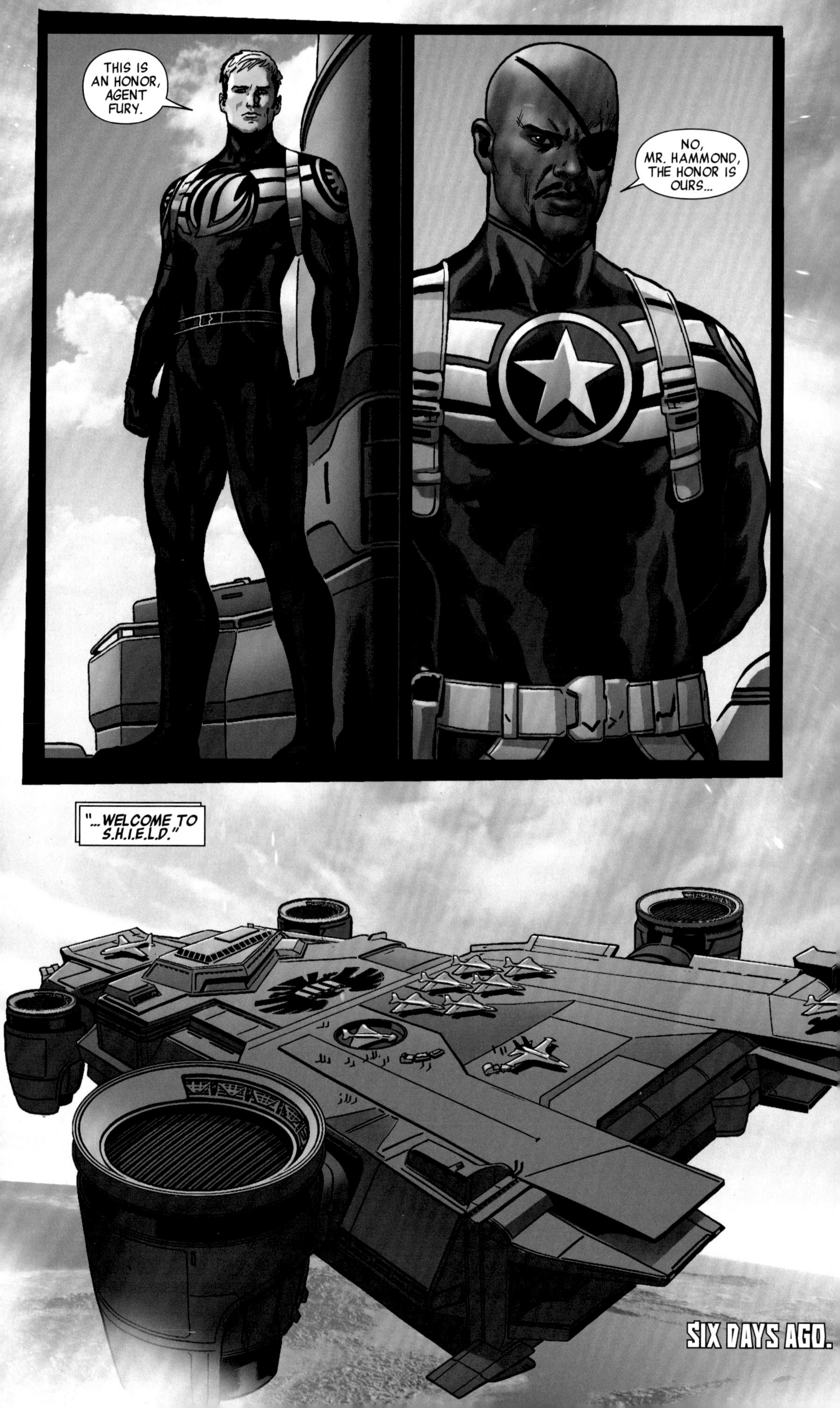
THIS IS AN HONOR, AGENT FURY.
NO, MR. HAMMOND, THE HONOR IS OURS...
"...WELCOME TO S.H.I.E.L.D."
SIX DAYS AGO.

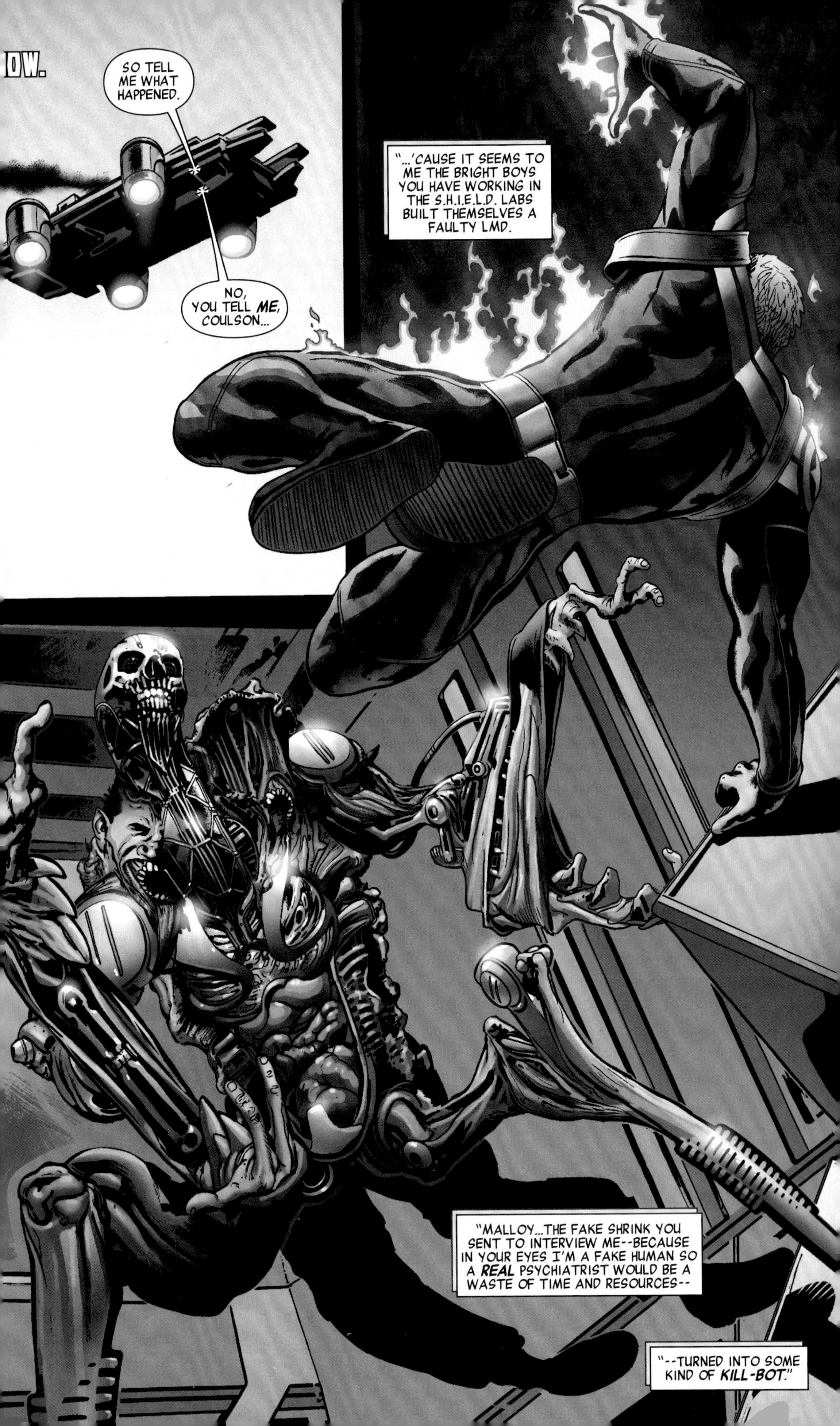
OW.
SO TELL ME WHAT HAPPENED.
NO, YOU TELL **ME**, COULSON...
"...'CAUSE IT SEEMS TO ME THE BRIGHT BOYS YOU HAVE WORKING IN THE S.H.I.E.L.D. LABS BUILT THEMSELVES A FAULTY LMD.
"MALLOY...THE FAKE SHRINK YOU SENT TO INTERVIEW ME--BECAUSE IN YOUR EYES I'M A FAKE HUMAN SO A **REAL** PSYCHIATRIST WOULD BE A WASTE OF TIME AND RESOURCES--
"--TURNED INTO SOME KIND OF **KILL-BOT**."

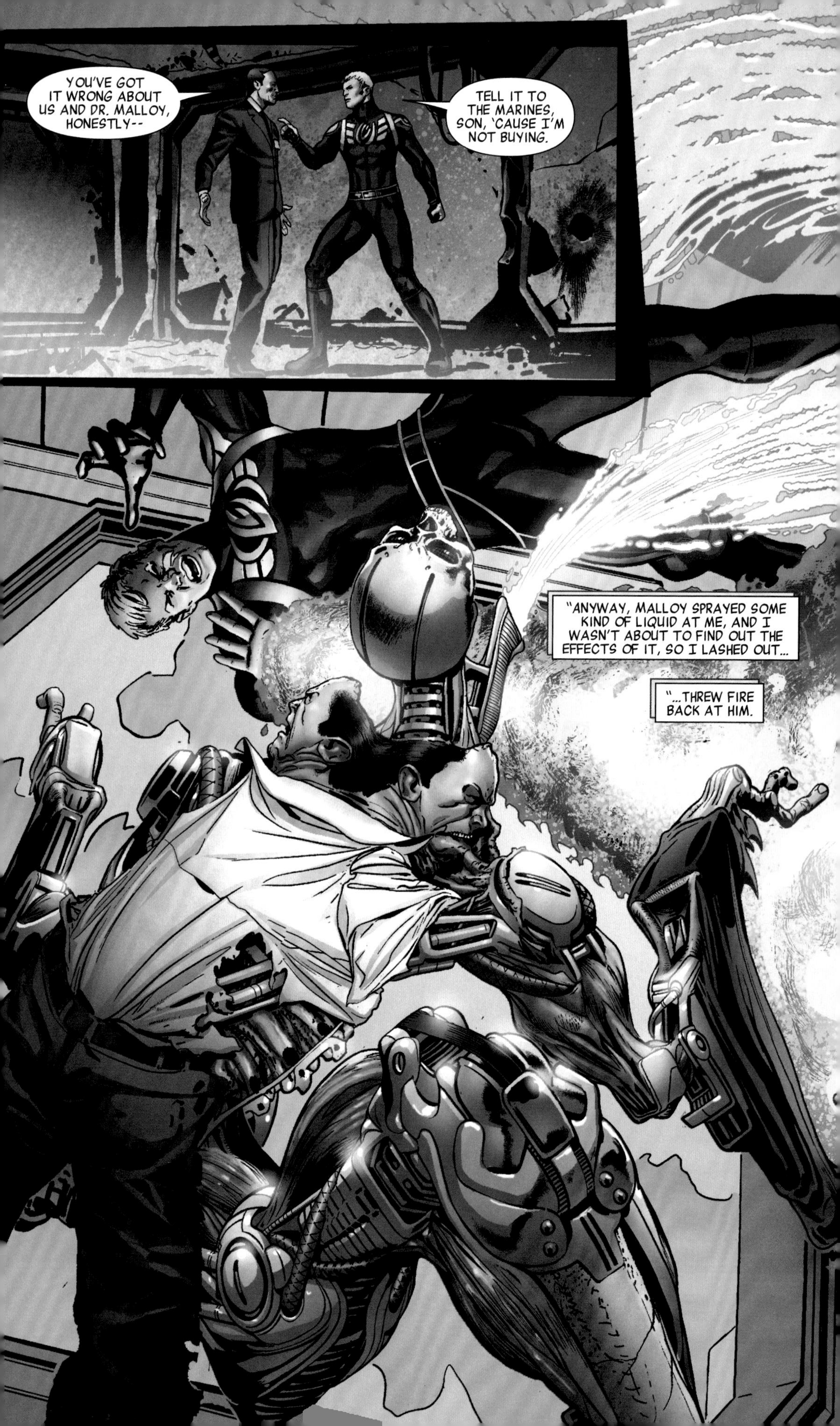
YOU'VE GOT IT WRONG ABOUT US AND DR. MALLOY, HONESTLY--
TELL IT TO THE MARINES, SON, 'CAUSE I'M NOT BUYING.
"ANYWAY, MALLOY SPRAYED SOME KIND OF LIQUID AT ME, AND I WASN'T ABOUT TO FIND OUT THE EFFECTS OF IT, SO I LASHED OUT...
"...THREW FIRE BACK AT HIM.

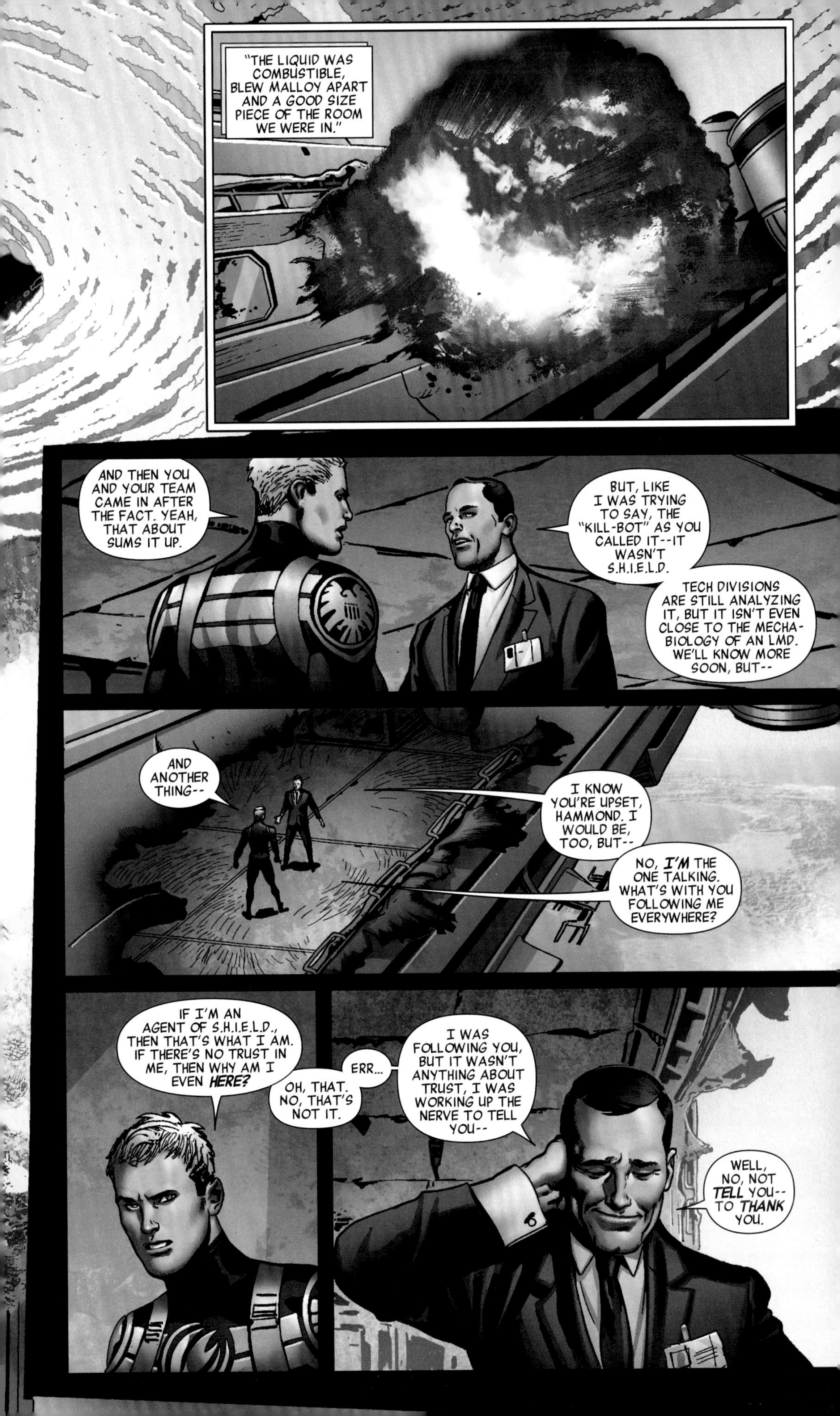
"THE LIQUID WAS COMBUSTIBLE, BLEW MALLOY APART AND A GOOD SIZE PIECE OF THE ROOM WE WERE IN."
AND THEN YOU AND YOUR TEAM CAME IN AFTER THE FACT. YEAH, THAT ABOUT SUMS IT UP.
BUT, LIKE I WAS TRYING TO SAY, THE "KILL-BOT" AS YOU CALLED IT--IT WASN'T S.H.I.E.L.D.
TECH DIVISIONS ARE STILL ANALYZING IT, BUT IT ISN'T EVEN CLOSE TO THE MECHA-BIOLOGY OF AN LMD. WE'LL KNOW MORE SOON, BUT--
AND ANOTHER THING--
I KNOW YOU'RE UPSET, HAMMOND. I WOULD BE, TOO, BUT--
NO, *I'M* THE ONE TALKING. WHAT'S WITH YOU FOLLOWING ME EVERYWHERE?
IF I'M AN AGENT OF S.H.I.E.L.D., THEN THAT'S WHAT I AM. IF THERE'S NO TRUST IN ME, THEN WHY AM I EVEN *HERE?*
ERR...
OH, THAT. NO, THAT'S NOT IT.
I WAS FOLLOWING YOU, BUT IT WASN'T ANYTHING ABOUT TRUST, I WAS WORKING UP THE NERVE TO TELL YOU--
WELL, NO, NOT *TELL* YOU--TO *THANK* YOU.

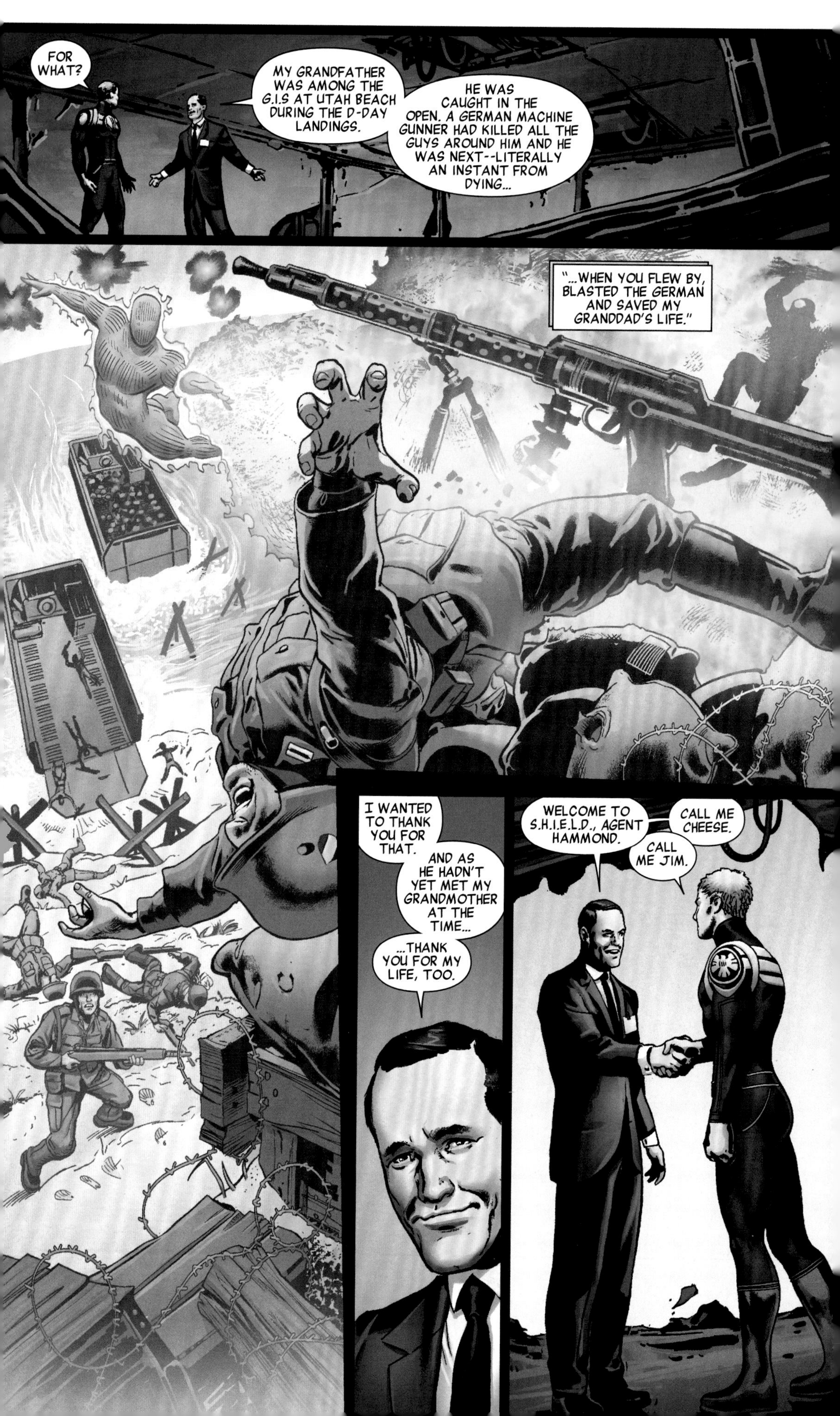
FOR WHAT?
MY GRANDFATHER WAS AMONG THE G.I.S AT UTAH BEACH DURING THE D-DAY LANDINGS.
HE WAS CAUGHT IN THE OPEN. A GERMAN MACHINE GUNNER HAD KILLED ALL THE GUYS AROUND HIM AND HE WAS NEXT--LITERALLY AN INSTANT FROM DYING...
"...WHEN YOU FLEW BY, BLASTED THE GERMAN AND SAVED MY GRANDDAD'S LIFE."
I WANTED TO THANK YOU FOR THAT.
AND AS HE HADN'T YET MET MY GRANDMOTHER AT THE TIME...
...THANK YOU FOR MY LIFE, TOO.
WELCOME TO S.H.I.E.L.D., AGENT HAMMOND.
CALL ME CHEESE.
CALL ME JIM.

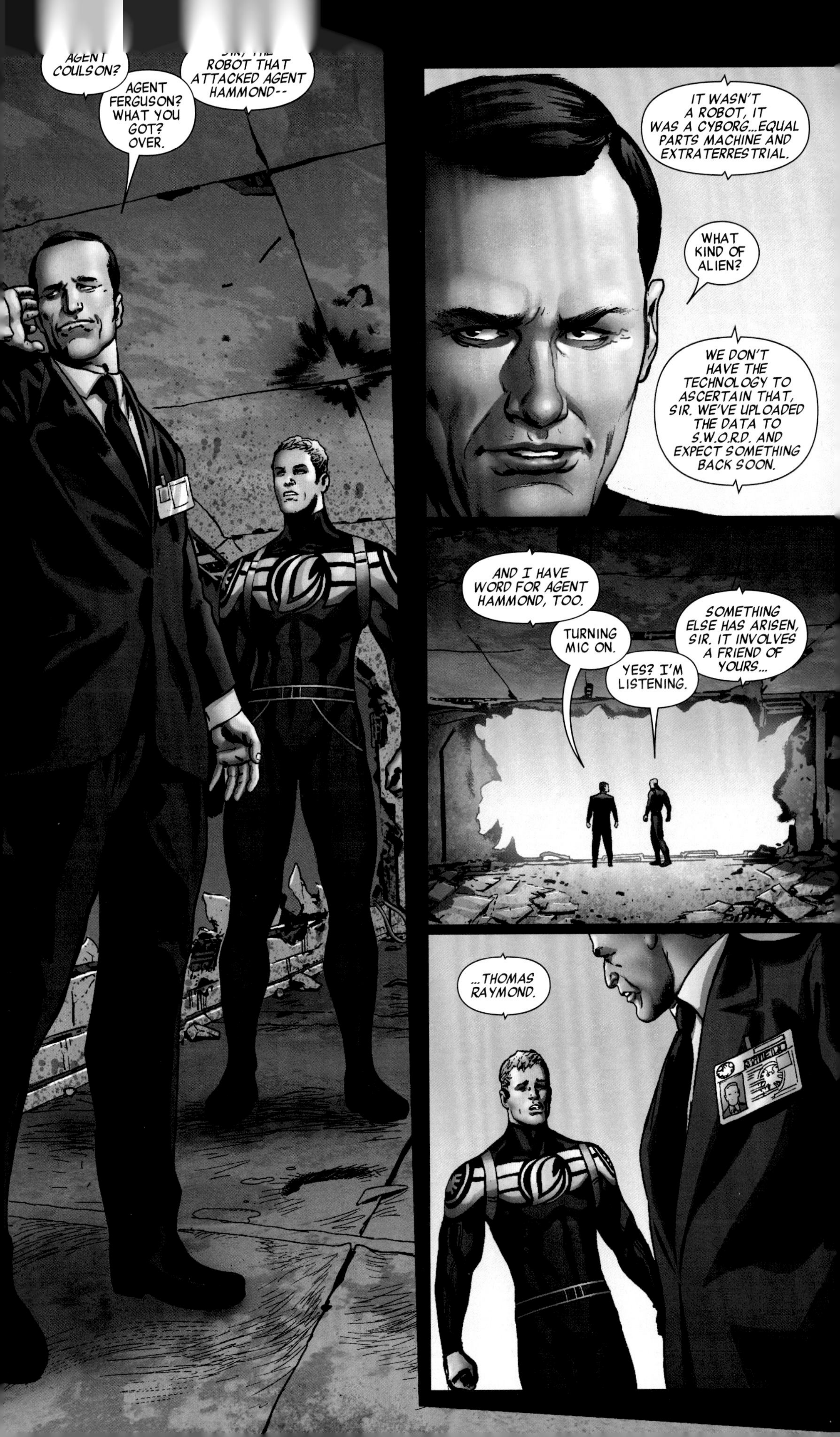
AGENT COULSON?
AGENT FERGUSON? WHAT YOU GOT? OVER.
ROBOT THAT ATTACKED AGENT HAMMOND--
IT WASN'T A ROBOT, IT WAS A CYBORG...EQUAL PARTS MACHINE AND EXTRATERRESTRIAL.
WHAT KIND OF ALIEN?
WE DON'T HAVE THE TECHNOLOGY TO ASCERTAIN THAT, SIR. WE'VE UPLOADED THE DATA TO S.W.O.R.D. AND EXPECT SOMETHING BACK SOON.
AND I HAVE WORD FOR AGENT HAMMOND, TOO.
TURNING MIC ON.
YES? I'M LISTENING.
SOMETHING ELSE HAS ARISEN, SIR. IT INVOLVES A FRIEND OF YOURS...
...THOMAS RAYMOND.

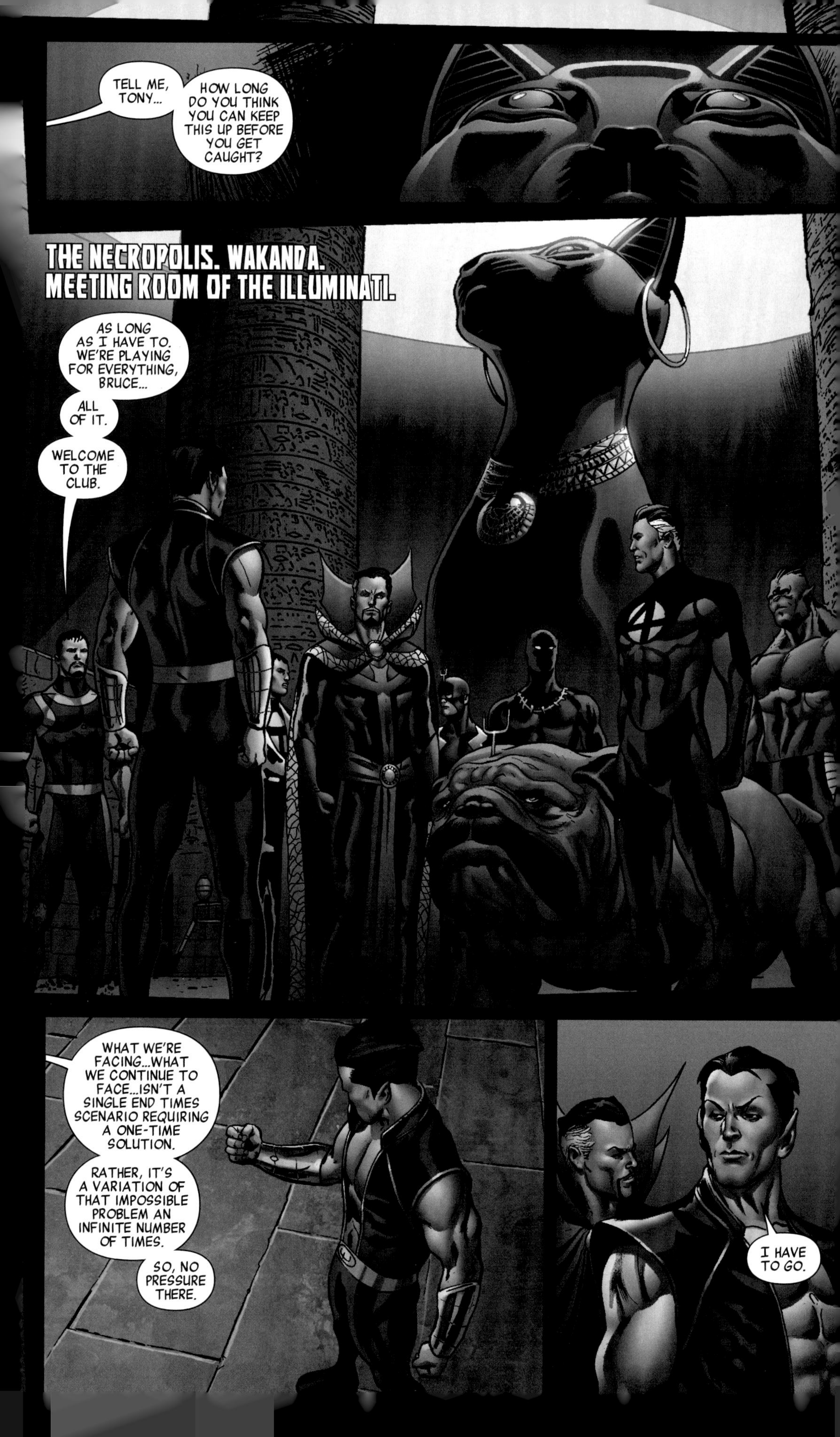
TELL ME, TONY...
HOW LONG DO YOU THINK YOU CAN KEEP THIS UP BEFORE YOU GET CAUGHT?
THE NECROPOLIS. WAKANDA. MEETING ROOM OF THE ILLUMINATI.
AS LONG AS I HAVE TO. WE'RE PLAYING FOR EVERYTHING, BRUCE...
ALL OF IT.
WELCOME TO THE CLUB.
WHAT WE'RE FACING...WHAT WE CONTINUE TO FACE...ISN'T A SINGLE END TIMES SCENARIO REQUIRING A ONE-TIME SOLUTION.
RATHER, IT'S A VARIATION OF THAT IMPOSSIBLE PROBLEM AN INFINITE NUMBER OF TIMES.
SO, NO PRESSURE THERE.
I HAVE TO GO.

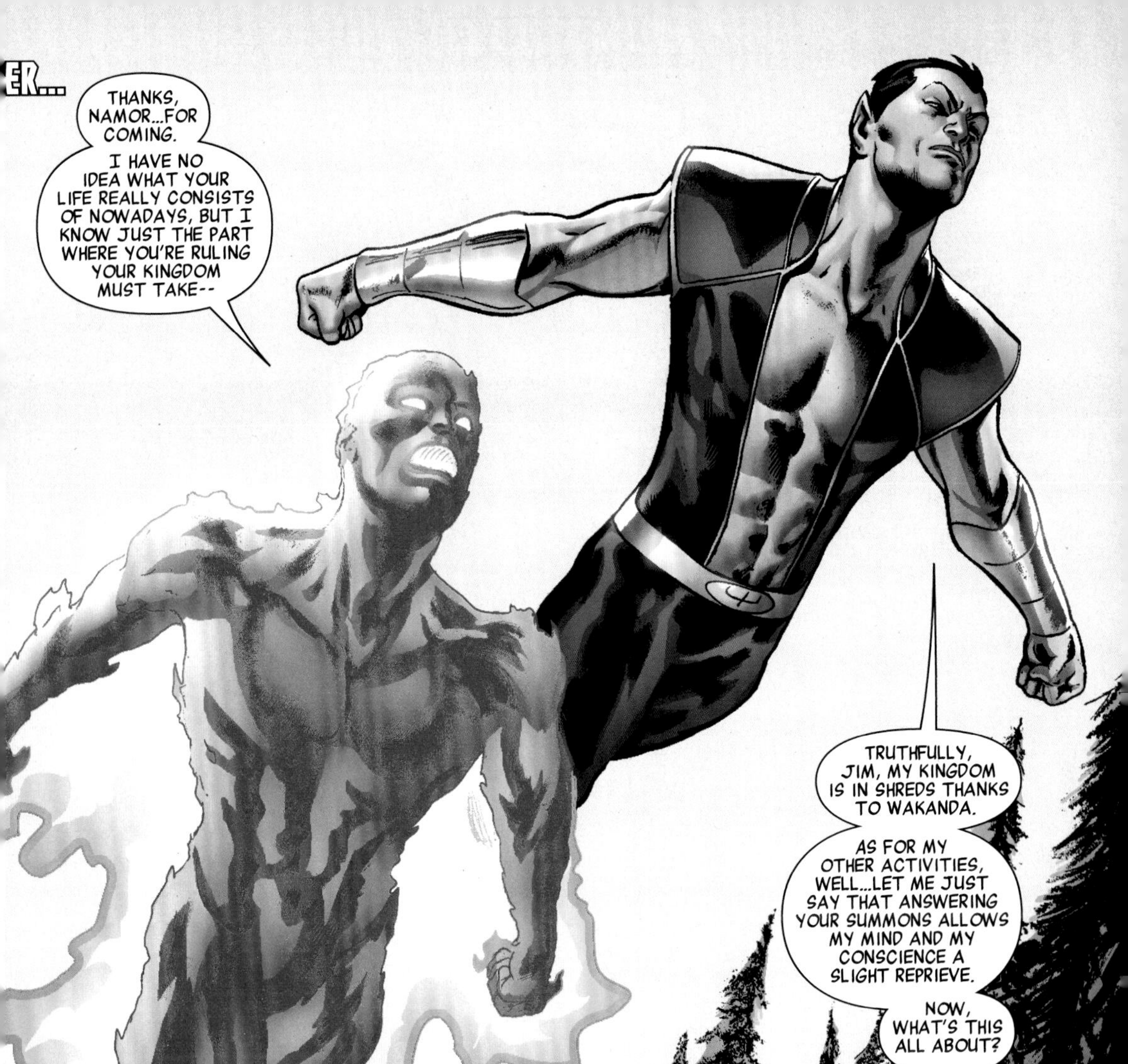
ER...
THANKS, NAMOR...FOR COMING.
I HAVE NO IDEA WHAT YOUR LIFE REALLY CONSISTS OF NOWADAYS, BUT I KNOW JUST THE PART WHERE YOU'RE RULING YOUR KINGDOM MUST TAKE--
TRUTHFULLY, JIM, MY KINGDOM IS IN SHREDS THANKS TO WAKANDA.
AS FOR MY OTHER ACTIVITIES, WELL...LET ME JUST SAY THAT ANSWERING YOUR SUMMONS ALLOWS MY MIND AND MY CONSCIENCE A SLIGHT REPRIEVE.
NOW, WHAT'S THIS ALL ABOUT?

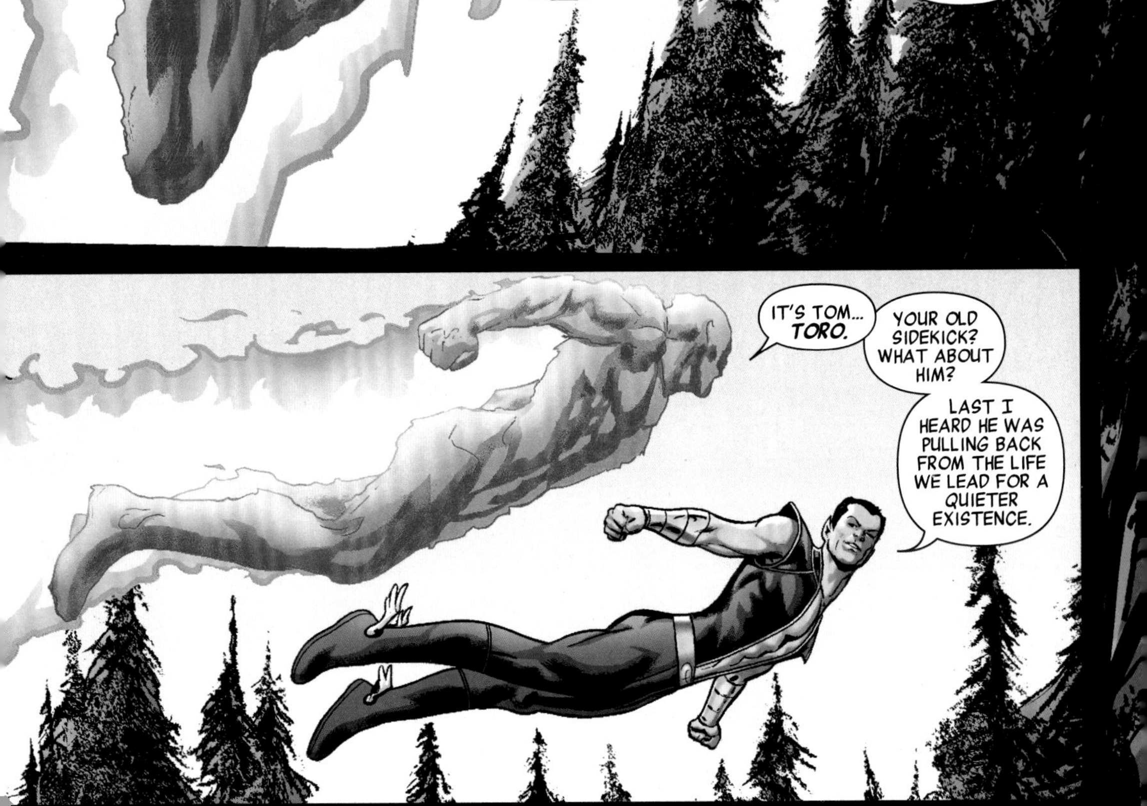
IT'S TOM... ***TORO.***
YOUR OLD SIDEKICK? WHAT ABOUT HIM?
LAST I HEARD HE WAS PULLING BACK FROM THE LIFE WE LEAD FOR A QUIETER EXISTENCE.

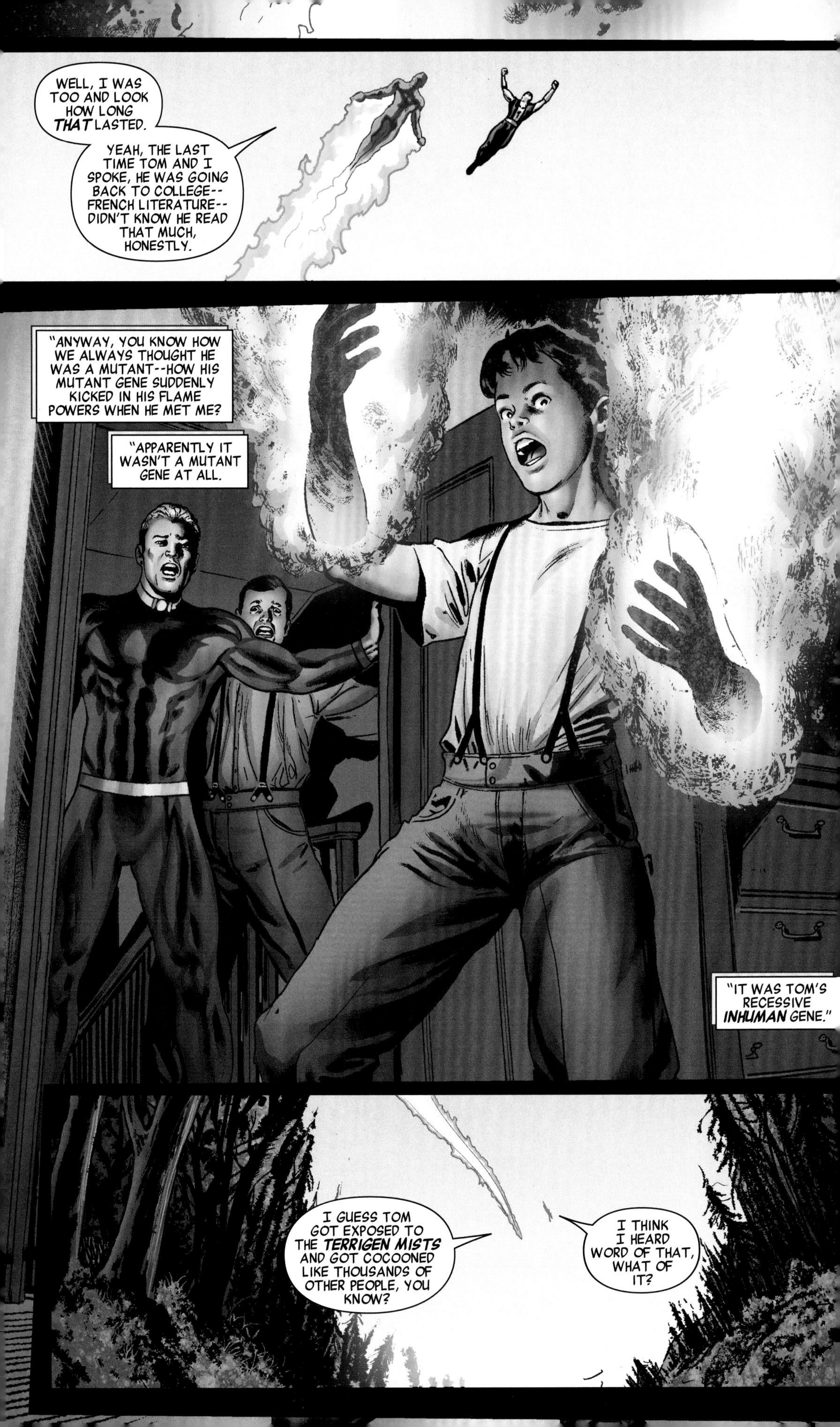
WELL, I WAS TOO AND LOOK HOW LONG *THAT* LASTED.
YEAH, THE LAST TIME TOM AND I SPOKE, HE WAS GOING BACK TO COLLEGE-- FRENCH LITERATURE-- DIDN'T KNOW HE READ THAT MUCH, HONESTLY.
"ANYWAY, YOU KNOW HOW WE ALWAYS THOUGHT HE WAS A MUTANT--HOW HIS MUTANT GENE SUDDENLY KICKED IN HIS FLAME POWERS WHEN HE MET ME?
"APPARENTLY IT WASN'T A MUTANT GENE AT ALL.
"IT WAS TOM'S RECESSIVE *INHUMAN* GENE."
I GUESS TOM GOT EXPOSED TO THE *TERRIGEN MISTS* AND GOT COCOONED LIKE THOUSANDS OF OTHER PEOPLE, YOU KNOW?
I THINK I HEARD WORD OF THAT, WHAT OF IT?

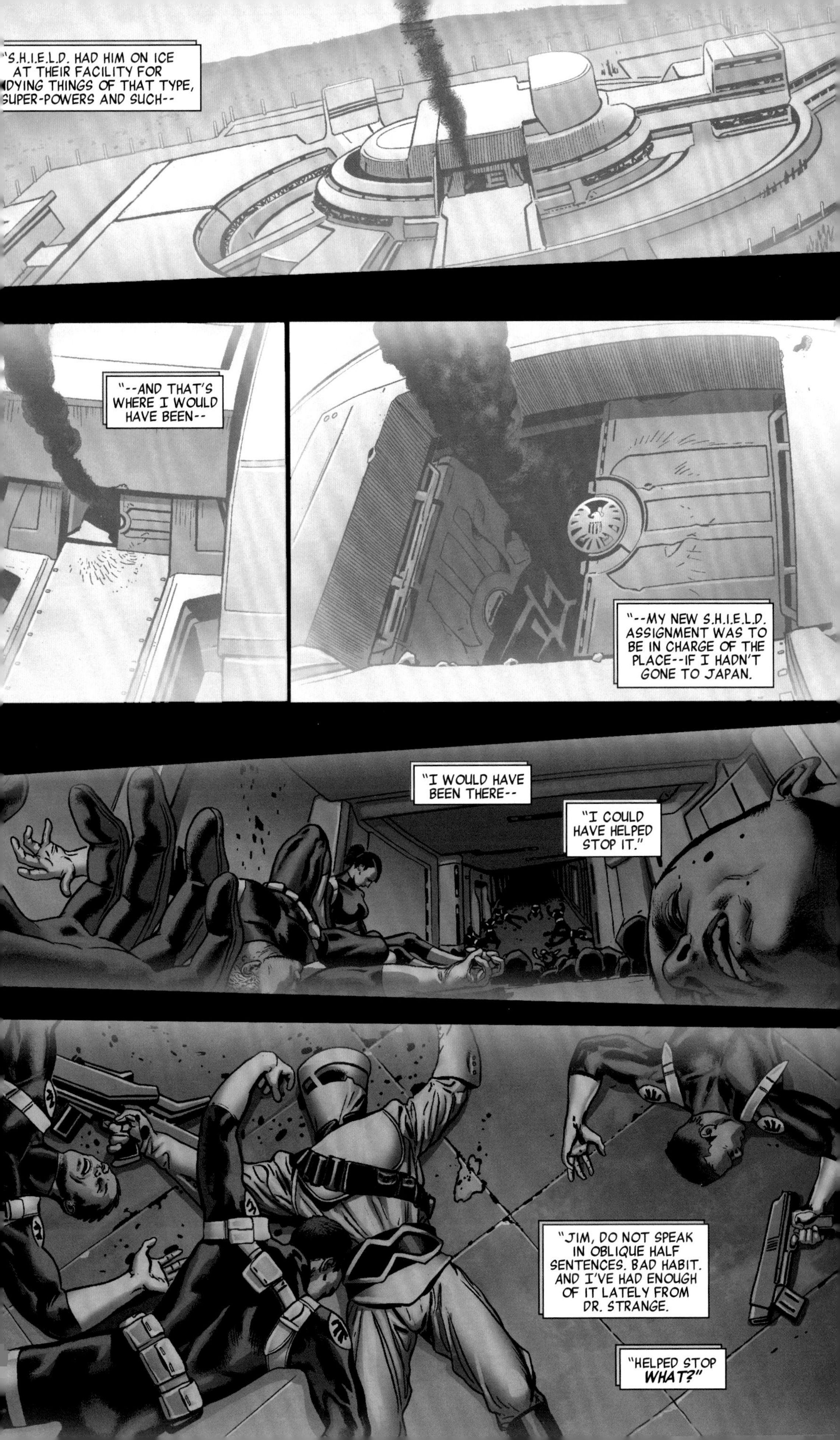
"S.H.I.E.L.D. HAD HIM ON ICE AT THEIR FACILITY FOR DYING THINGS OF THAT TYPE, SUPER-POWERS AND SUCH--
"--AND THAT'S WHERE I WOULD HAVE BEEN--
"--MY NEW S.H.I.E.L.D. ASSIGNMENT WAS TO BE IN CHARGE OF THE PLACE--IF I HADN'T GONE TO JAPAN.
"I WOULD HAVE BEEN THERE--
"I COULD HAVE HELPED STOP IT."
"JIM, DO NOT SPEAK IN OBLIQUE HALF SENTENCES. BAD HABIT. AND I'VE HAD ENOUGH OF IT LATELY FROM DR. STRANGE.
"HELPED STOP *WHAT?*"

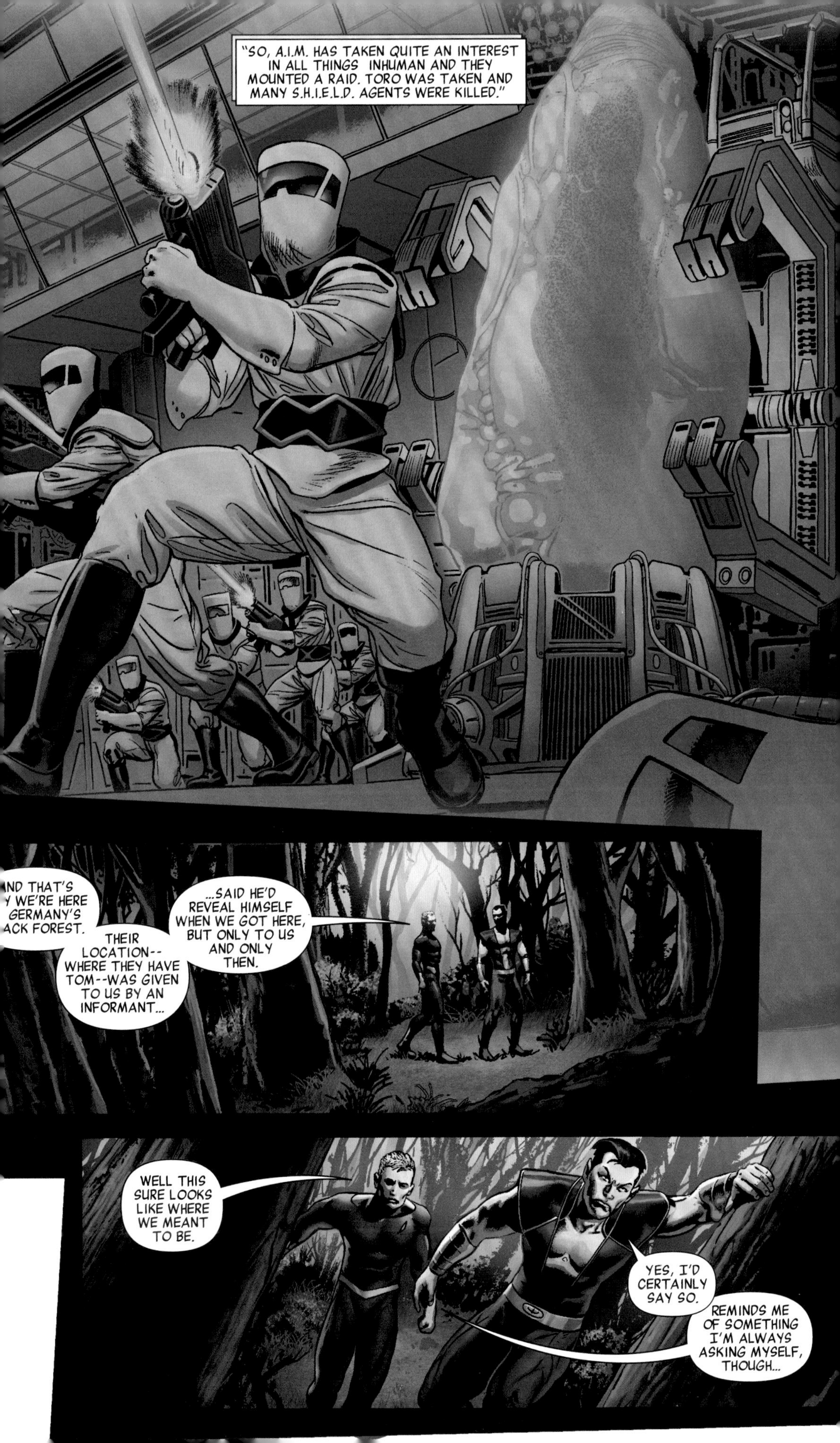

"SO, A.I.M. HAS TAKEN QUITE AN INTEREST IN ALL THINGS INHUMAN AND THEY MOUNTED A RAID. TORO WAS TAKEN AND MANY S.H.I.E.L.D. AGENTS WERE KILLED."
ND THAT'S Y WE'RE HERE GERMANY'S ACK FOREST.
THEIR LOCATION--WHERE THEY HAVE TOM--WAS GIVEN TO US BY AN INFORMANT...
...SAID HE'D REVEAL HIMSELF WHEN WE GOT HERE, BUT ONLY TO US AND ONLY THEN.
WELL THIS SURE LOOKS LIKE WHERE WE MEANT TO BE.
YES, I'D CERTAINLY SAY SO.
REMINDS ME OF SOMETHING I'M ALWAYS ASKING MYSELF, THOUGH...

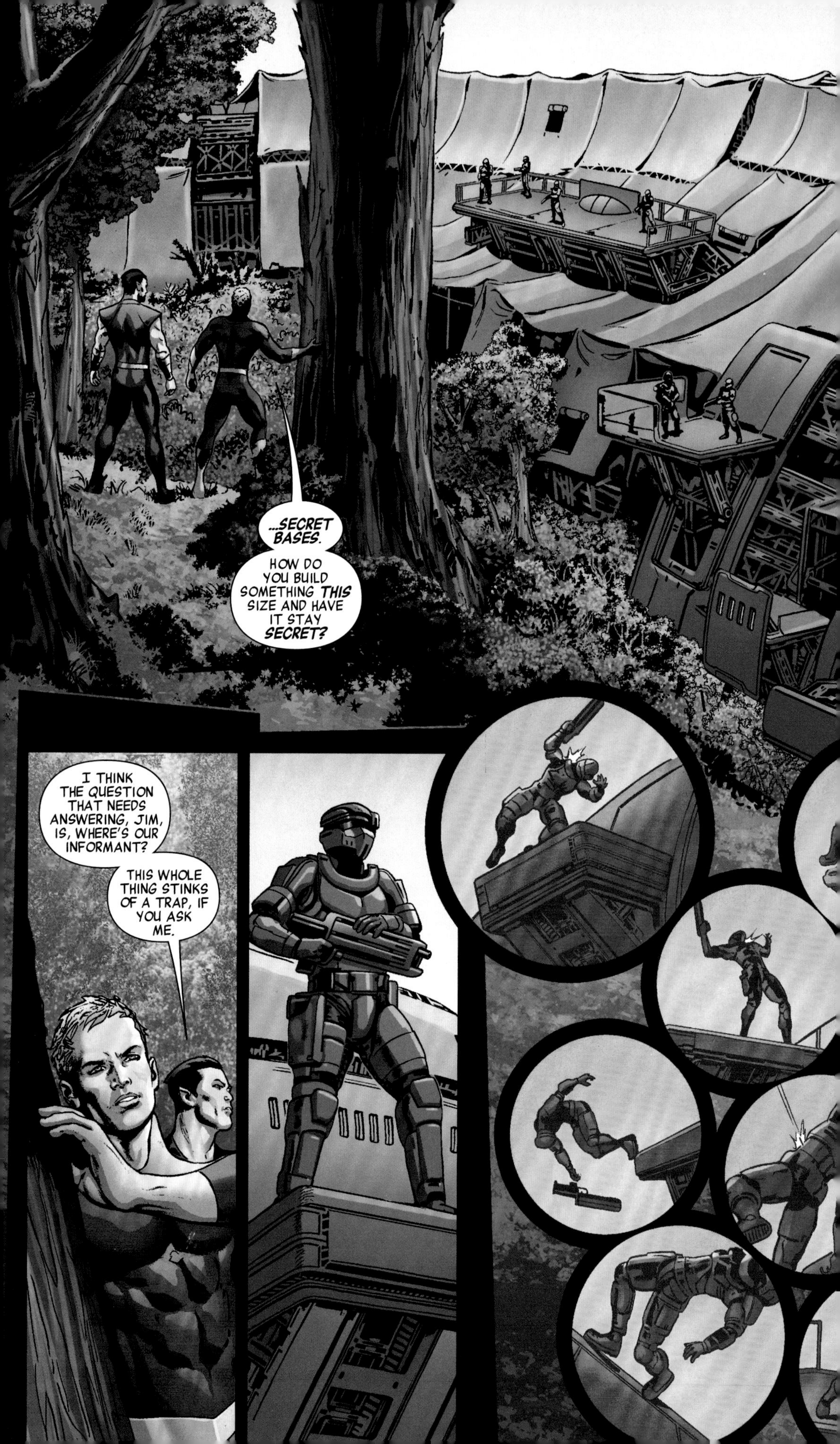
...SECRET BASES.
HOW DO YOU BUILD SOMETHING THIS SIZE AND HAVE IT STAY SECRET?
I THINK THE QUESTION THAT NEEDS ANSWERING, JIM, IS, WHERE'S OUR INFORMANT?
THIS WHOLE THING STINKS OF A TRAP, IF YOU ASK ME.

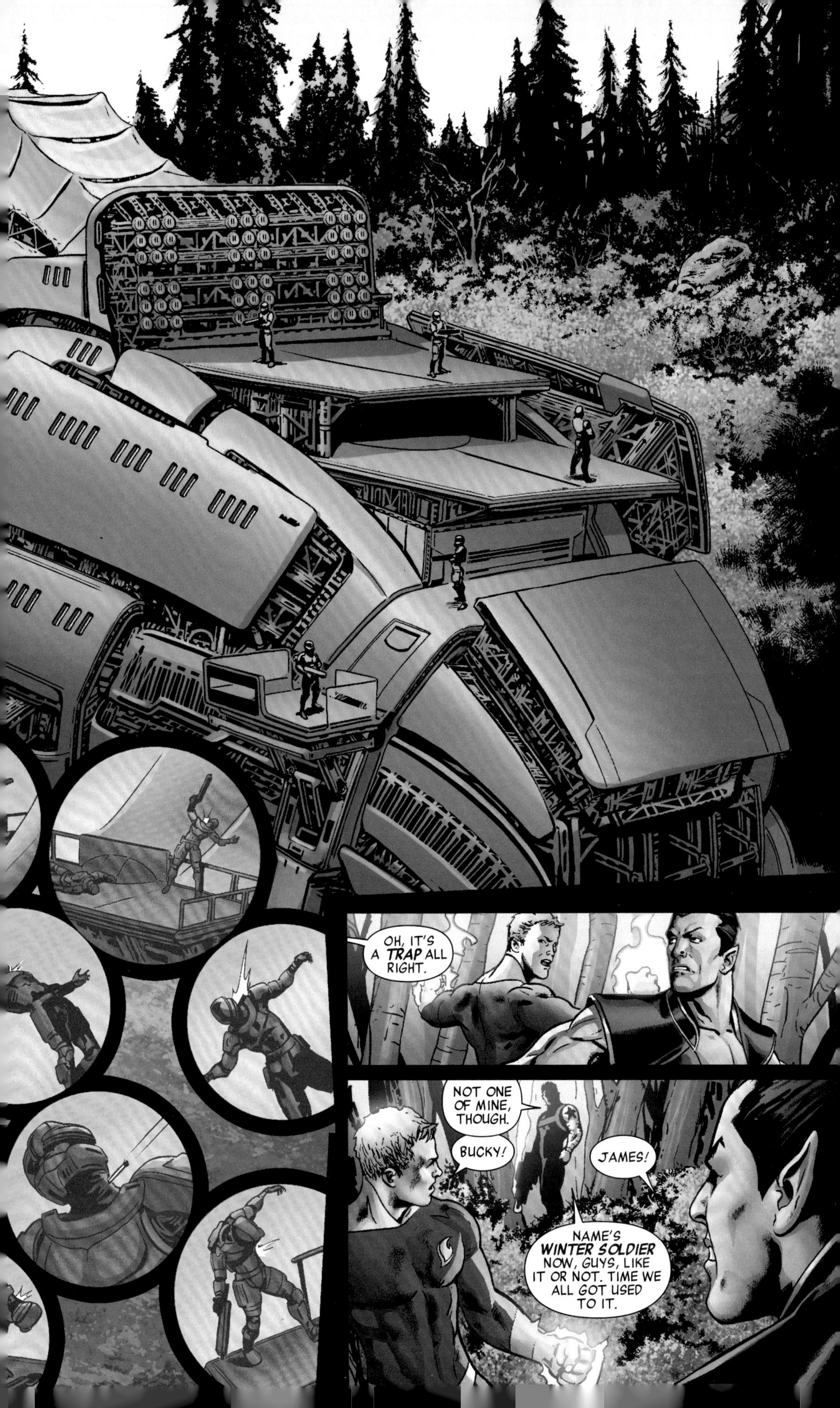
OH, IT'S A TRAP ALL RIGHT.
NOT ONE OF MINE, THOUGH.
BUCKY!
JAMES!
NAME'S WINTER SOLDIER NOW, GUYS, LIKE IT OR NOT. TIME WE ALL GOT USED TO IT.

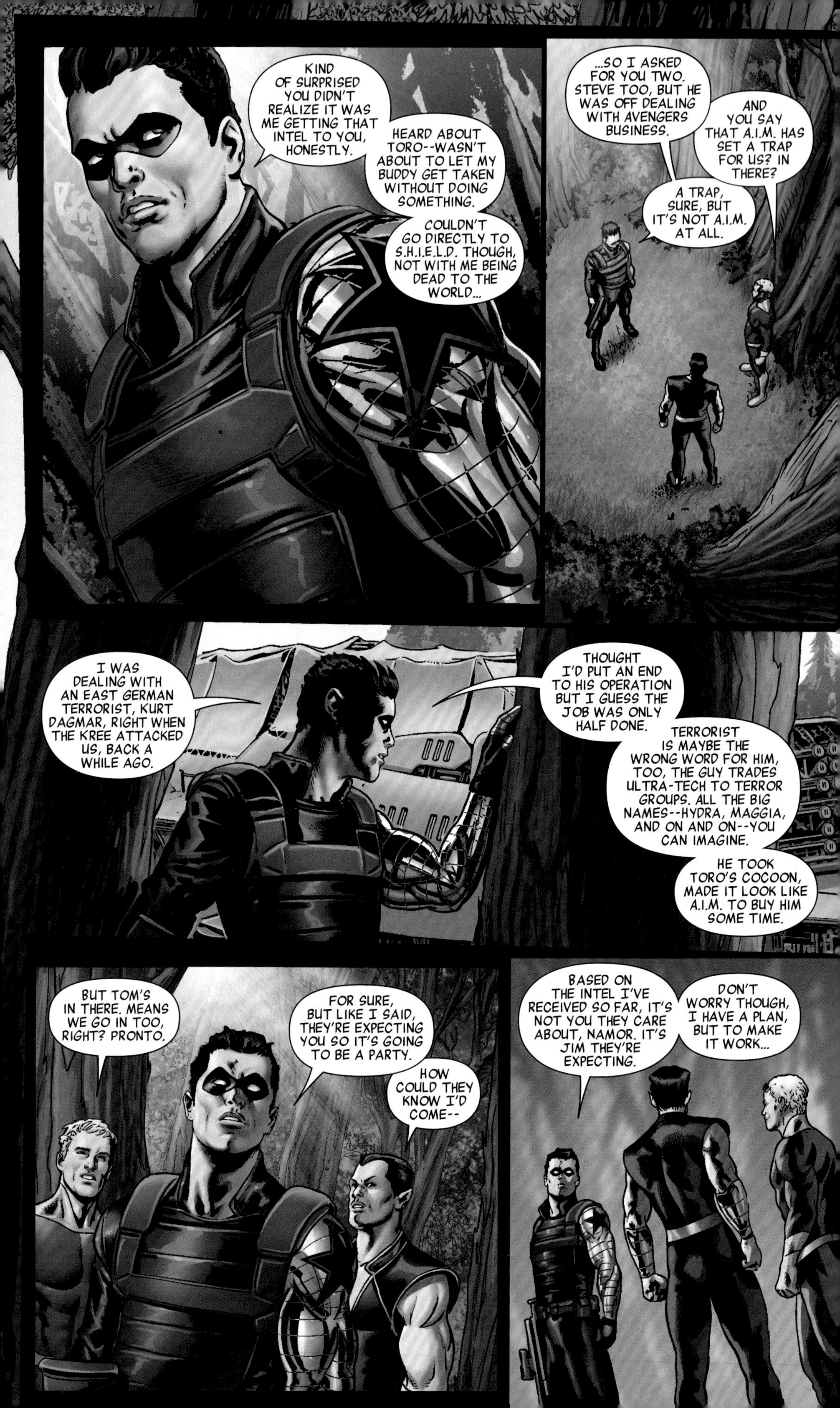
KIND OF SURPRISED YOU DIDN'T REALIZE IT WAS ME GETTING THAT INTEL TO YOU, HONESTLY.
HEARD ABOUT TORO--WASN'T ABOUT TO LET MY BUDDY GET TAKEN WITHOUT DOING SOMETHING.
COULDN'T GO DIRECTLY TO S.H.I.E.L.D. THOUGH, NOT WITH ME BEING DEAD TO THE WORLD...
...SO I ASKED FOR YOU TWO. STEVE TOO, BUT HE WAS OFF DEALING WITH AVENGERS BUSINESS.
AND YOU SAY THAT A.I.M. HAS SET A TRAP FOR US? IN THERE?
A TRAP, SURE, BUT IT'S NOT A.I.M. AT ALL.
I WAS DEALING WITH AN EAST GERMAN TERRORIST, KURT DAGMAR, RIGHT WHEN THE KREE ATTACKED US, BACK A WHILE AGO.
THOUGHT I'D PUT AN END TO HIS OPERATION BUT I GUESS THE JOB WAS ONLY HALF DONE.
TERRORIST IS MAYBE THE WRONG WORD FOR HIM, TOO, THE GUY TRADES ULTRA-TECH TO TERROR GROUPS. ALL THE BIG NAMES--HYDRA, MAGGIA, AND ON AND ON--YOU CAN IMAGINE.
HE TOOK TORO'S COCOON, MADE IT LOOK LIKE A.I.M. TO BUY HIM SOME TIME.
BUT TOM'S IN THERE. MEANS WE GO IN TOO, RIGHT? PRONTO.
FOR SURE, BUT LIKE I SAID, THEY'RE EXPECTING YOU SO IT'S GOING TO BE A PARTY.
HOW COULD THEY KNOW I'D COME--
BASED ON THE INTEL I'VE RECEIVED SO FAR, IT'S NOT YOU THEY CARE ABOUT, NAMOR. IT'S JIM THEY'RE EXPECTING.
DON'T WORRY THOUGH, I HAVE A PLAN, BUT TO MAKE IT WORK...

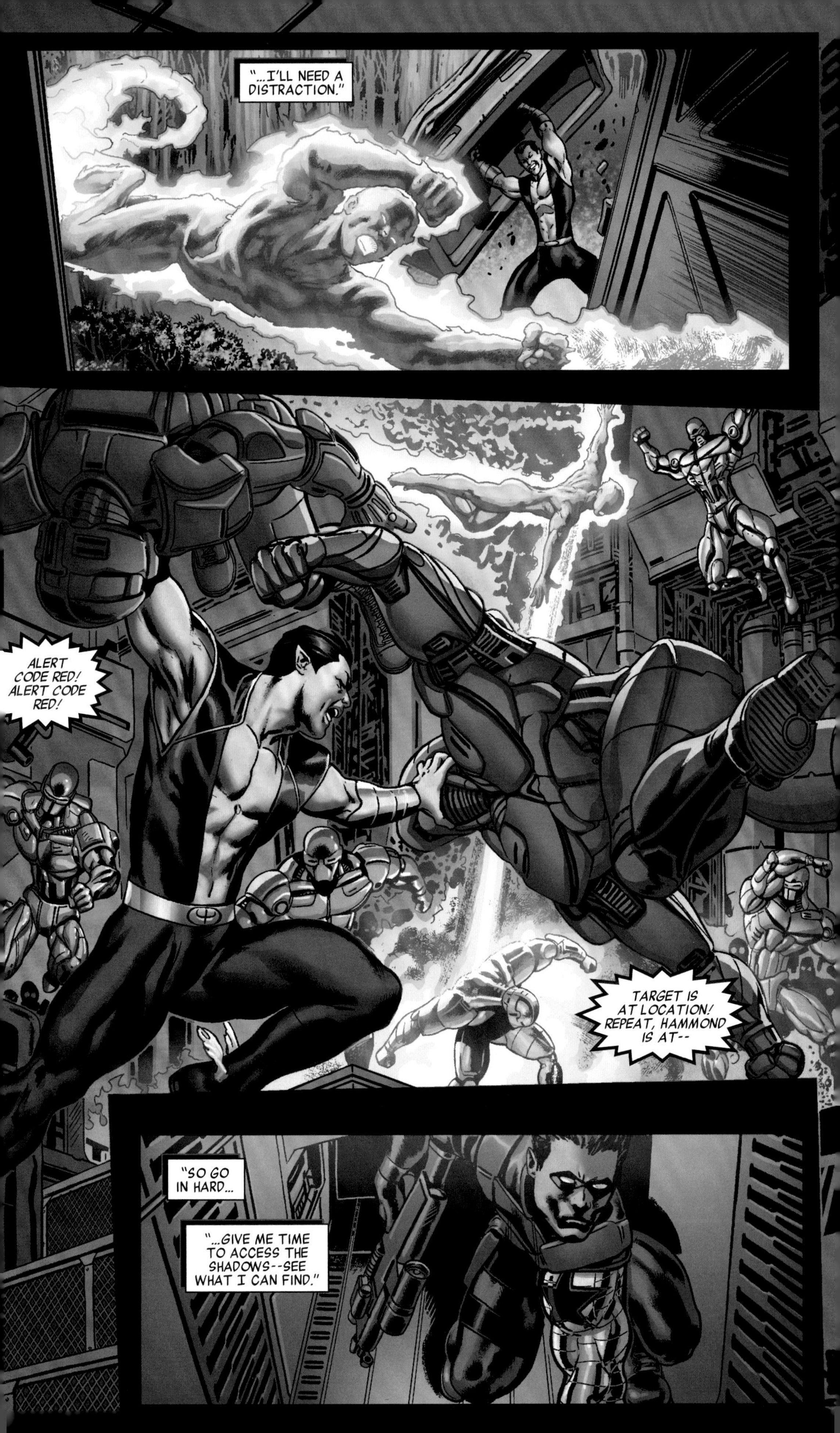
"...I'LL NEED A DISTRACTION."
ALERT CODE RED! ALERT CODE RED!
TARGET IS AT LOCATION! REPEAT, HAMMOND IS AT--
"SO GO IN HARD...
"...GIVE ME TIME TO ACCESS THE SHADOWS--SEE WHAT I CAN FIND."

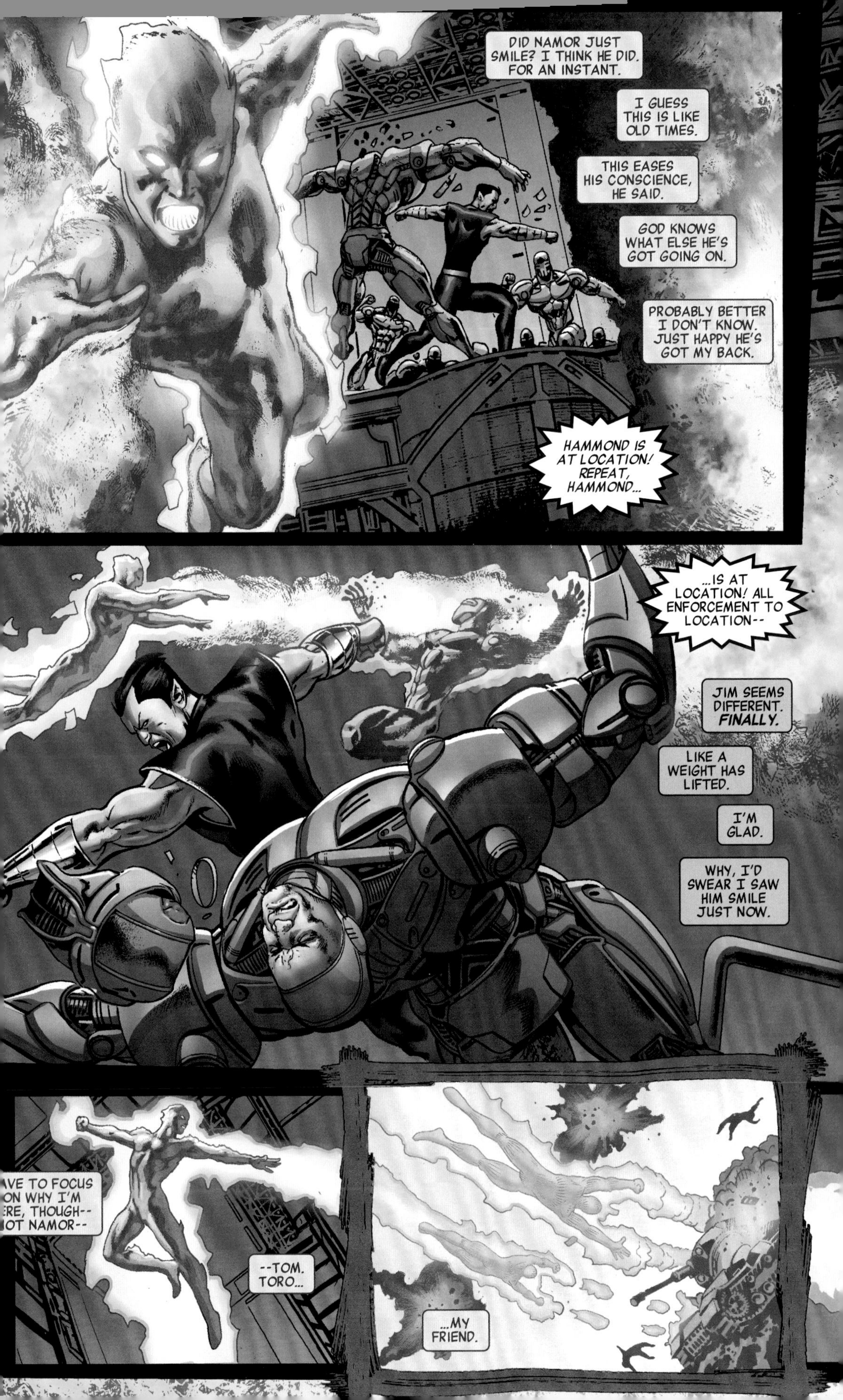

DID NAMOR JUST SMILE? I THINK HE DID. FOR AN INSTANT.
I GUESS THIS IS LIKE OLD TIMES.
THIS EASES HIS CONSCIENCE, HE SAID.
GOD KNOWS WHAT ELSE HE'S GOT GOING ON.
PROBABLY BETTER I DON'T KNOW. JUST HAPPY HE'S GOT MY BACK.
HAMMOND IS AT LOCATION! REPEAT, HAMMOND...
...IS AT LOCATION! ALL ENFORCEMENT TO LOCATION--
JIM SEEMS DIFFERENT. *FINALLY.*
LIKE A WEIGHT HAS LIFTED.
I'M GLAD.
WHY, I'D SWEAR I SAW HIM SMILE JUST NOW.
AVE TO FOCUS ON WHY I'M ERE, THOUGH-- OT NAMOR--
--TOM. TORO...
...MY FRIEND.

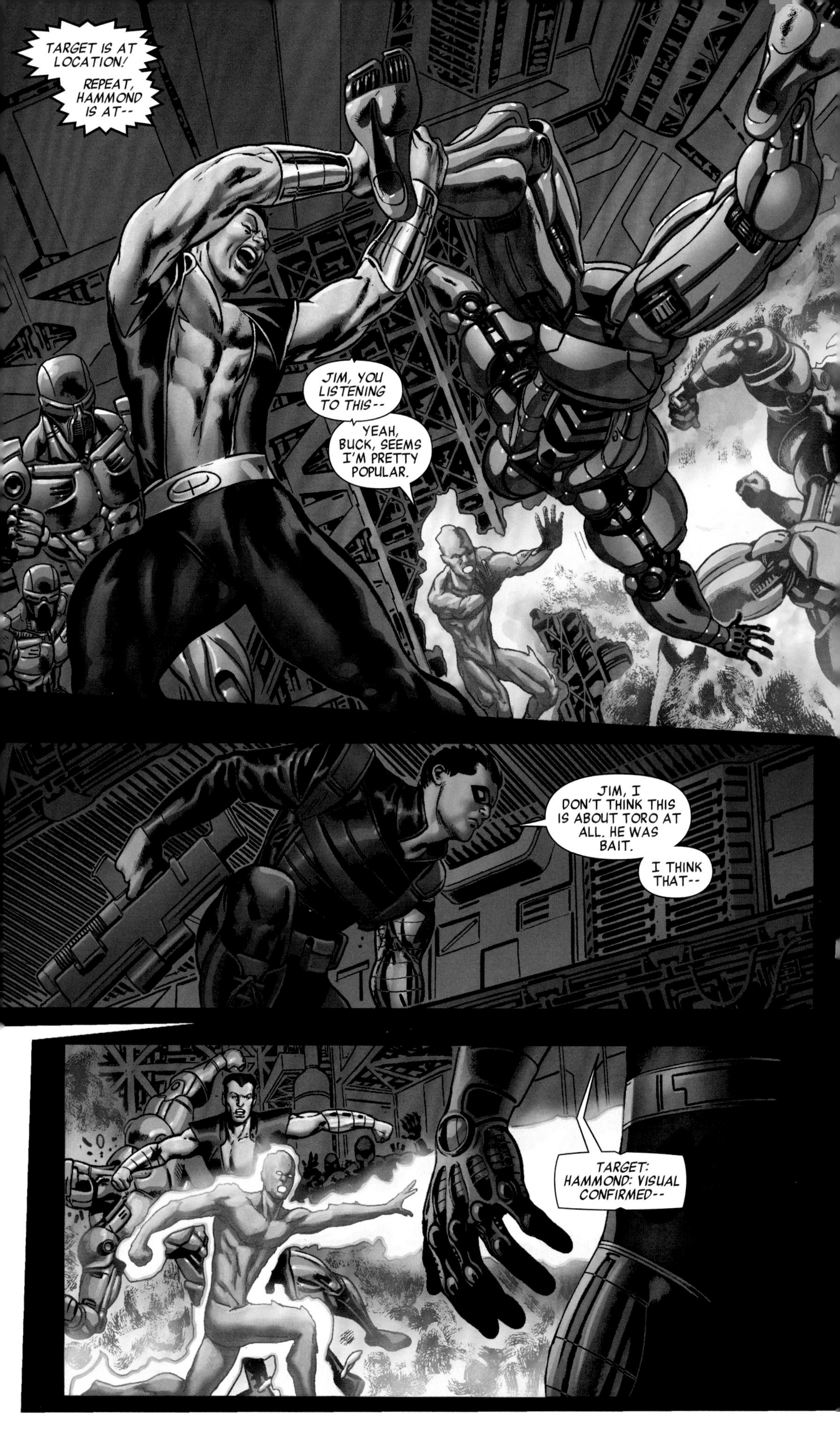
TARGET IS AT LOCATION!
REPEAT, HAMMOND IS AT--
JIM, YOU LISTENING TO THIS--
YEAH, BUCK, SEEMS I'M PRETTY POPULAR.
JIM, I DON'T THINK THIS IS ABOUT TORO AT ALL. HE WAS BAIT.
I THINK THAT--
TARGET: HAMMOND: VISUAL CONFIRMED--

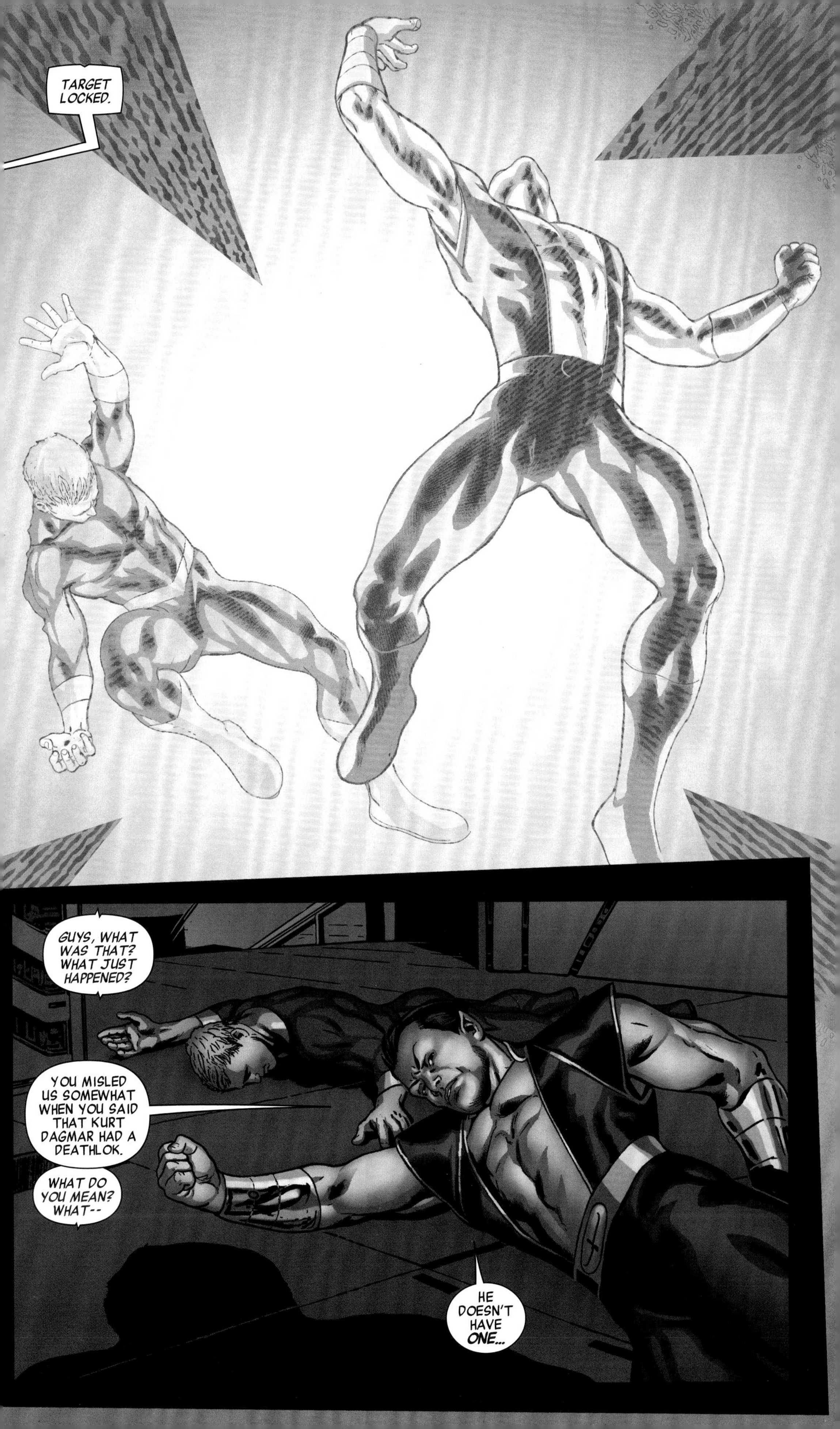
TARGET LOCKED.
GUYS, WHAT WAS THAT? WHAT JUST HAPPENED?
YOU MISLED US SOMEWHAT WHEN YOU SAID THAT KURT DAGMAR HAD A DEATHLOK.
WHAT DO YOU MEAN? WHAT--
HE DOESN'T HAVE ONE...

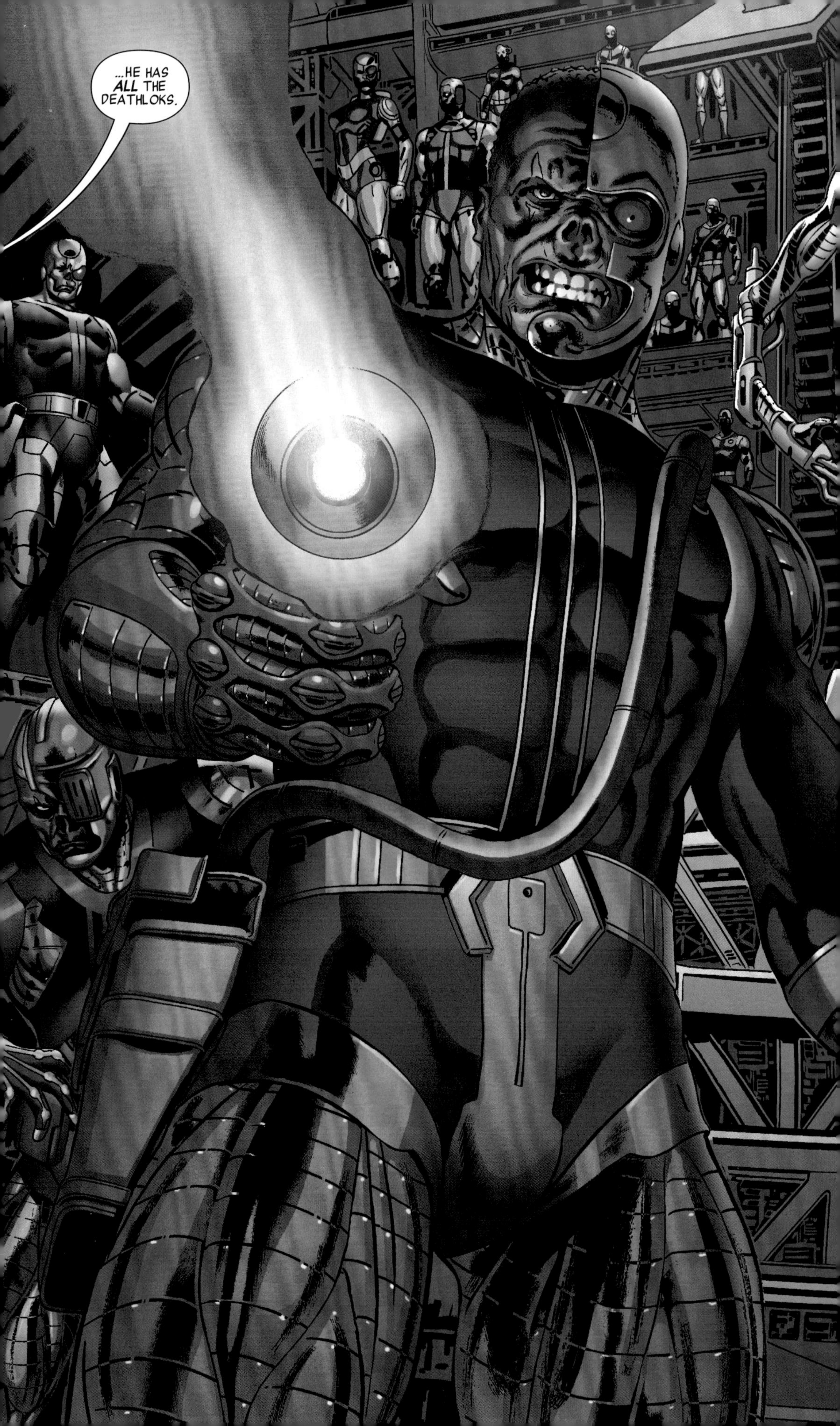
...HE HAS ALL THE DEATHLOKS.

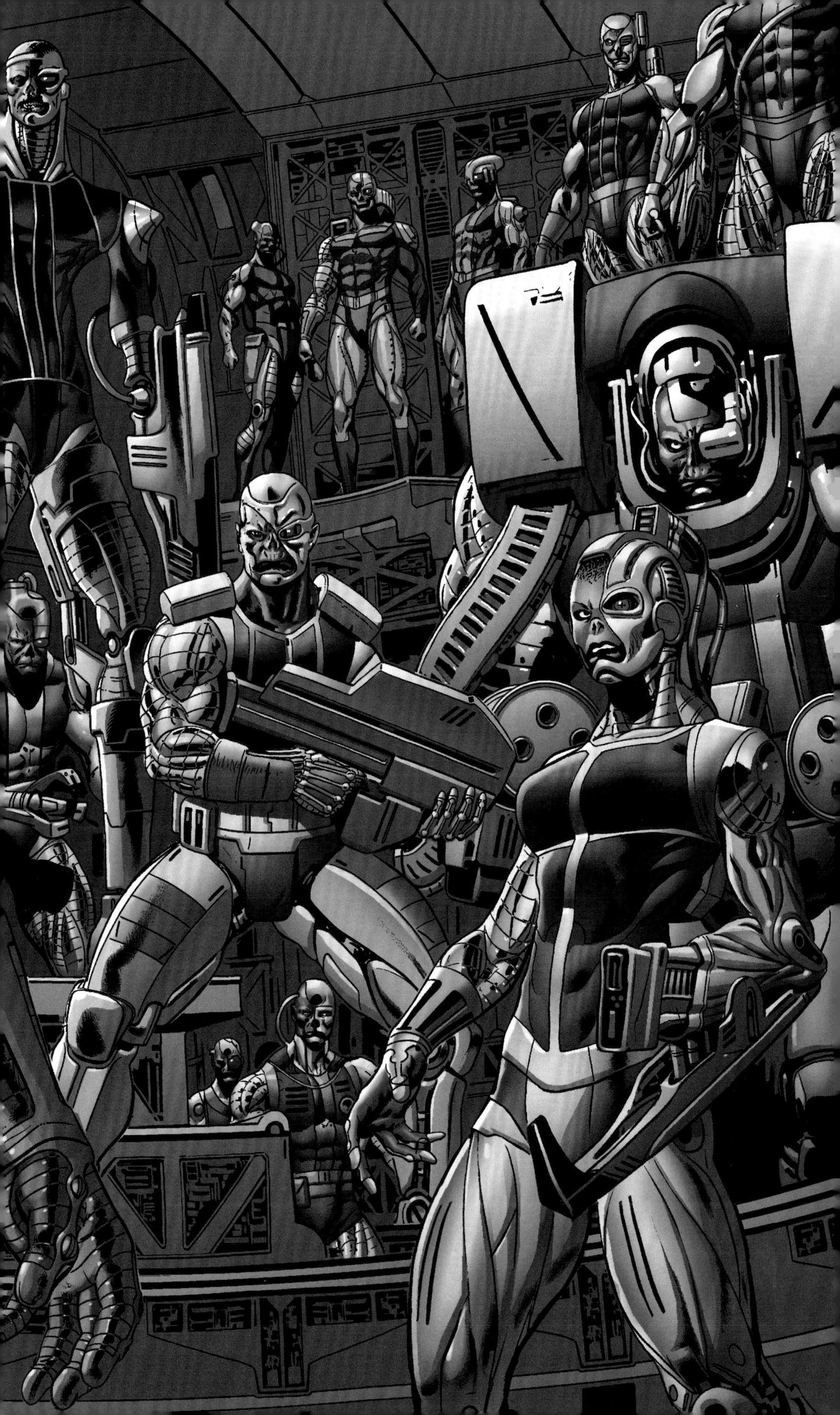

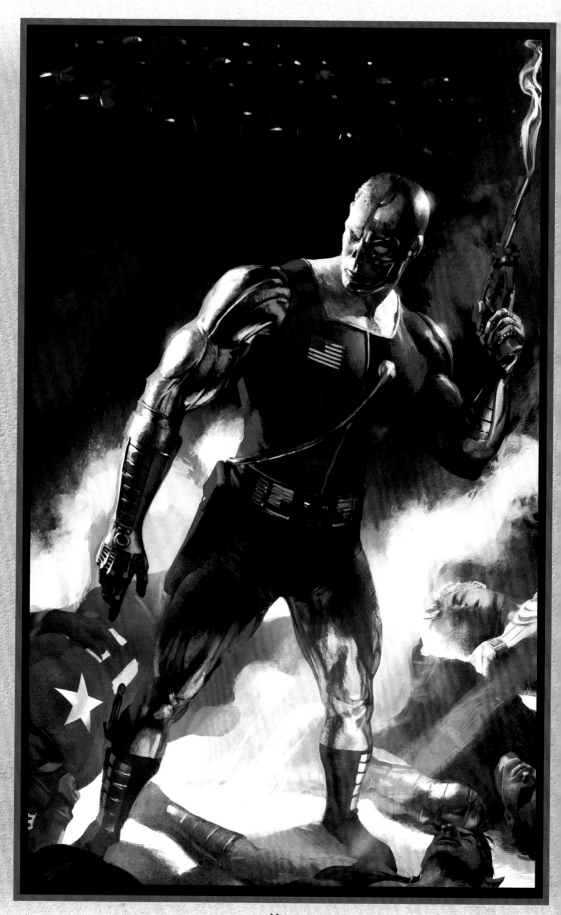

#9

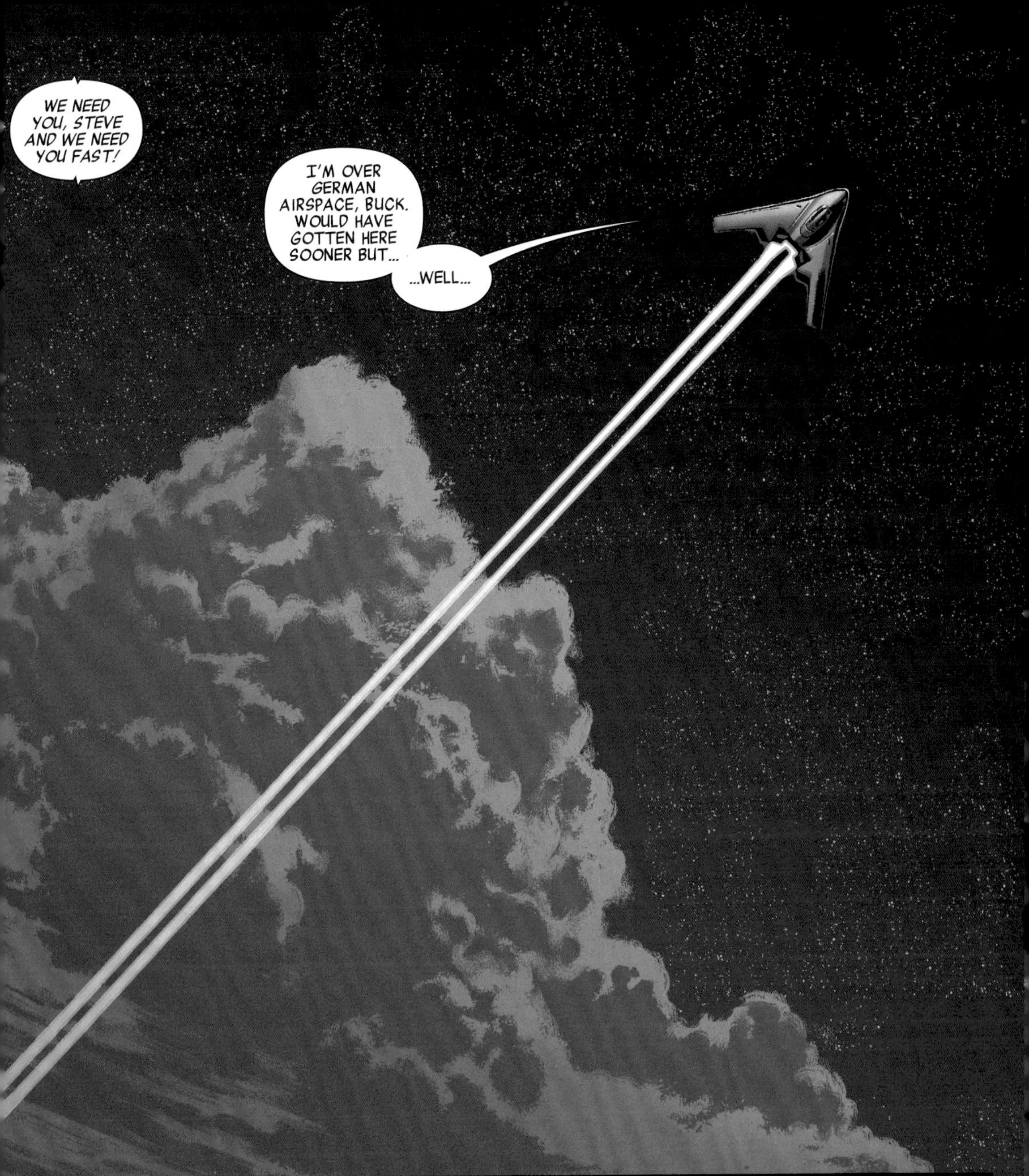
WE NEED YOU, STEVE AND WE NEED YOU FAST!
I'M OVER GERMAN AIRSPACE, BUCK. WOULD HAVE GOTTEN HERE SOONER BUT...
...WELL...

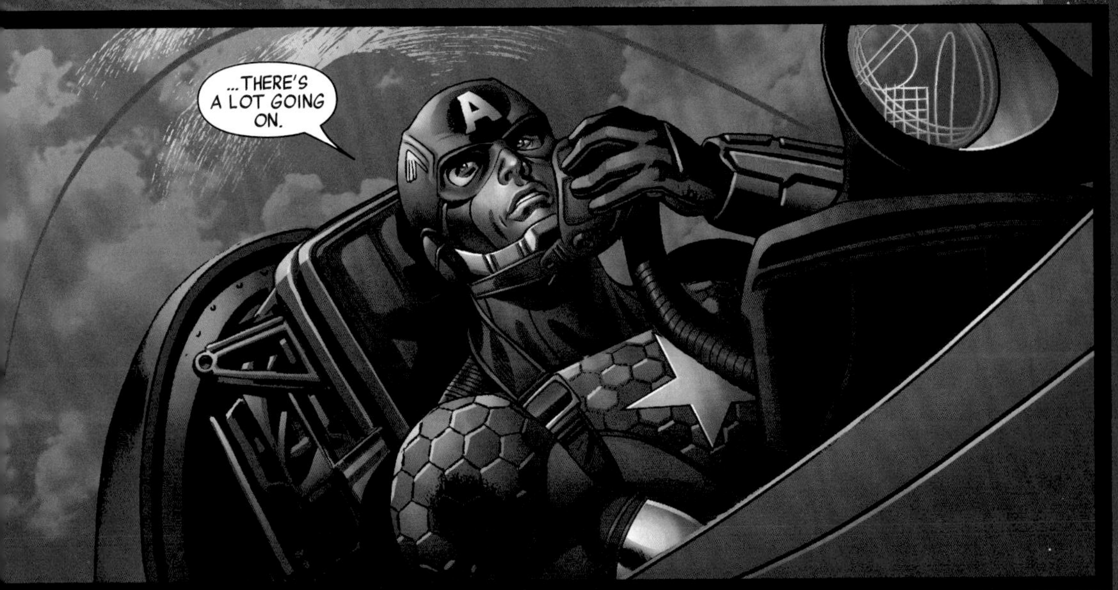
...THERE'S A LOT GOING ON.

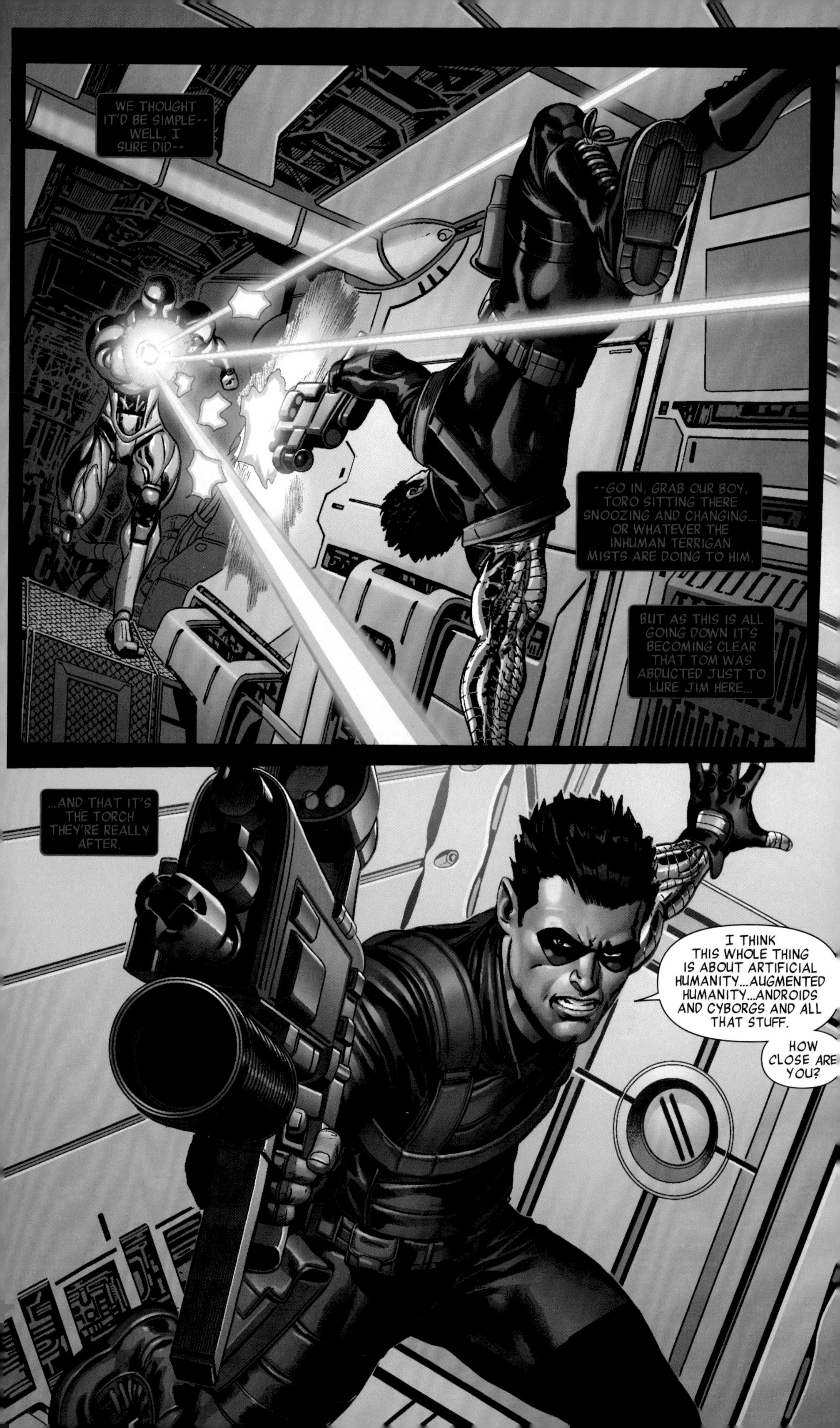

WE THOUGHT IT'D BE SIMPLE-- WELL, I SURE DID--
--GO IN, GRAB OUR BOY, TORO SITTING THERE SNOOZING AND CHANGING... OR WHATEVER THE INHUMAN TERRIGAN MISTS ARE DOING TO HIM.
BUT AS THIS IS ALL GOING DOWN IT'S BECOMING CLEAR THAT TOM WAS ABDUCTED JUST TO LURE JIM HERE...
...AND THAT IT'S THE TORCH THEY'RE REALLY AFTER.
I THINK THIS WHOLE THING IS ABOUT ARTIFICIAL HUMANITY...AUGMENTED HUMANITY...ANDROIDS AND CYBORGS AND ALL THAT STUFF.
HOW CLOSE ARE YOU?

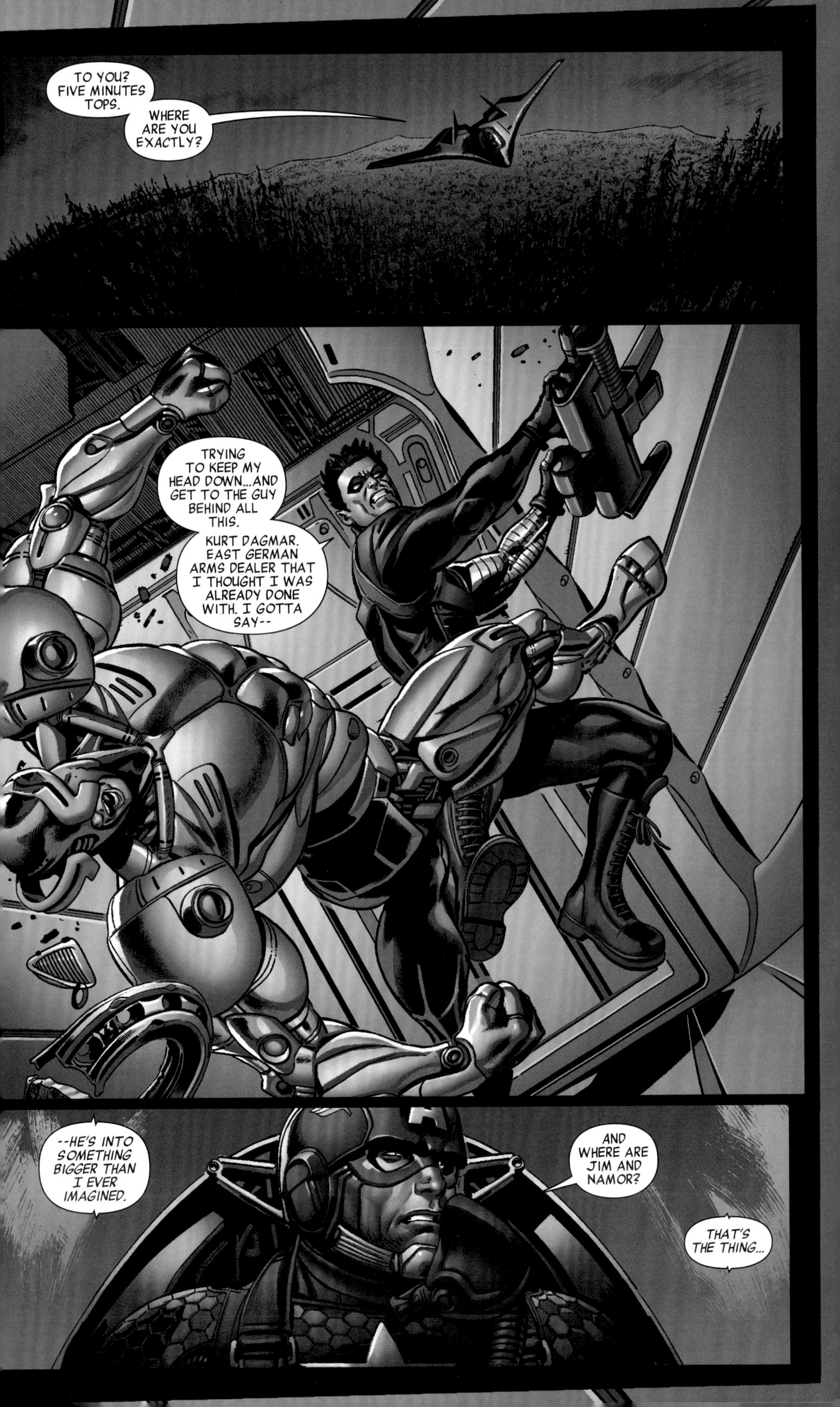
TO YOU? FIVE MINUTES TOPS.
WHERE ARE YOU EXACTLY?
TRYING TO KEEP MY HEAD DOWN...AND GET TO THE GUY BEHIND ALL THIS.
KURT DAGMAR. EAST GERMAN ARMS DEALER THAT I THOUGHT I WAS ALREADY DONE WITH. I GOTTA SAY--
--HE'S INTO SOMETHING BIGGER THAN I EVER IMAGINED.
AND WHERE ARE JIM AND NAMOR?
THAT'S THE THING...

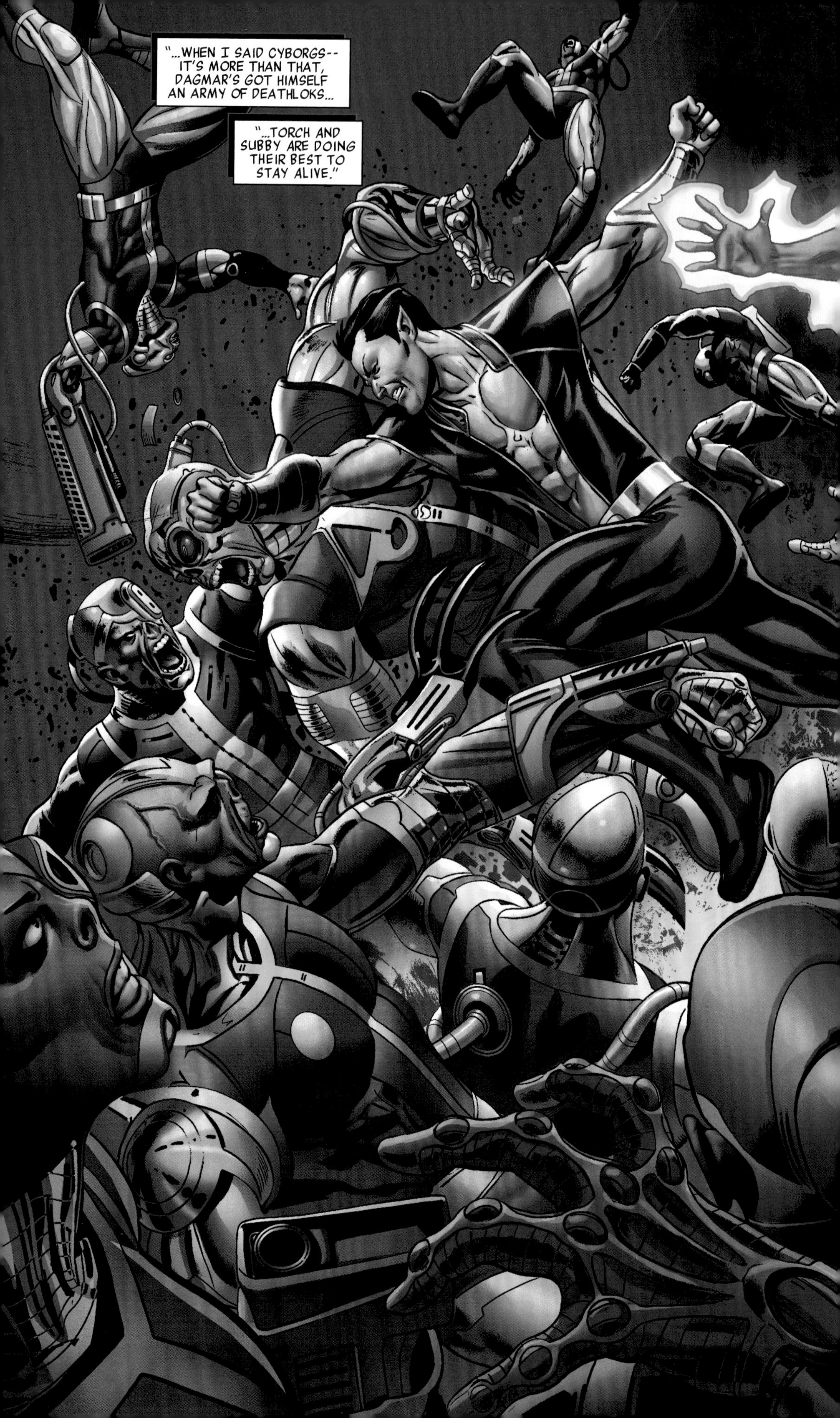
"...WHEN I SAID CYBORGS-- IT'S MORE THAN THAT, DAGMAR'S GOT HIMSELF AN ARMY OF DEATHLOKS...
"...TORCH AND SUBBY ARE DOING THEIR BEST TO STAY ALIVE."

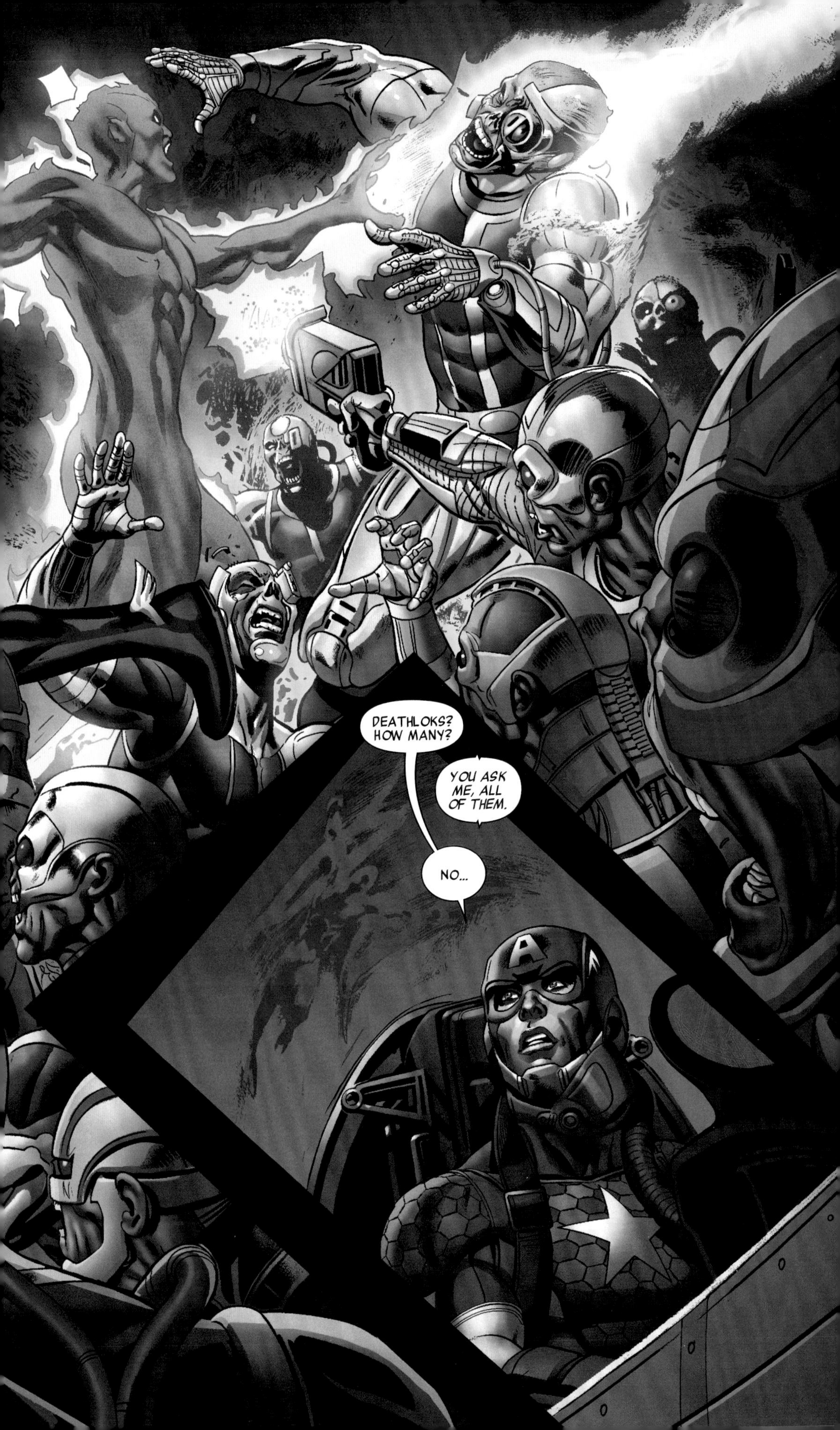
DEATHLOKS? HOW MANY?
YOU ASK ME, ALL OF THEM.
NO...

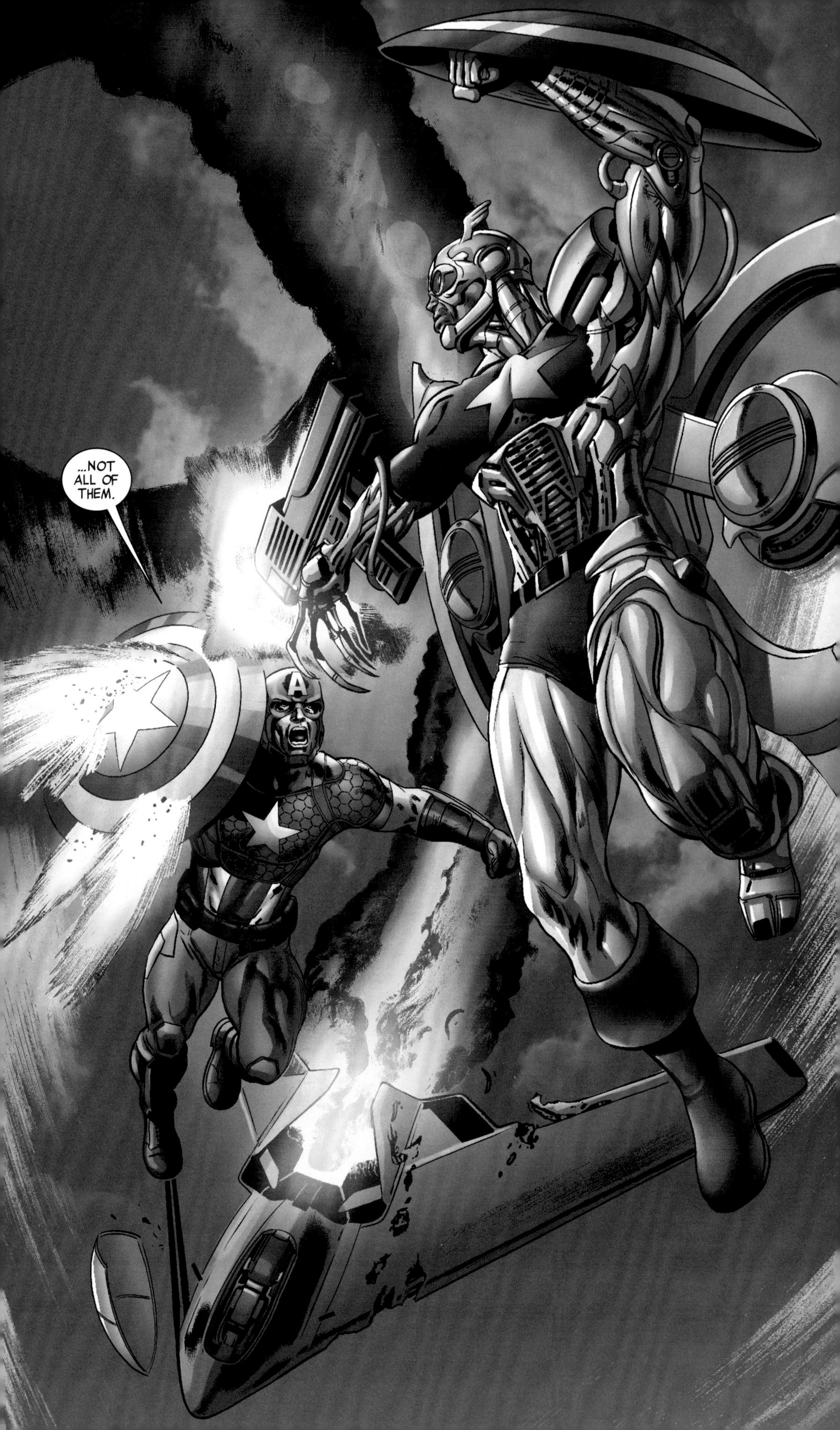
...NOT ALL OF THEM.

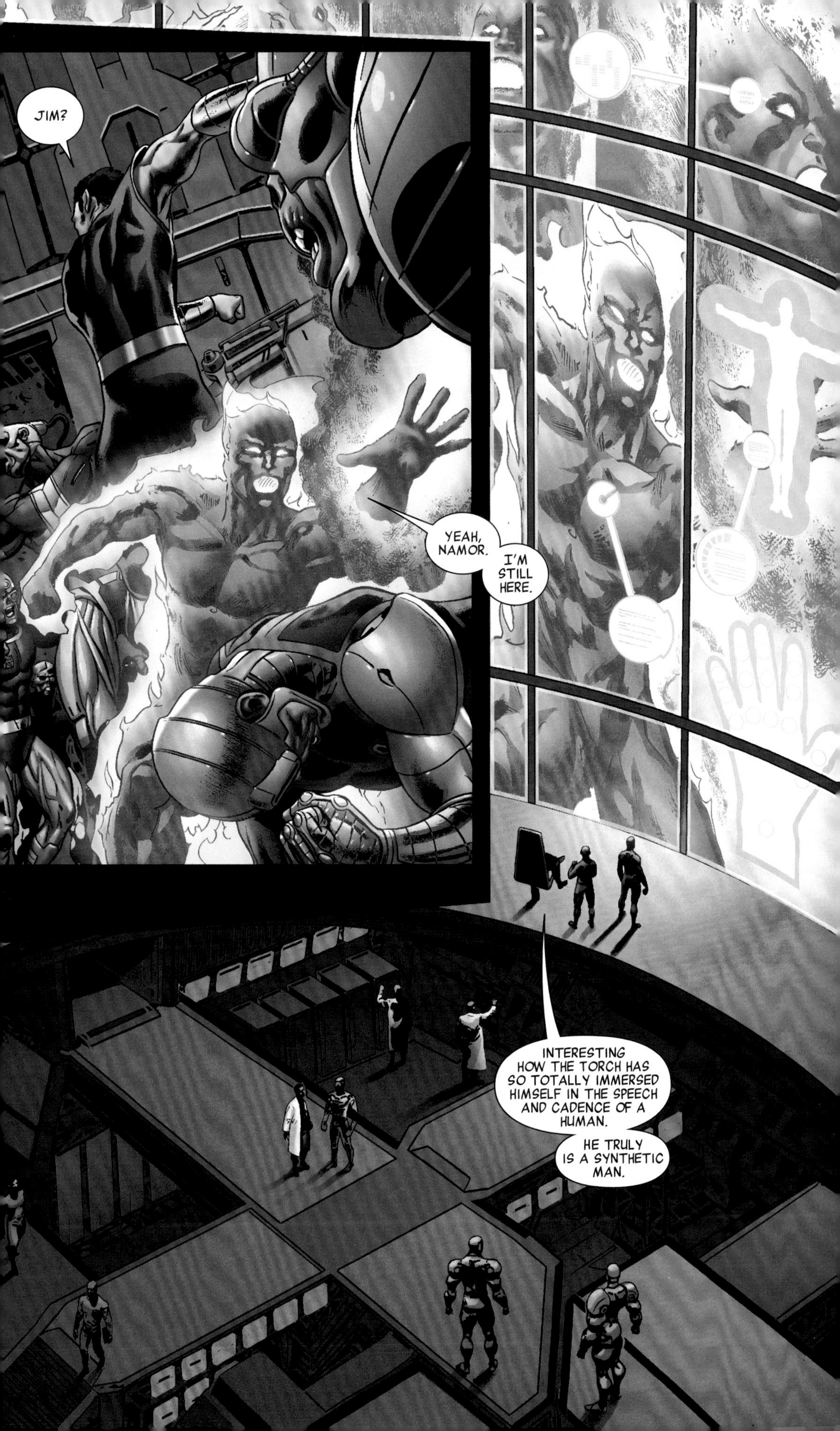

JIM?
YEAH, NAMOR.
I'M STILL HERE.
INTERESTING HOW THE TORCH HAS SO TOTALLY IMMERSED HIMSELF IN THE SPEECH AND CADENCE OF A HUMAN.
HE TRULY IS A SYNTHETIC MAN.

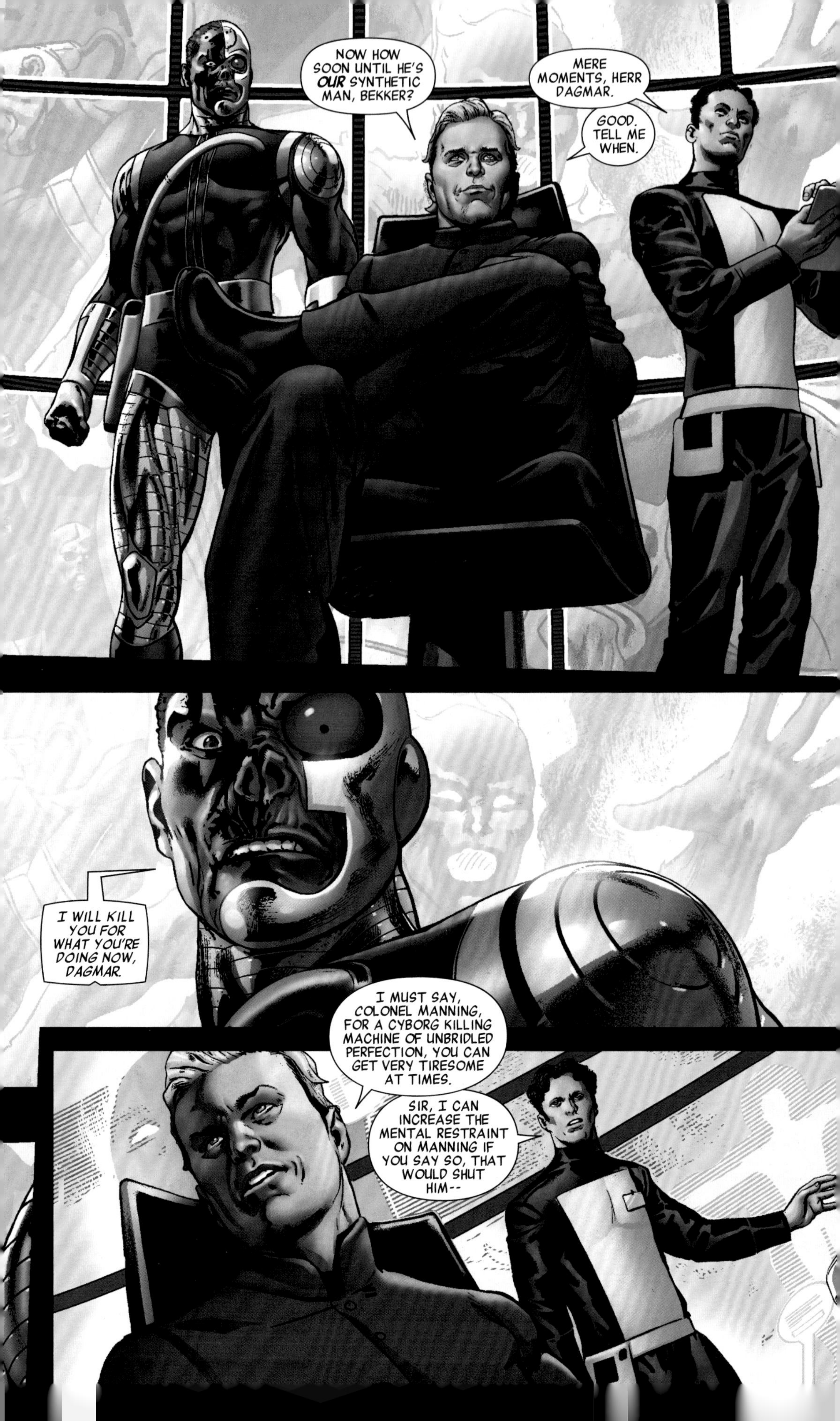
NOW HOW SOON UNTIL HE'S OUR SYNTHETIC MAN, BEKKER?
MERE MOMENTS, HERR DAGMAR.
GOOD. TELL ME WHEN.
I WILL KILL YOU FOR WHAT YOU'RE DOING NOW, DAGMAR.
I MUST SAY, COLONEL MANNING, FOR A CYBORG KILLING MACHINE OF UNBRIDLED PERFECTION, YOU CAN GET VERY TIRESOME AT TIMES.
SIR, I CAN INCREASE THE MENTAL RESTRAINT ON MANNING IF YOU SAY SO, THAT WOULD SHUT HIM--

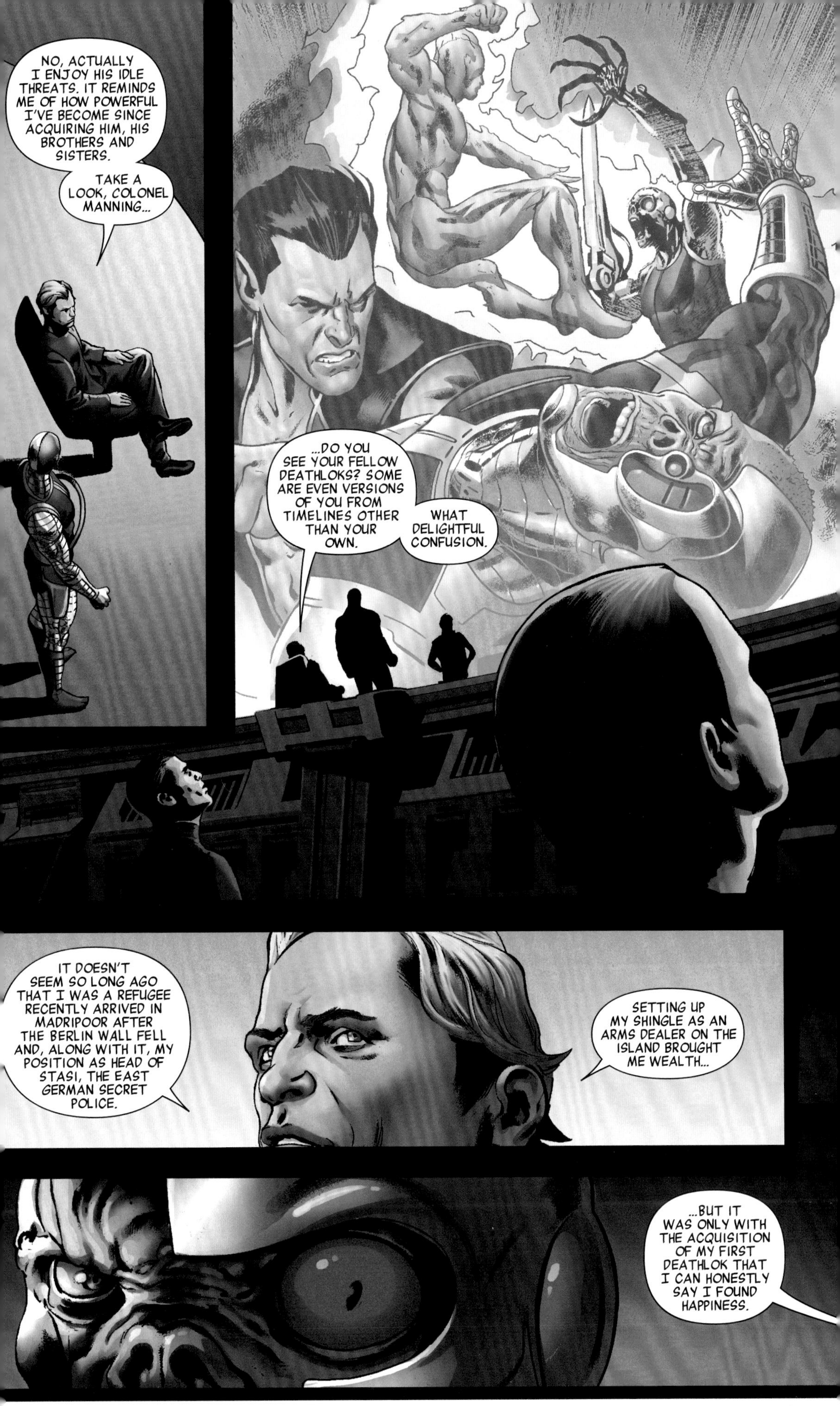

NO, ACTUALLY I ENJOY HIS IDLE THREATS. IT REMINDS ME OF HOW POWERFUL I'VE BECOME SINCE ACQUIRING HIM, HIS BROTHERS AND SISTERS.
TAKE A LOOK, COLONEL MANNING...
...DO YOU SEE YOUR FELLOW DEATHLOKS? SOME ARE EVEN VERSIONS OF YOU FROM TIMELINES OTHER THAN YOUR OWN.
WHAT DELIGHTFUL CONFUSION.
IT DOESN'T SEEM SO LONG AGO THAT I WAS A REFUGEE RECENTLY ARRIVED IN MADRIPOOR AFTER THE BERLIN WALL FELL AND, ALONG WITH IT, MY POSITION AS HEAD OF STASI, THE EAST GERMAN SECRET POLICE.
SETTING UP MY SHINGLE AS AN ARMS DEALER ON THE ISLAND BROUGHT ME WEALTH...
...BUT IT WAS ONLY WITH THE ACQUISITION OF MY FIRST DEATHLOK THAT I CAN HONESTLY SAY I FOUND HAPPINESS.

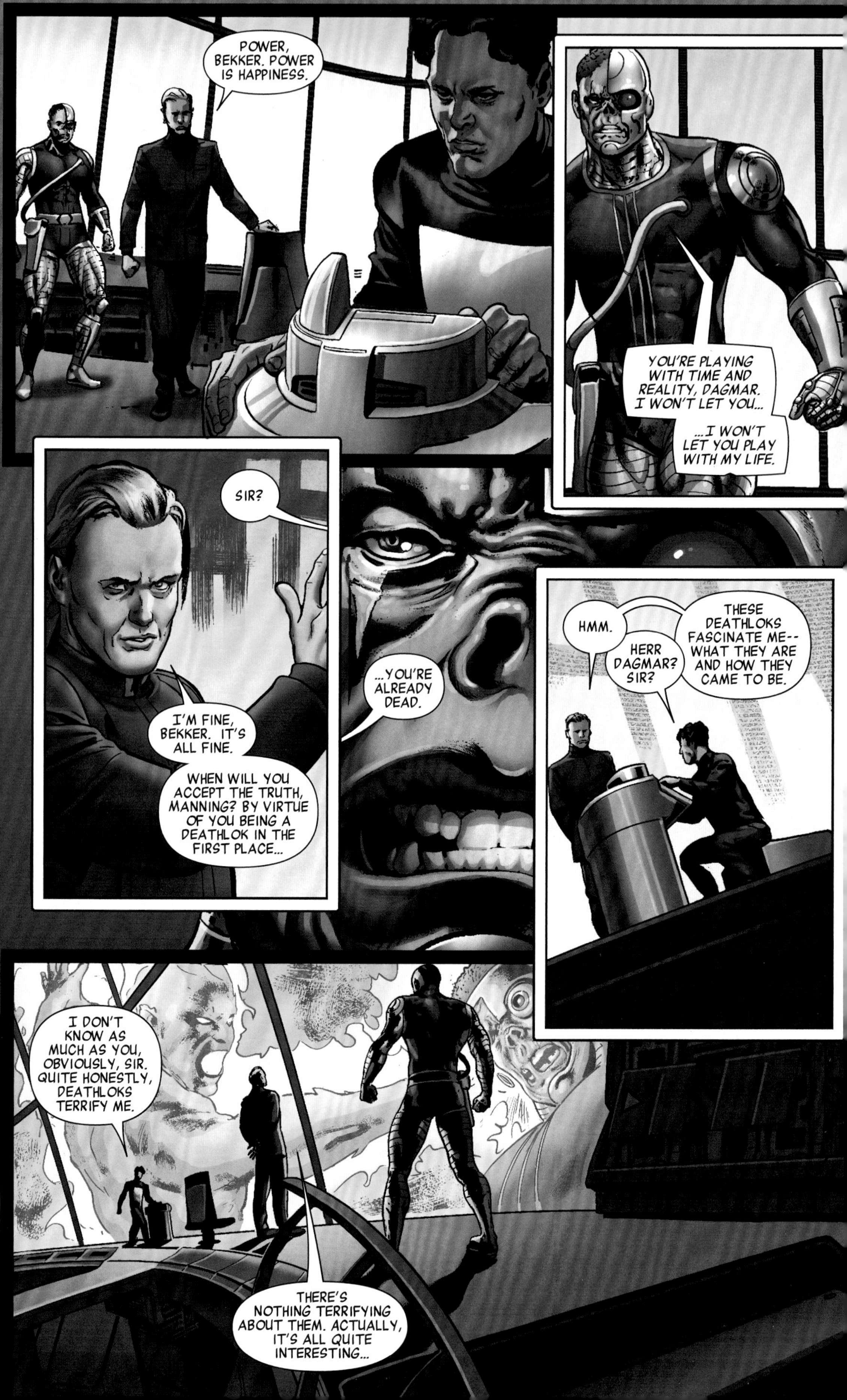
POWER, BEKKER. POWER IS HAPPINESS.
YOU'RE PLAYING WITH TIME AND REALITY, DAGMAR. I WON'T LET YOU...
...I WON'T LET YOU PLAY WITH MY LIFE.
SIR?
I'M FINE, BEKKER. IT'S ALL FINE.
WHEN WILL YOU ACCEPT THE TRUTH, MANNING? BY VIRTUE OF YOU BEING A DEATHLOK IN THE FIRST PLACE...
...YOU'RE ALREADY DEAD.
HMM.
HERR DAGMAR? SIR?
THESE DEATHLOKS FASCINATE ME--WHAT THEY ARE AND HOW THEY CAME TO BE.
I DON'T KNOW AS MUCH AS YOU, OBVIOUSLY, SIR. QUITE HONESTLY, DEATHLOKS TERRIFY ME.
THERE'S NOTHING TERRIFYING ABOUT THEM. ACTUALLY, IT'S ALL QUITE INTERESTING...

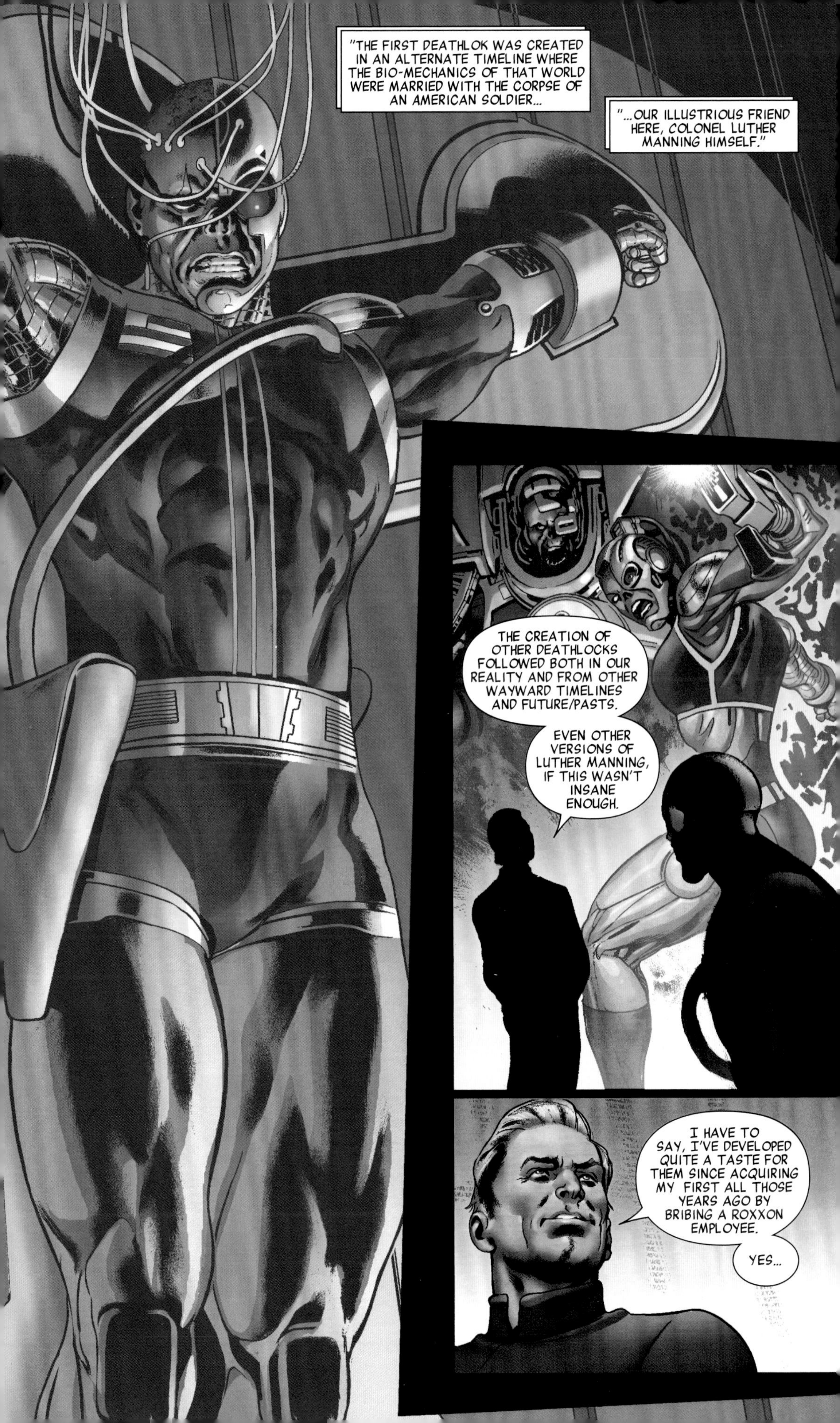
"THE FIRST DEATHLOK WAS CREATED IN AN ALTERNATE TIMELINE WHERE THE BIO-MECHANICS OF THAT WORLD WERE MARRIED WITH THE CORPSE OF AN AMERICAN SOLDIER...
"...OUR ILLUSTRIOUS FRIEND HERE, COLONEL LUTHER MANNING HIMSELF."
THE CREATION OF OTHER DEATHLOCKS FOLLOWED BOTH IN OUR REALITY AND FROM OTHER WAYWARD TIMELINES AND FUTURE/PASTS.
EVEN OTHER VERSIONS OF LUTHER MANNING, IF THIS WASN'T INSANE ENOUGH.
I HAVE TO SAY, I'VE DEVELOPED QUITE A TASTE FOR THEM SINCE ACQUIRING MY FIRST ALL THOSE YEARS AGO BY BRIBING A ROXXON EMPLOYEE.
YES...

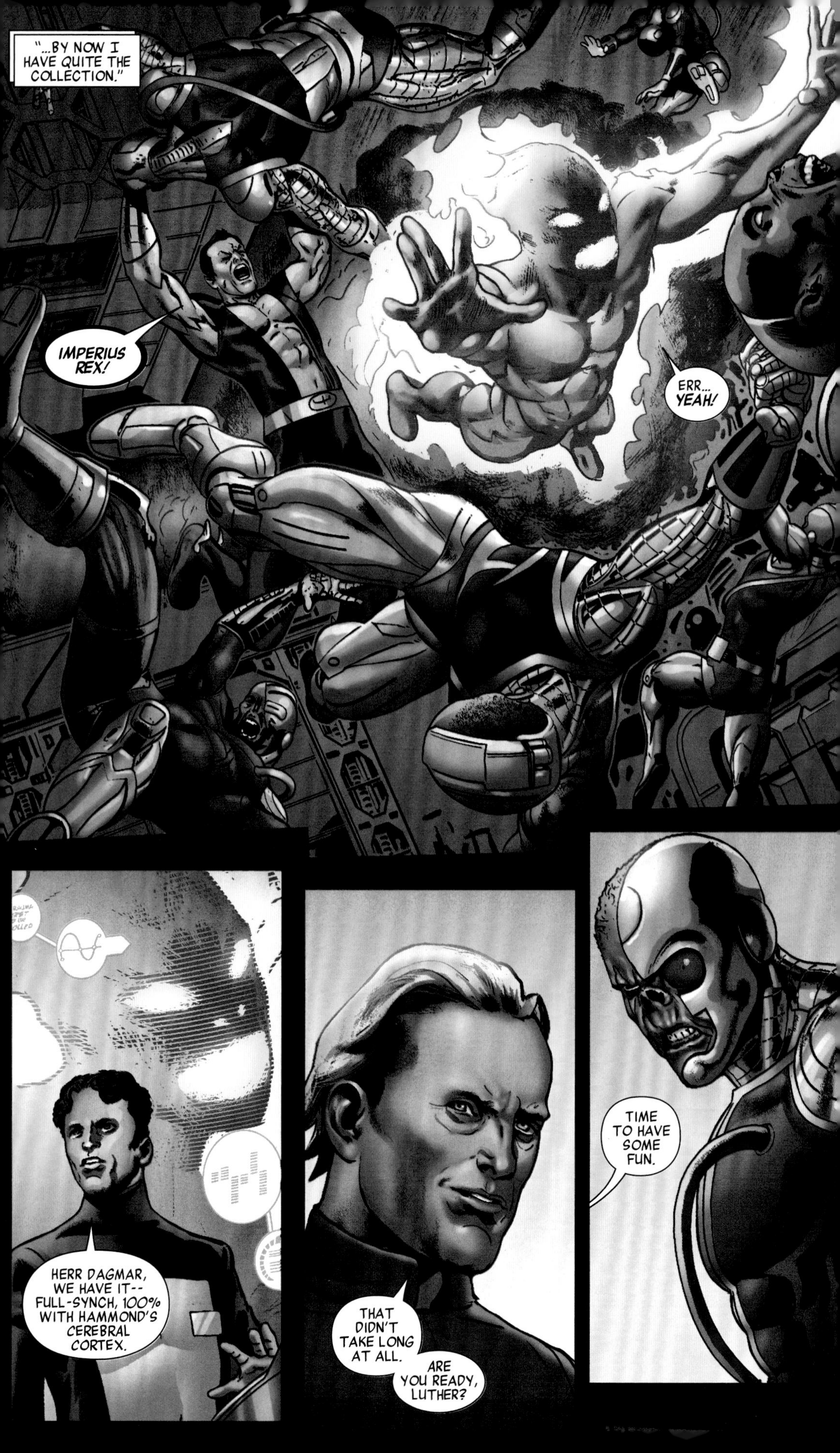

"...BY NOW I HAVE QUITE THE COLLECTION."
IMPERIUS REX!
ERR... YEAH!
HERR DAGMAR, WE HAVE IT-- FULL-SYNCH, 100% WITH HAMMOND'S CEREBRAL CORTEX.
THAT DIDN'T TAKE LONG AT ALL.
ARE YOU READY, LUTHER?
TIME TO HAVE SOME FUN.

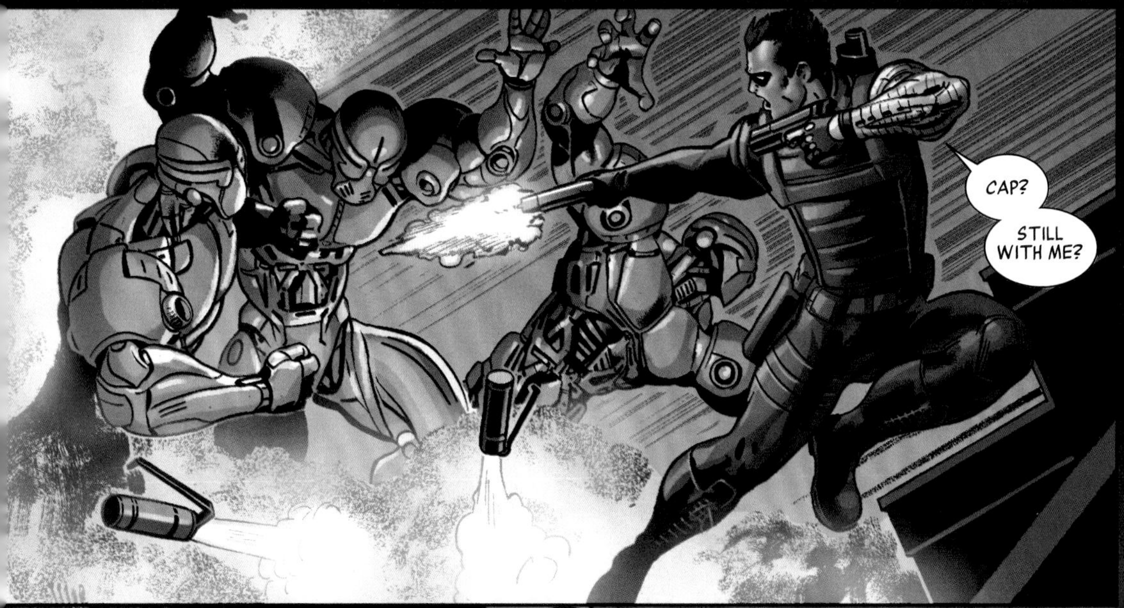
CAP?
STILL WITH ME?

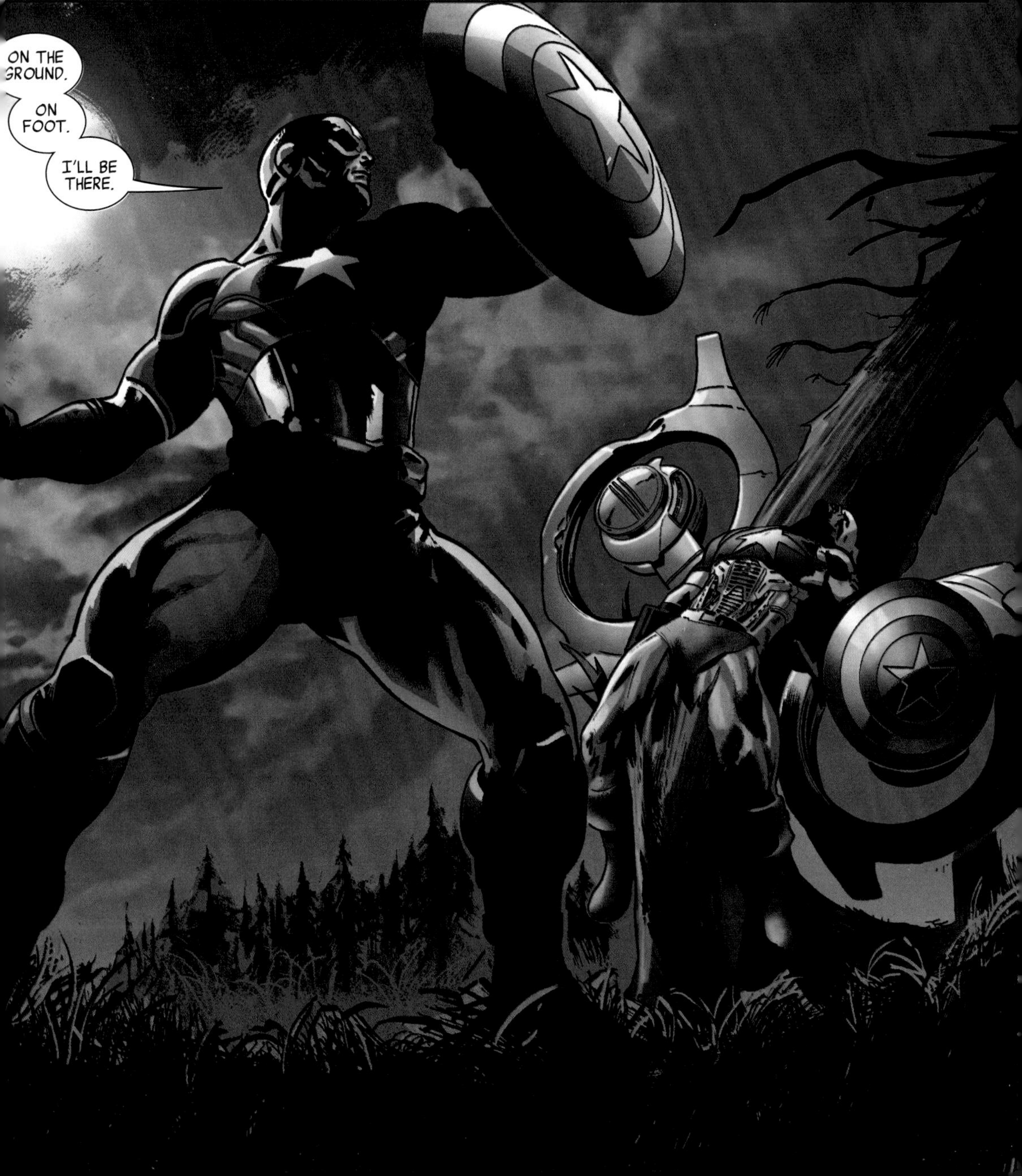
ON THE GROUND.
ON FOOT.
I'LL BE THERE.

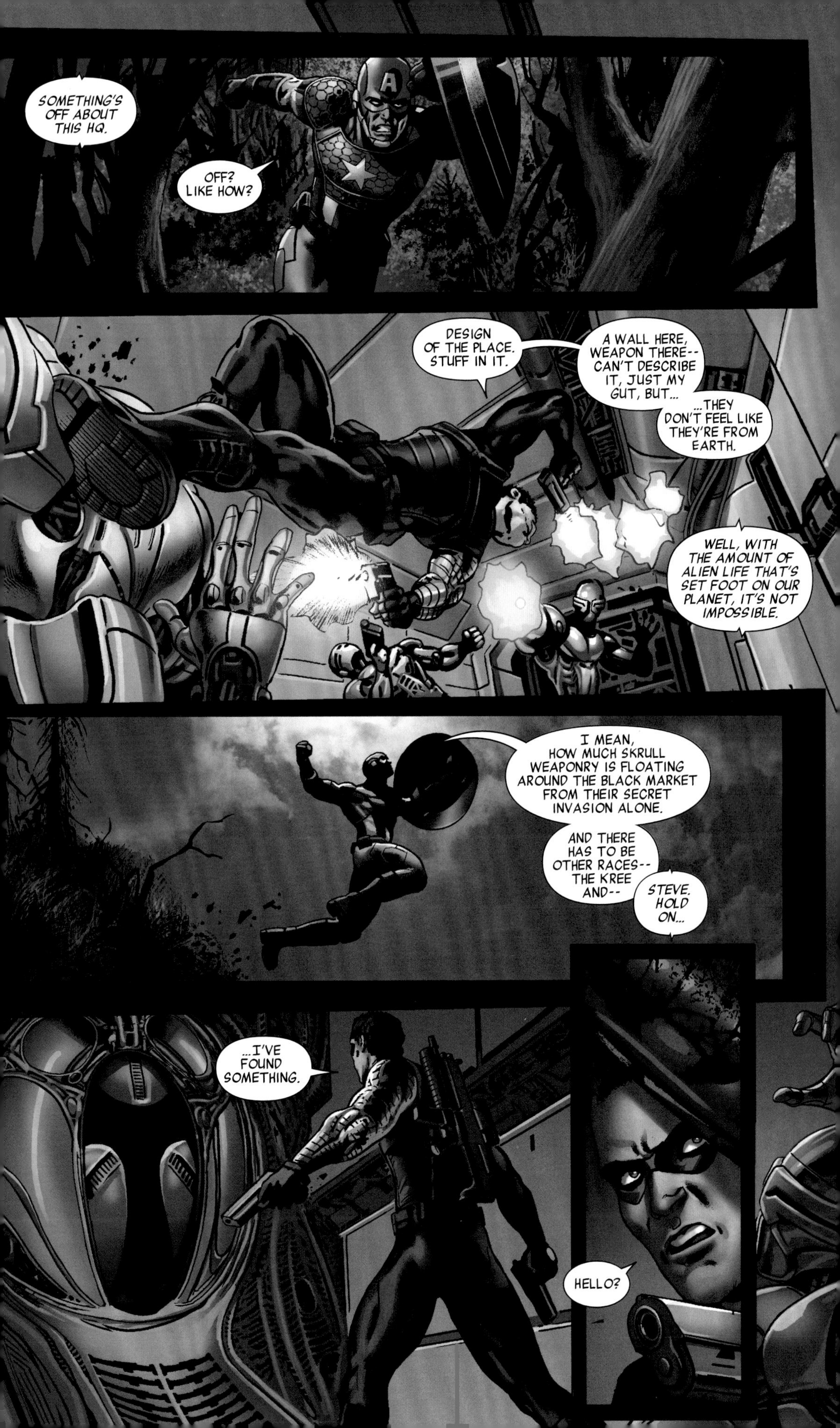
SOMETHING'S OFF ABOUT THIS HQ.
OFF? LIKE HOW?
DESIGN OF THE PLACE. STUFF IN IT.
A WALL HERE, WEAPON THERE-- CAN'T DESCRIBE IT, JUST MY GUT, BUT...
...THEY DON'T FEEL LIKE THEY'RE FROM EARTH.
WELL, WITH THE AMOUNT OF ALIEN LIFE THAT'S SET FOOT ON OUR PLANET, IT'S NOT IMPOSSIBLE.
I MEAN, HOW MUCH SKRULL WEAPONRY IS FLOATING AROUND THE BLACK MARKET FROM THEIR SECRET INVASION ALONE.
AND THERE HAS TO BE OTHER RACES-- THE KREE AND--
STEVE. HOLD ON...
...I'VE FOUND SOMETHING.
HELLO?

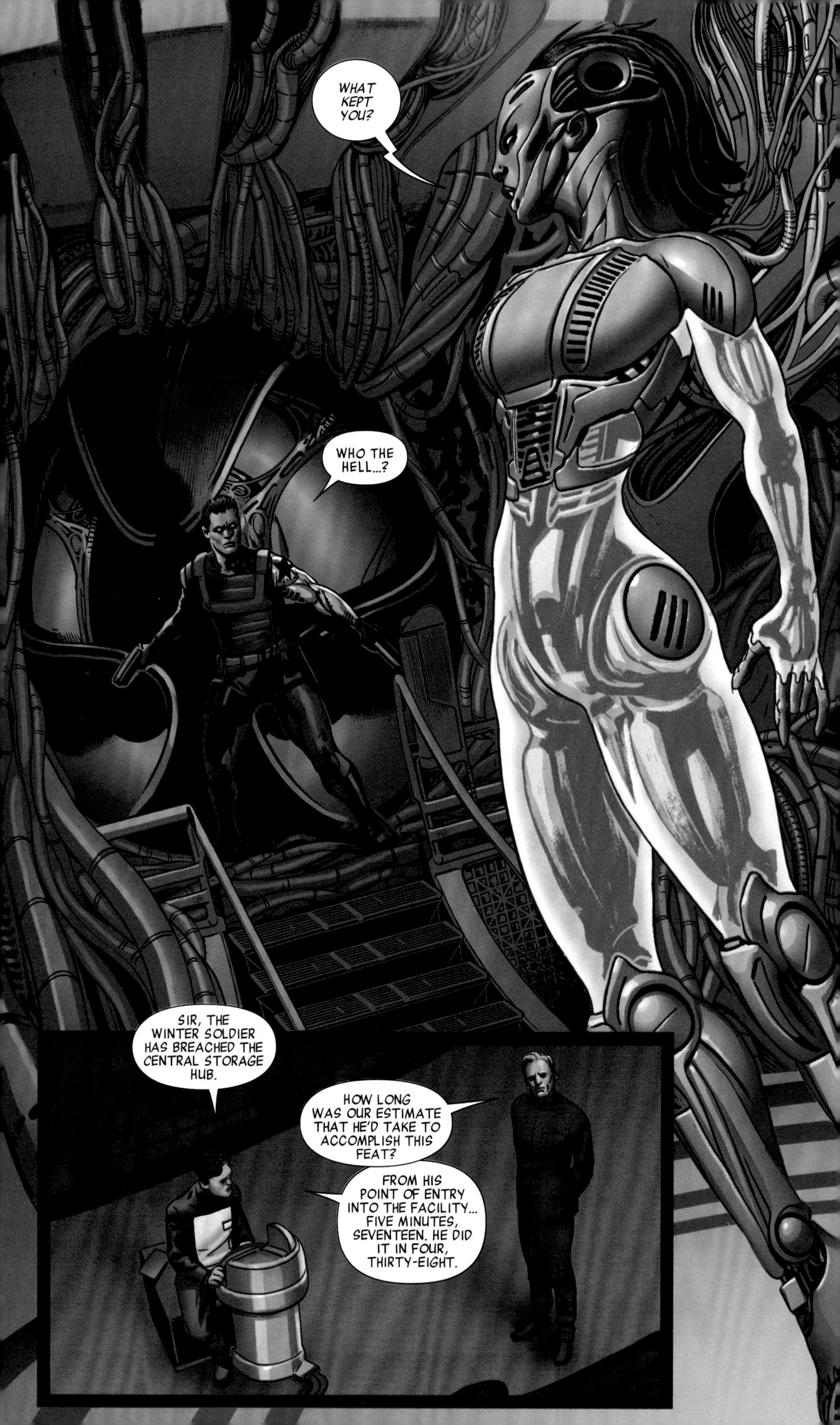
WHAT KEPT YOU?
WHO THE HELL...?
SIR, THE WINTER SOLDIER HAS BREACHED THE CENTRAL STORAGE HUB.
HOW LONG WAS OUR ESTIMATE THAT HE'D TAKE TO ACCOMPLISH THIS FEAT?
FROM HIS POINT OF ENTRY INTO THE FACILITY... FIVE MINUTES, SEVENTEEN. HE DID IT IN FOUR, THIRTY-EIGHT.

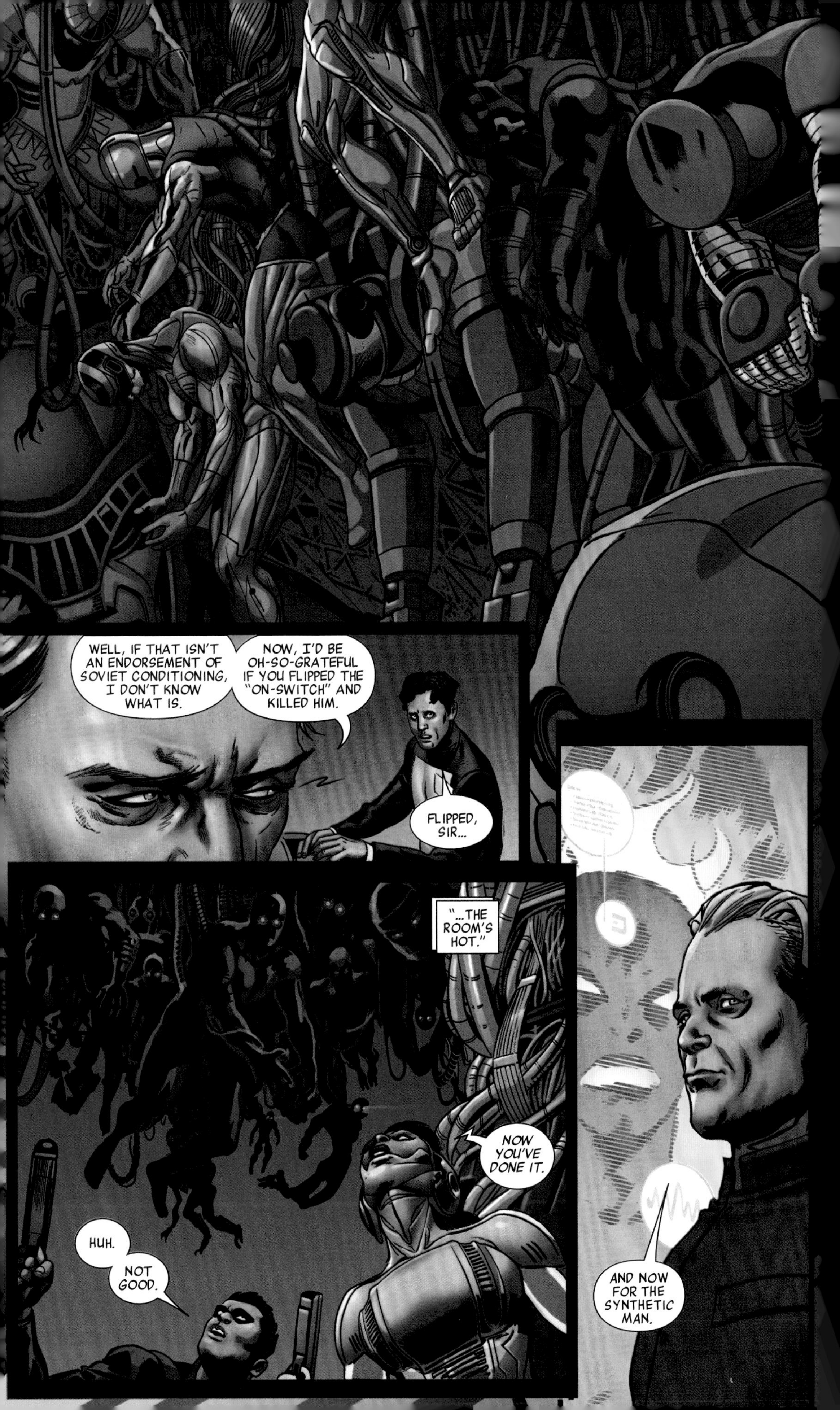
WELL, IF THAT ISN'T AN ENDORSEMENT OF SOVIET CONDITIONING, I DON'T KNOW WHAT IS.
NOW, I'D BE OH-SO-GRATEFUL IF YOU FLIPPED THE "ON-SWITCH" AND KILLED HIM.
FLIPPED, SIR...
"...THE ROOM'S HOT."
NOW YOU'VE DONE IT.
HUH.
NOT GOOD.
AND NOW FOR THE SYNTHETIC MAN.

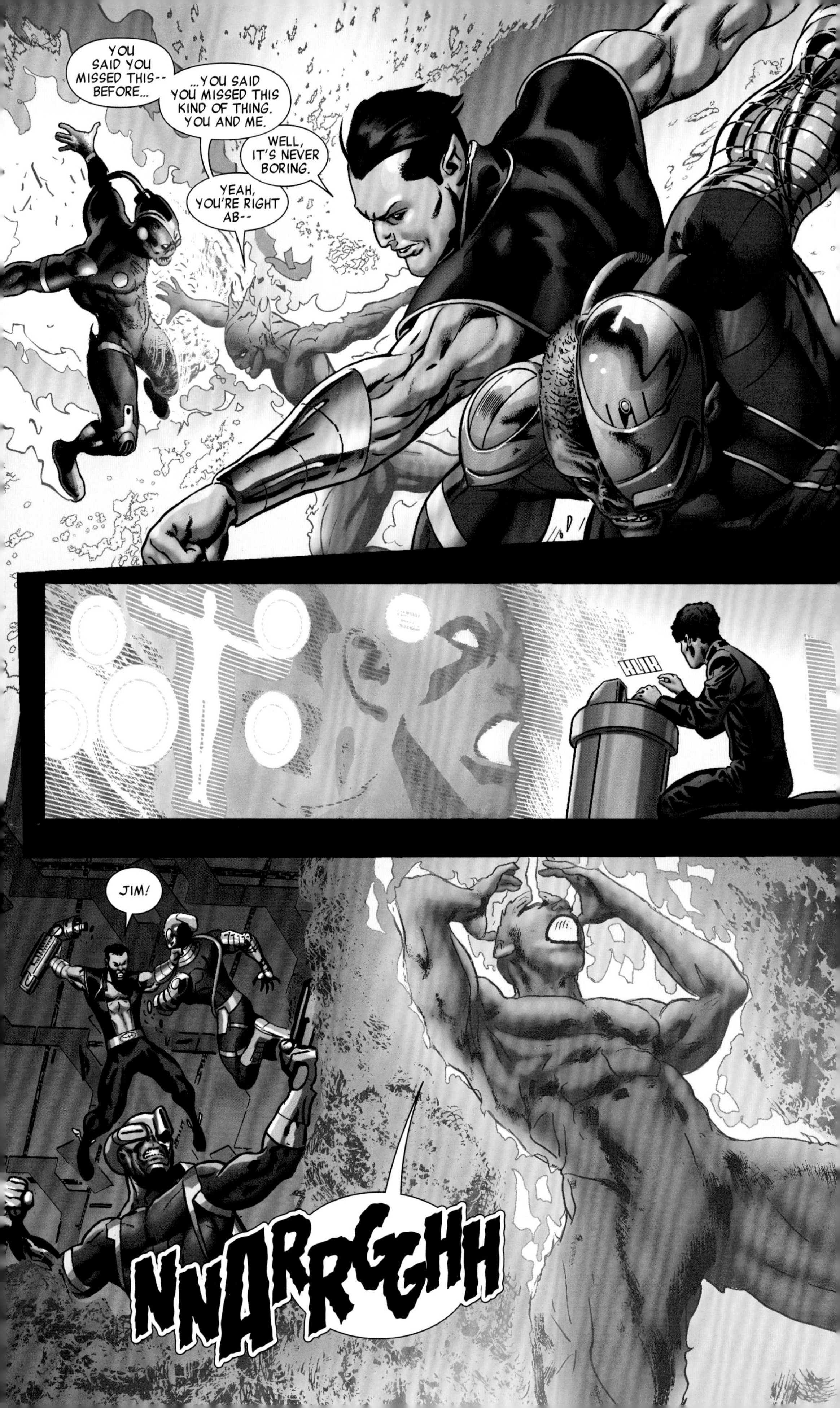
YOU SAID YOU MISSED THIS-- BEFORE...
...YOU SAID YOU MISSED THIS KIND OF THING. YOU AND ME.
WELL, IT'S NEVER BORING.
YEAH, YOU'RE RIGHT AB--
KLIK
JIM!
NNARRGGHH

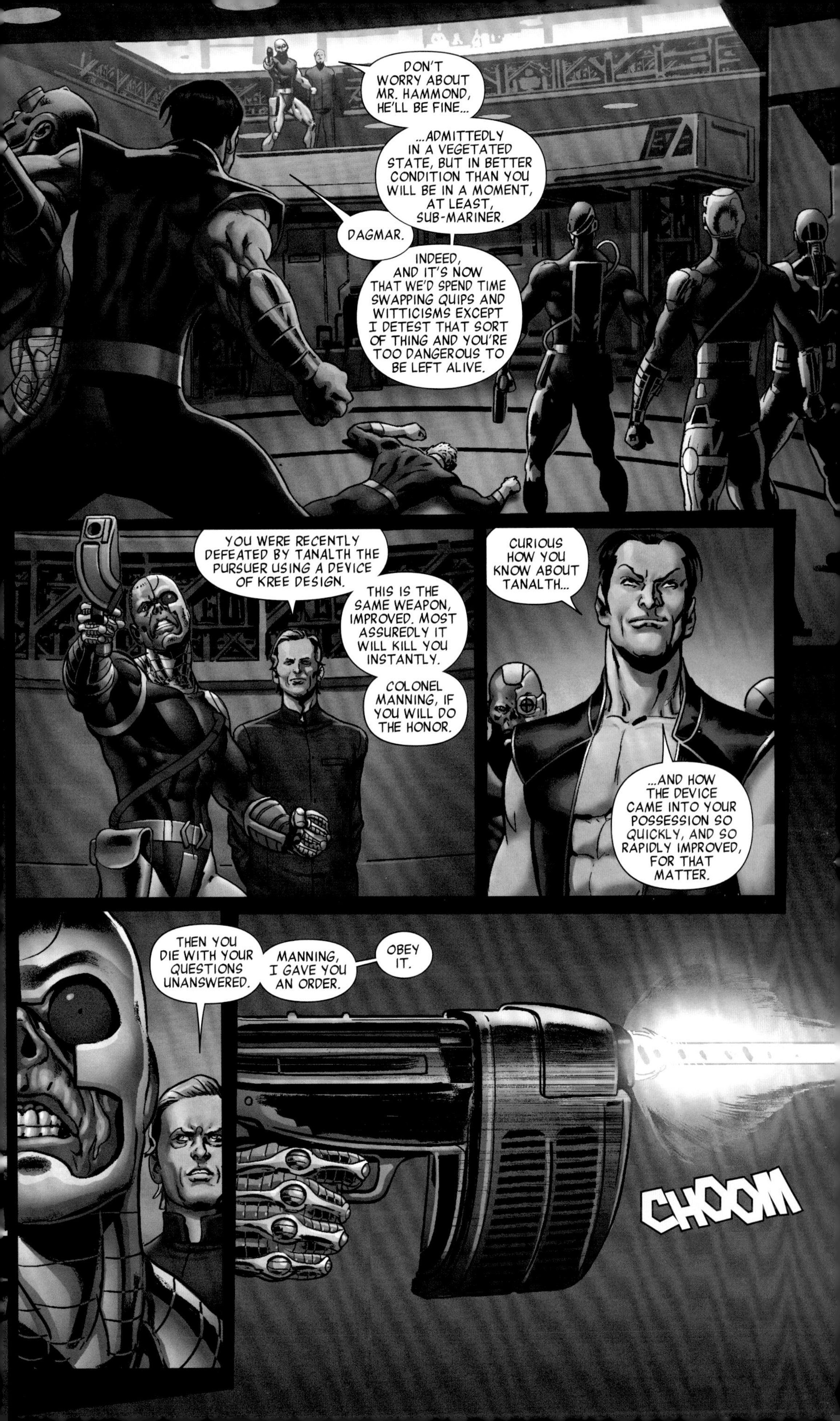
DON'T WORRY ABOUT MR. HAMMOND, HE'LL BE FINE...
...ADMITTEDLY IN A VEGETATED STATE, BUT IN BETTER CONDITION THAN YOU WILL BE IN A MOMENT, AT LEAST, SUB-MARINER.
DAGMAR.
INDEED, AND IT'S NOW THAT WE'D SPEND TIME SWAPPING QUIPS AND WITTICISMS EXCEPT I DETEST THAT SORT OF THING AND YOU'RE TOO DANGEROUS TO BE LEFT ALIVE.
YOU WERE RECENTLY DEFEATED BY TANALTH THE PURSUER USING A DEVICE OF KREE DESIGN.
THIS IS THE SAME WEAPON, IMPROVED. MOST ASSUREDLY IT WILL KILL YOU INSTANTLY.
COLONEL MANNING, IF YOU WILL DO THE HONOR.
CURIOUS HOW YOU KNOW ABOUT TANALTH...
...AND HOW THE DEVICE CAME INTO YOUR POSSESSION SO QUICKLY, AND SO RAPIDLY IMPROVED, FOR THAT MATTER.
THEN YOU DIE WITH YOUR QUESTIONS UNANSWERED.
MANNING, I GAVE YOU AN ORDER.
OBEY IT.
CHOOOM

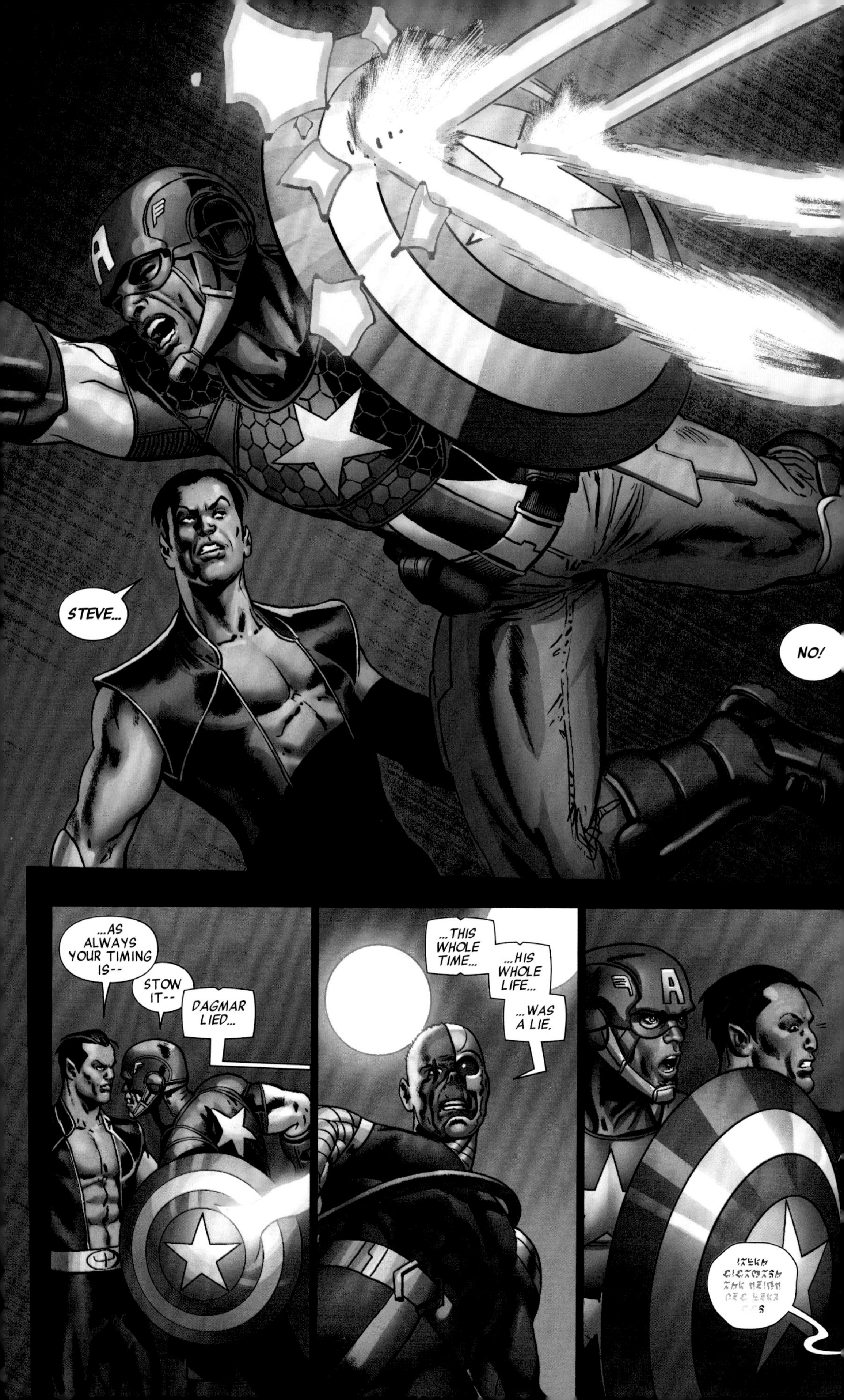
STEVE...
NO!
...AS ALWAYS YOUR TIMING IS--
STOW IT--
DAGMAR LIED...
...THIS WHOLE TIME...
...HIS WHOLE LIFE...
...WAS A LIE.

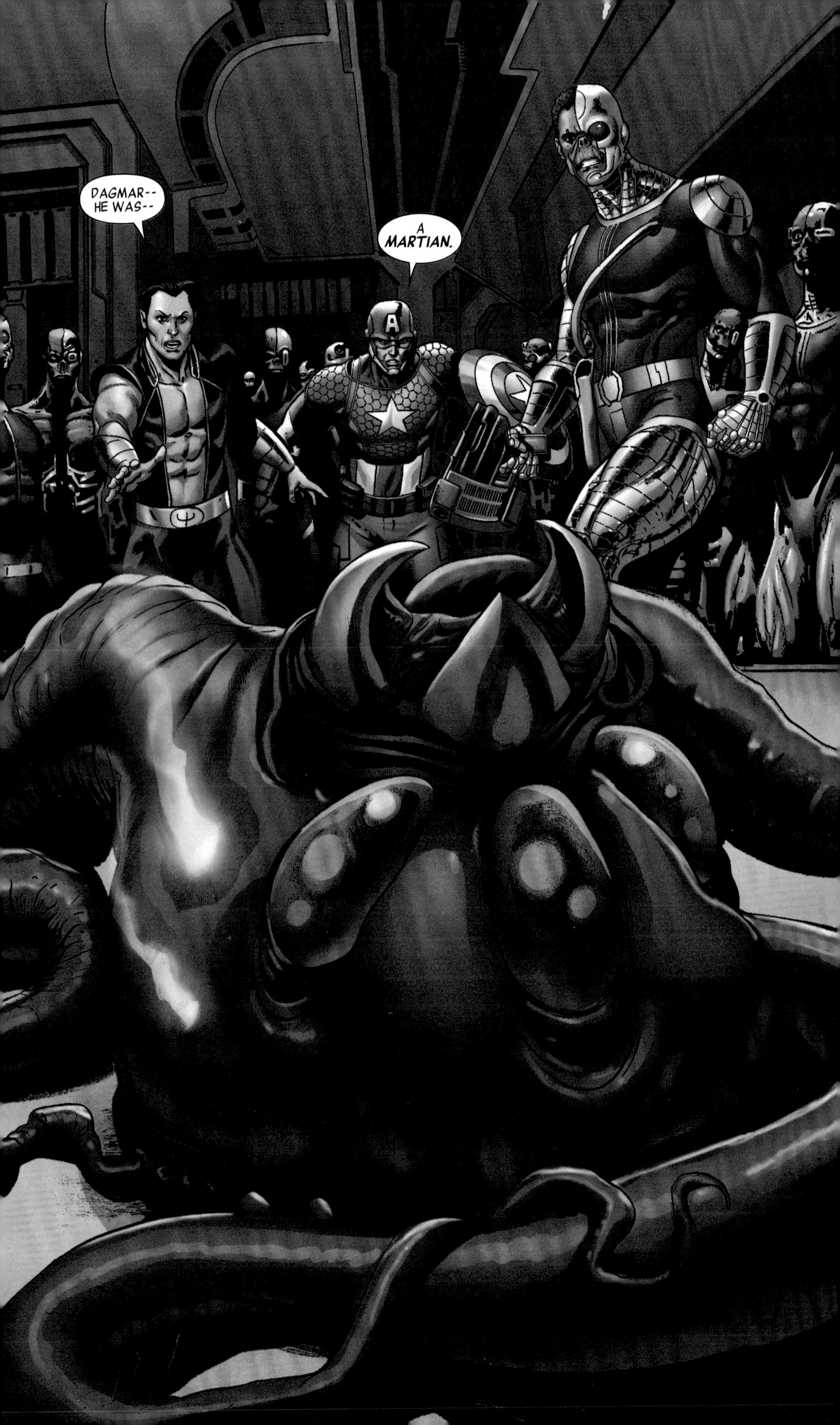
DAGMAR-- HE WAS--
A MARTIAN.

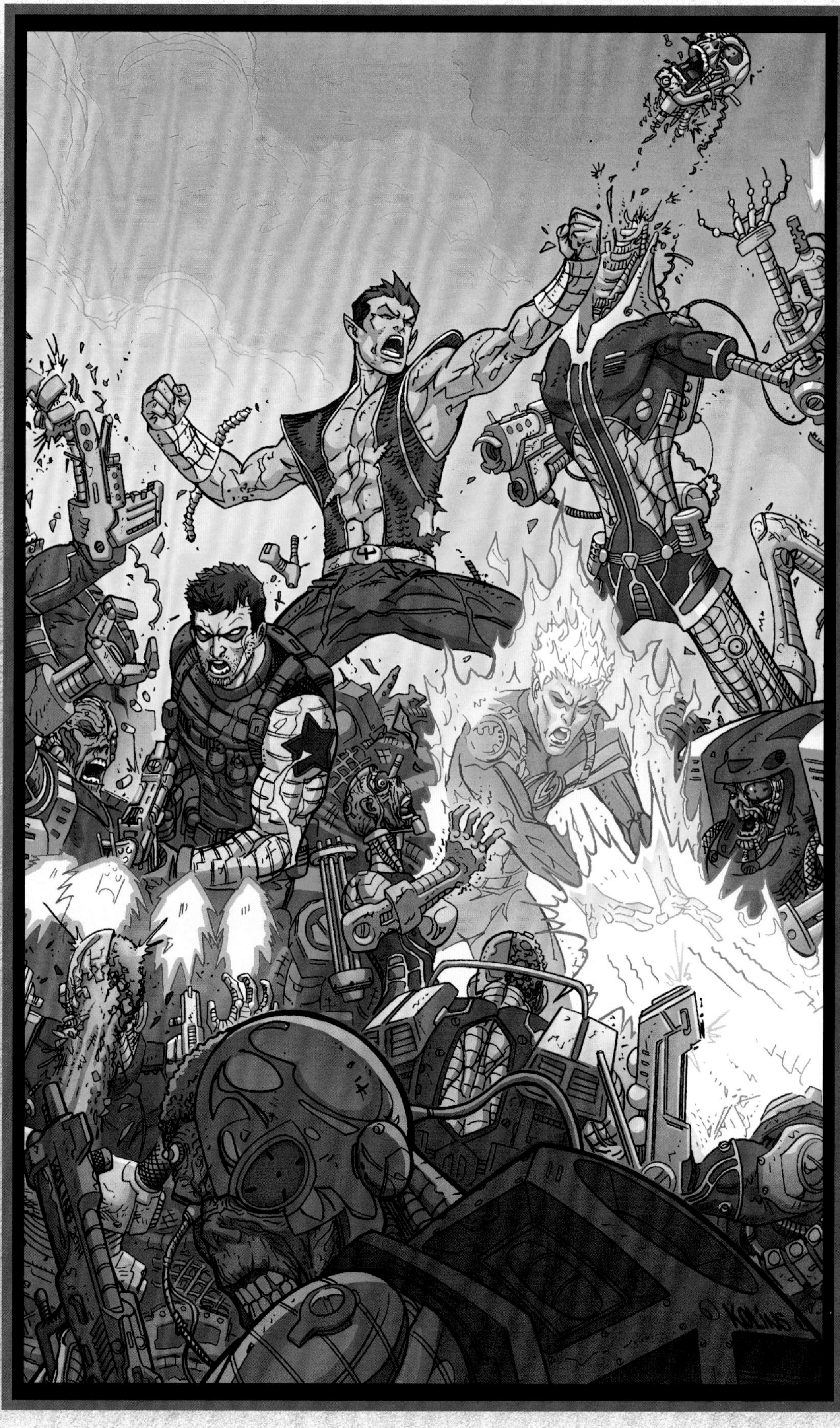

#10

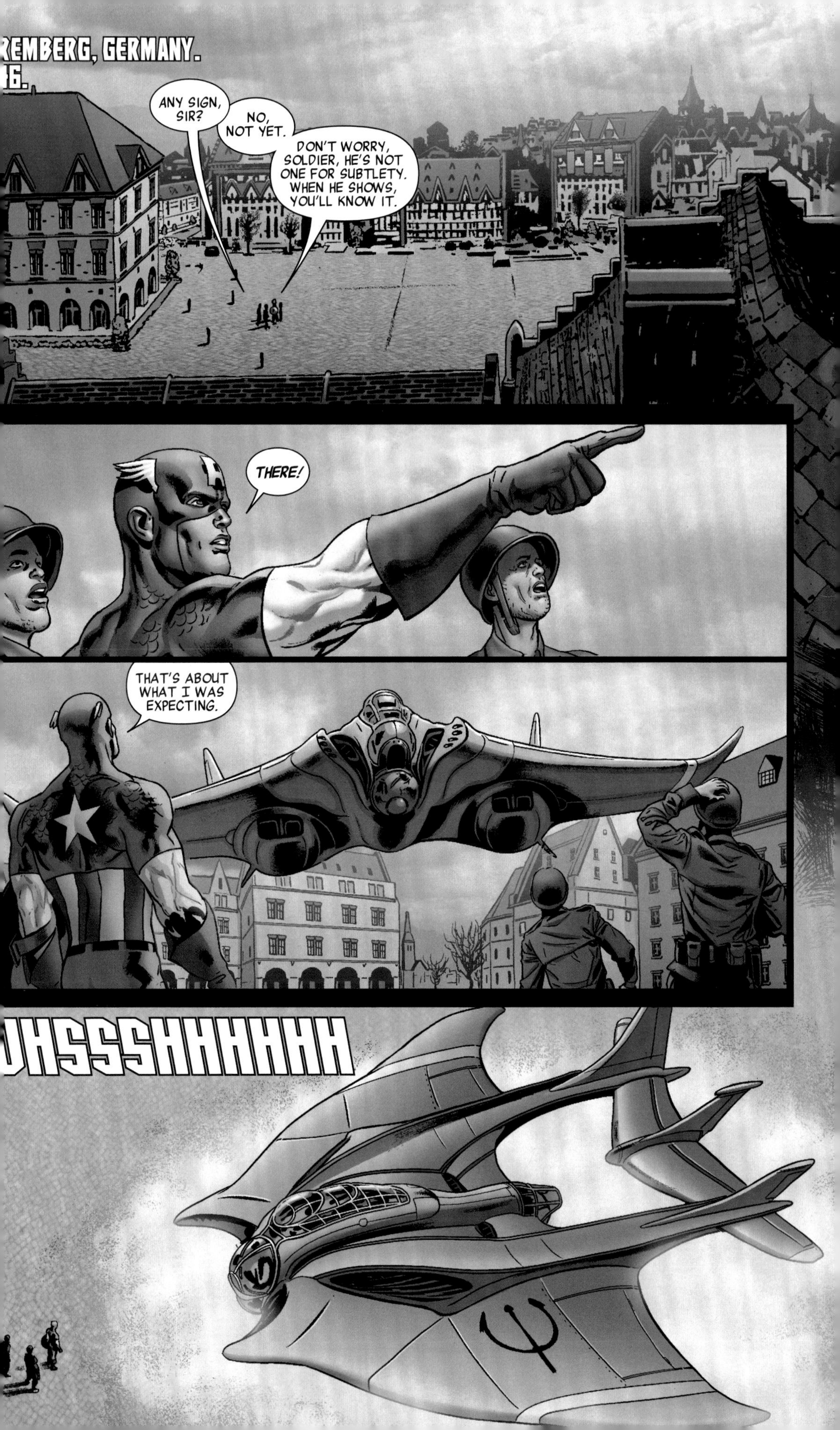
REMBERG, GERMANY.
46.
ANY SIGN, SIR?
NO, NOT YET.
DON'T WORRY, SOLDIER, HE'S NOT ONE FOR SUBTLETY. WHEN HE SHOWS, YOU'LL KNOW IT.
THERE!
THAT'S ABOUT WHAT I WAS EXPECTING.
VHSSSHHHHHH

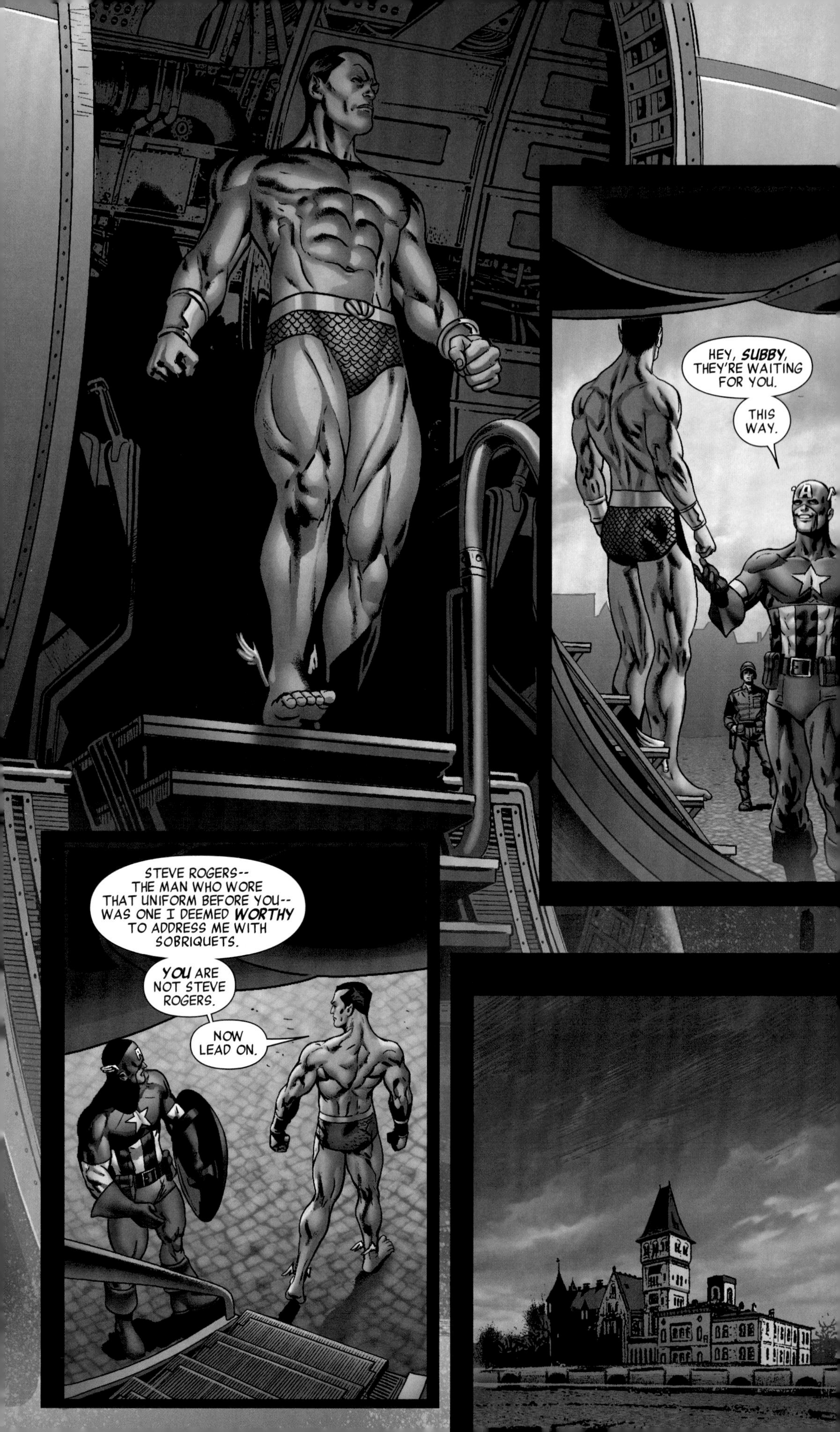

HEY, SUBBY, THEY'RE WAITING FOR YOU.
THIS WAY.
STEVE ROGERS-- THE MAN WHO WORE THAT UNIFORM BEFORE YOU-- WAS ONE I DEEMED WORTHY TO ADDRESS ME WITH SOBRIQUETS.
YOU ARE NOT STEVE ROGERS.
NOW LEAD ON.

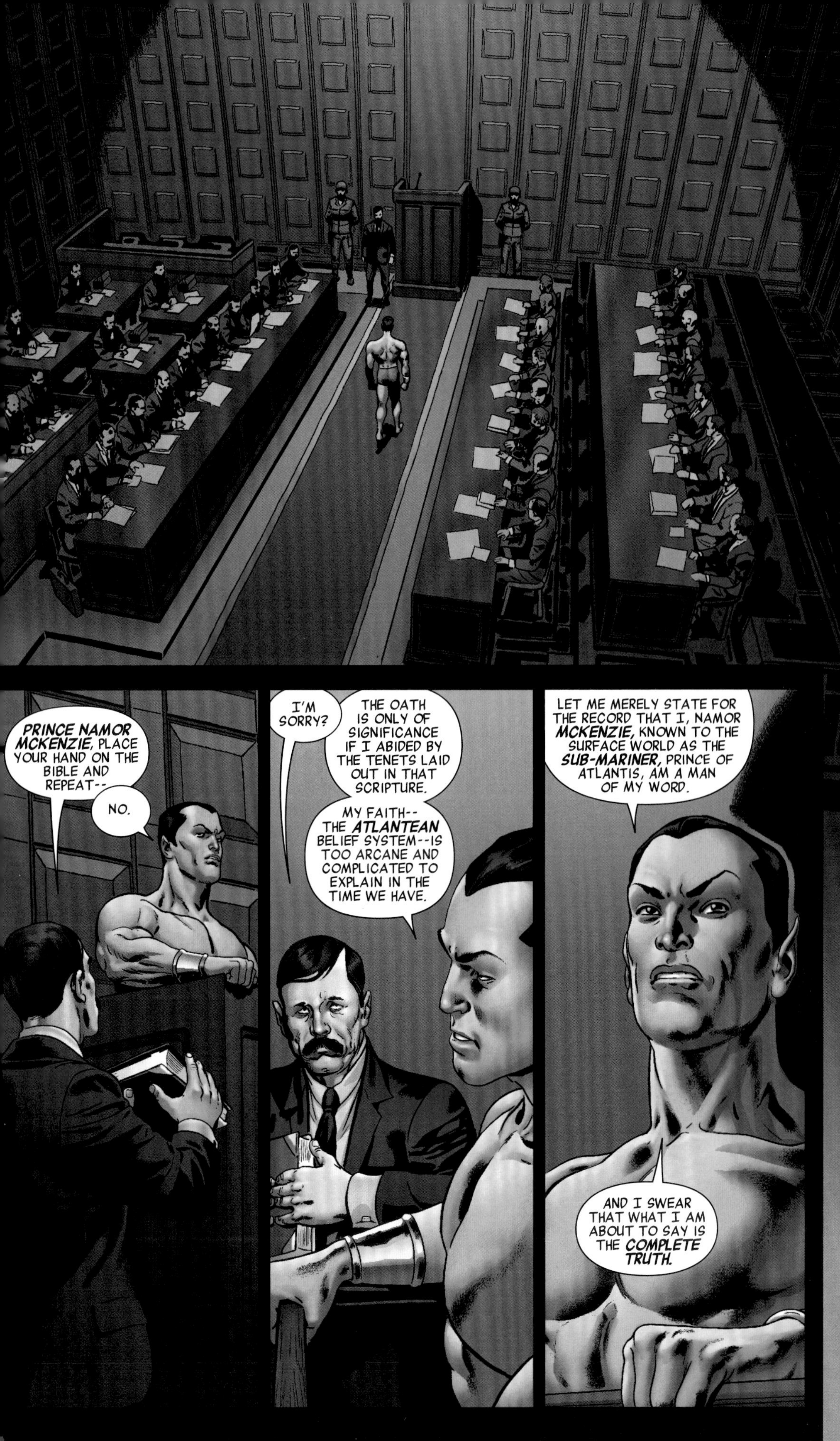
PRINCE NAMOR MCKENZIE, PLACE YOUR HAND ON THE BIBLE AND REPEAT--
NO.
I'M SORRY?
THE OATH IS ONLY OF SIGNIFICANCE IF I ABIDED BY THE TENETS LAID OUT IN THAT SCRIPTURE.
MY FAITH-- THE ATLANTEAN BELIEF SYSTEM--IS TOO ARCANE AND COMPLICATED TO EXPLAIN IN THE TIME WE HAVE.
LET ME MERELY STATE FOR THE RECORD THAT I, NAMOR MCKENZIE, KNOWN TO THE SURFACE WORLD AS THE SUB-MARINER, PRINCE OF ATLANTIS, AM A MAN OF MY WORD.
AND I SWEAR THAT WHAT I AM ABOUT TO SAY IS THE COMPLETE TRUTH.

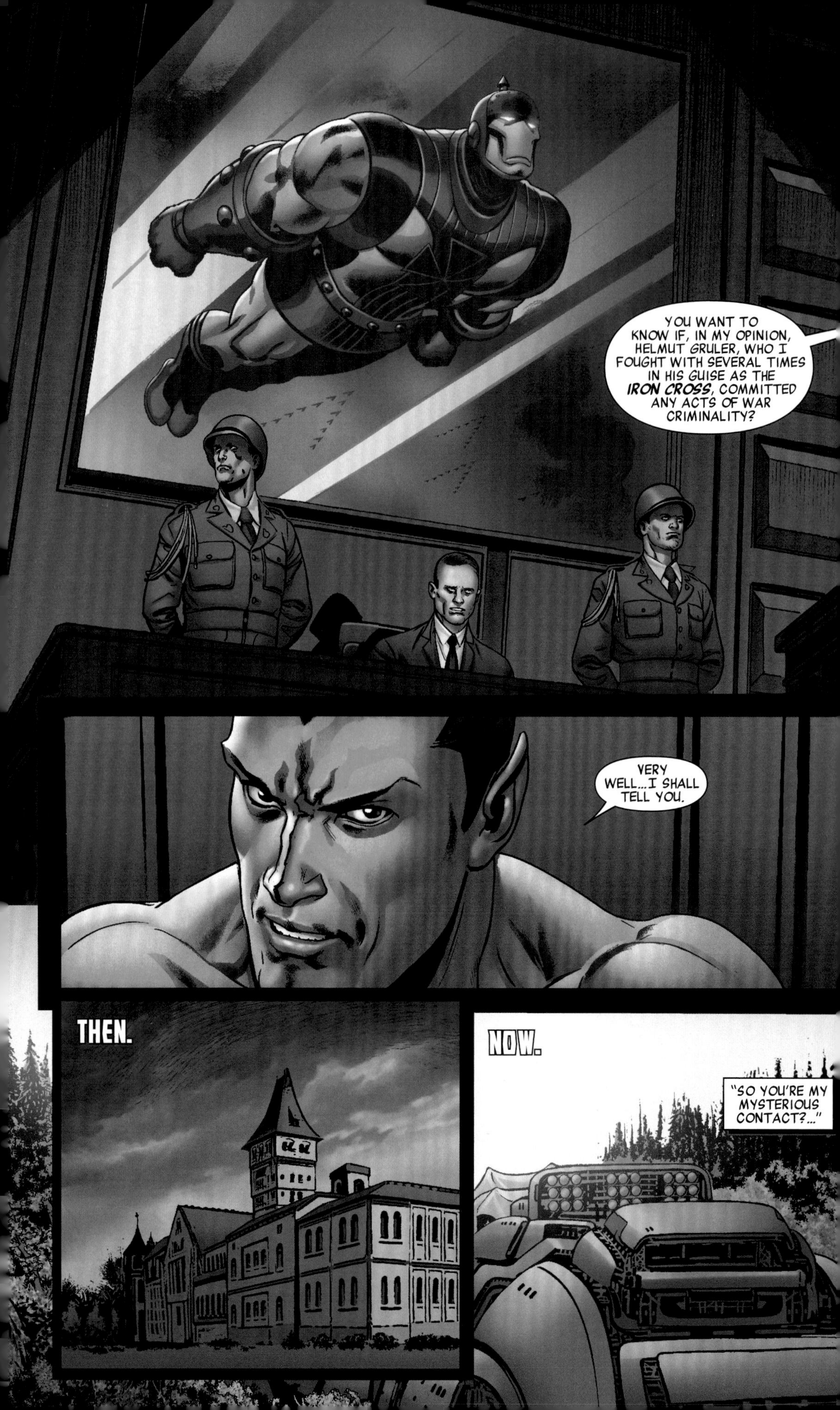
YOU WANT TO KNOW IF, IN MY OPINION, HELMUT GRULER, WHO I FOUGHT WITH SEVERAL TIMES IN HIS GUISE AS THE IRON CROSS, COMMITTED ANY ACTS OF WAR CRIMINALITY?
VERY WELL...I SHALL TELL YOU.
THEN.
NOW.
"SO YOU'RE MY MYSTERIOUS CONTACT?..."

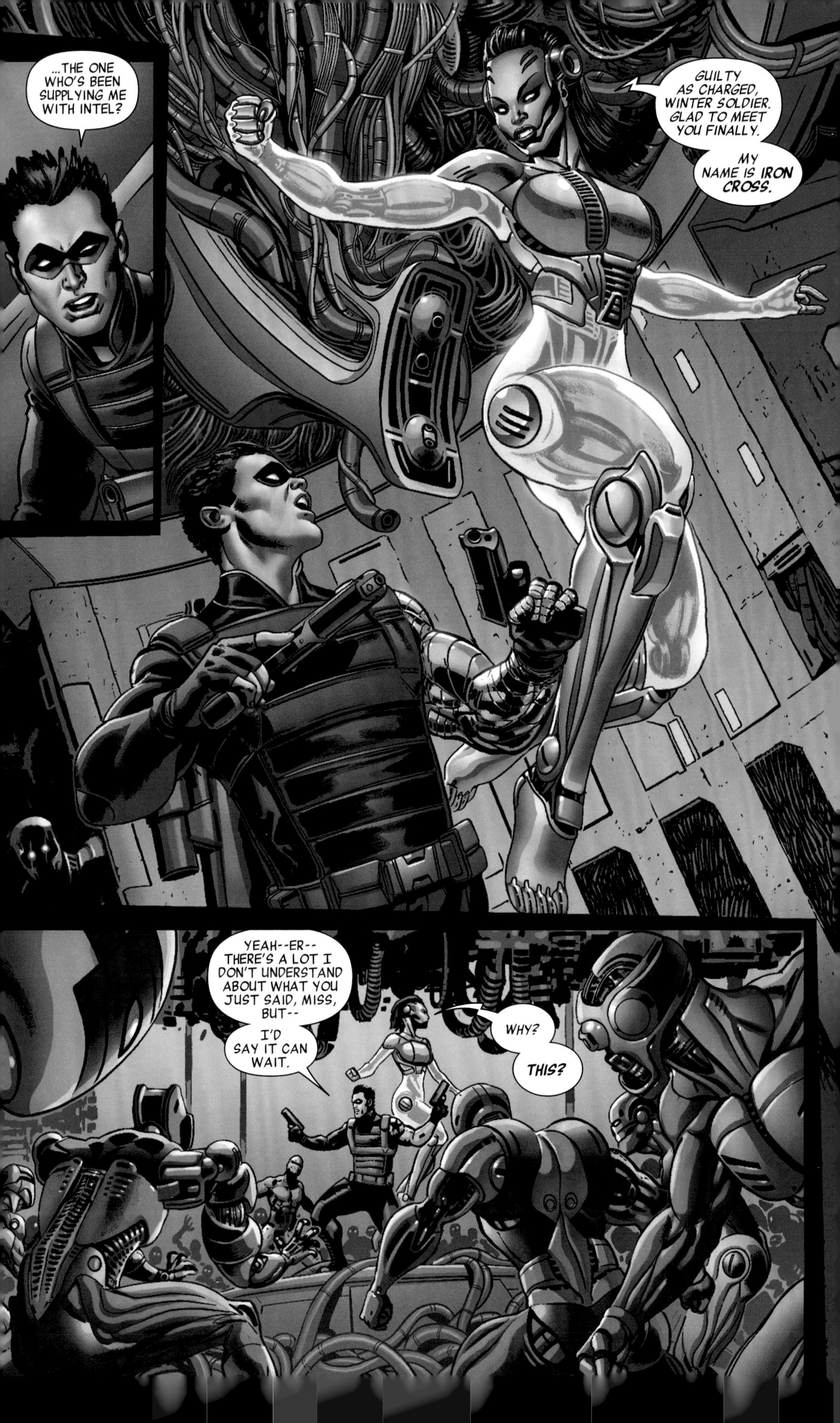
...THE ONE WHO'S BEEN SUPPLYING ME WITH INTEL?
GUILTY AS CHARGED, WINTER SOLDIER. GLAD TO MEET YOU FINALLY.
MY NAME IS IRON CROSS.
YEAH--ER-- THERE'S A LOT I DON'T UNDERSTAND ABOUT WHAT YOU JUST SAID, MISS, BUT--
I'D SAY IT CAN WAIT.
WHY?
THIS?

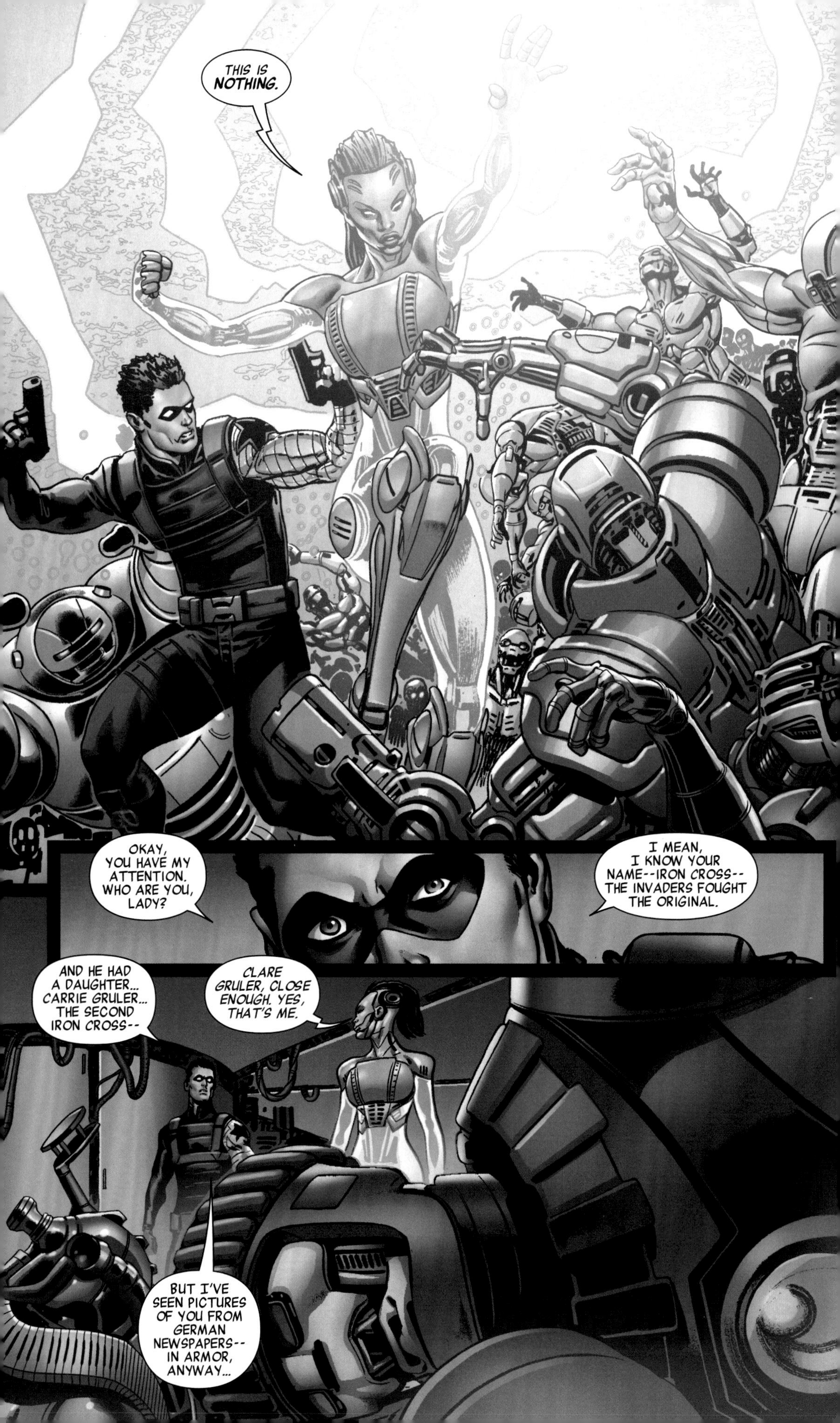
THIS IS NOTHING.
OKAY, YOU HAVE MY ATTENTION. WHO ARE YOU, LADY?
I MEAN, I KNOW YOUR NAME--IRON CROSS--THE INVADERS FOUGHT THE ORIGINAL.
AND HE HAD A DAUGHTER... CARRIE GRULER... THE SECOND IRON CROSS--
CLARE GRULER, CLOSE ENOUGH. YES, THAT'S ME.
BUT I'VE SEEN PICTURES OF YOU FROM GERMAN NEWSPAPERS--IN ARMOR, ANYWAY...

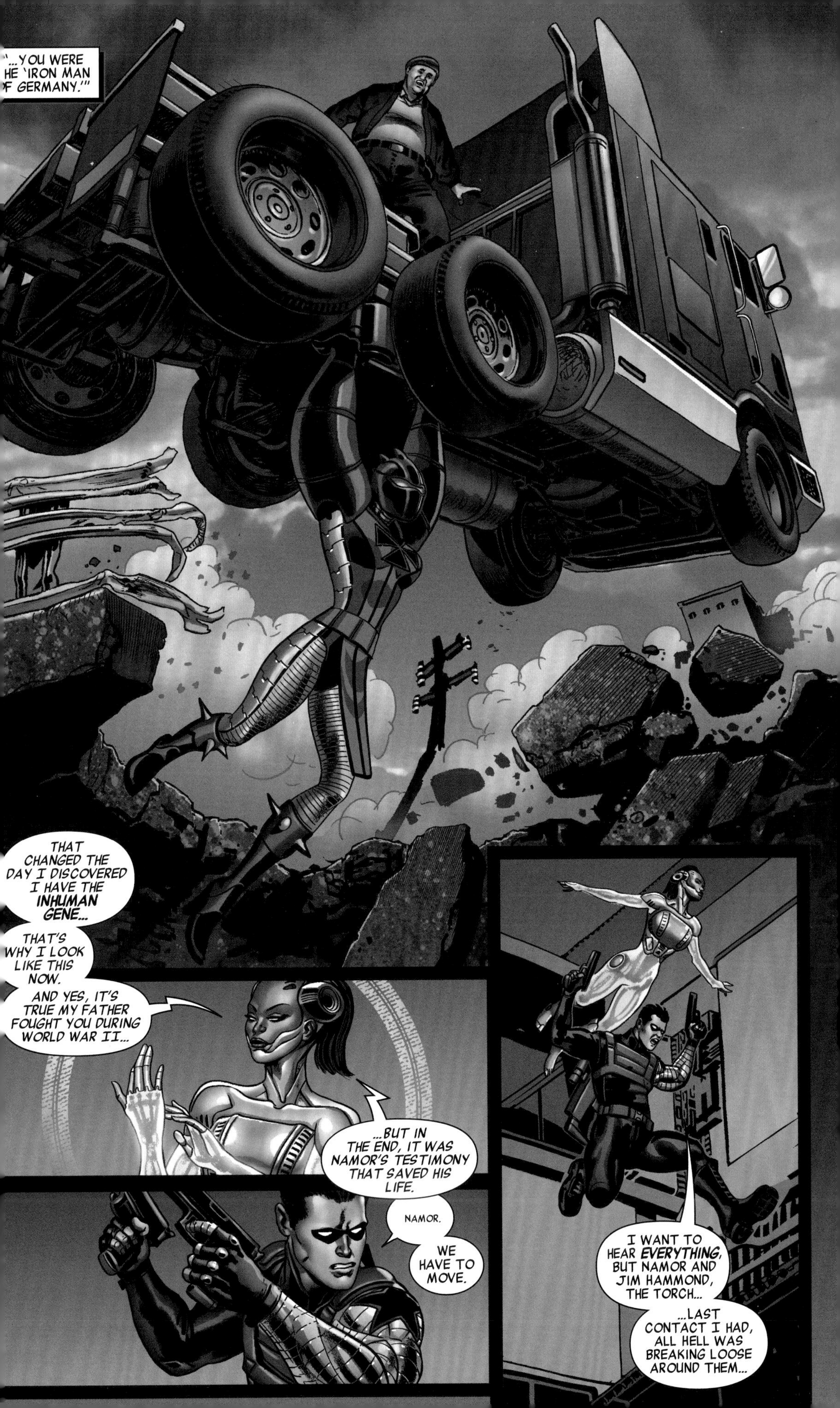
"...YOU WERE
HE 'IRON MAN
F GERMANY.'"
THAT CHANGED THE DAY I DISCOVERED I HAVE THE **INHUMAN GENE...**
THAT'S WHY I LOOK LIKE THIS NOW.
AND YES, IT'S TRUE MY FATHER FOUGHT YOU DURING WORLD WAR II...
...BUT IN THE END, IT WAS NAMOR'S TESTIMONY THAT SAVED HIS LIFE.
NAMOR.
WE HAVE TO MOVE.
I WANT TO HEAR **EVERYTHING**, BUT NAMOR AND JIM HAMMOND, THE TORCH...
...LAST CONTACT I HAD, ALL HELL WAS BREAKING LOOSE AROUND THEM...

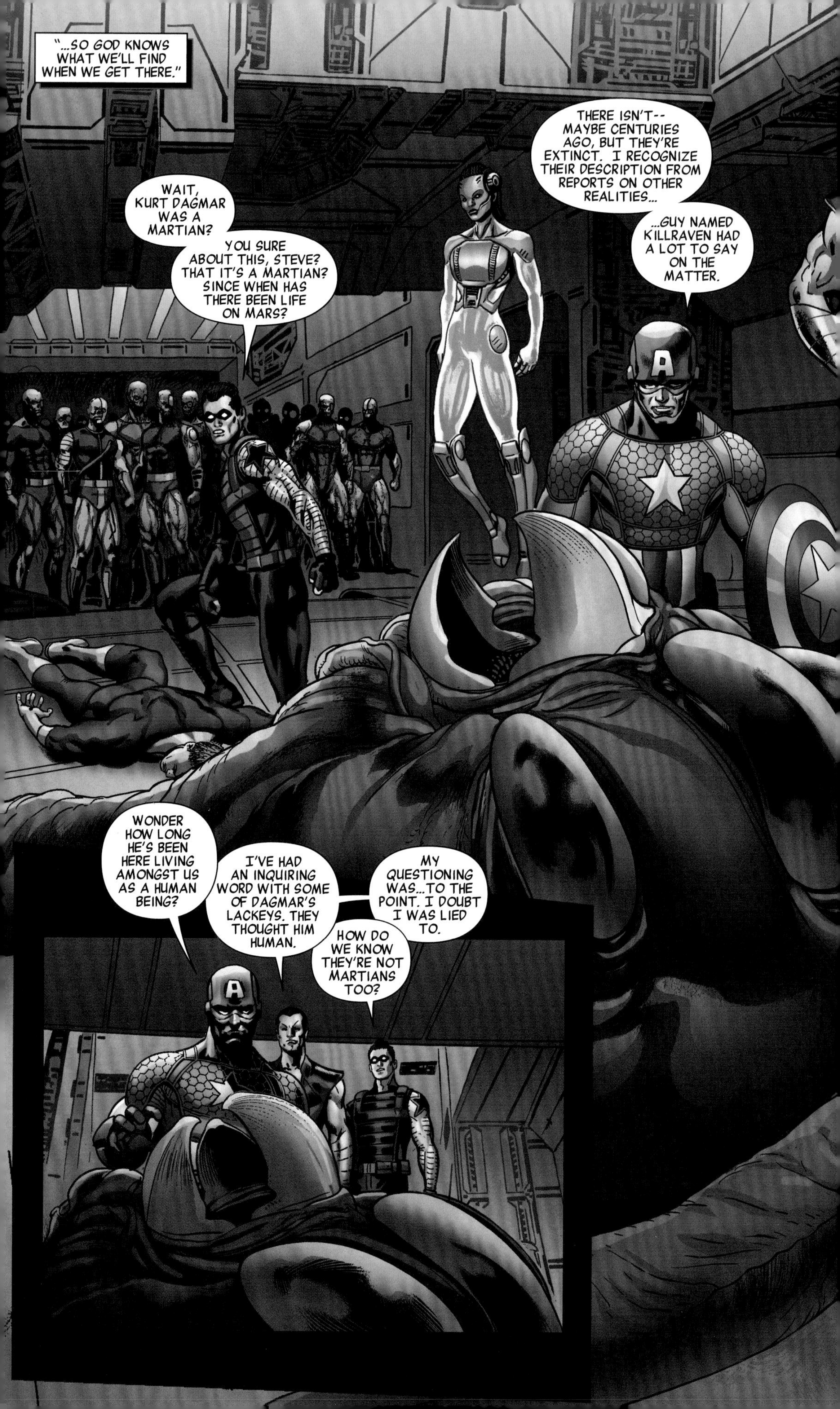
"...SO GOD KNOWS WHAT WE'LL FIND WHEN WE GET THERE."
WAIT, KURT DAGMAR WAS A MARTIAN?
YOU SURE ABOUT THIS, STEVE? THAT IT'S A MARTIAN? SINCE WHEN HAS THERE BEEN LIFE ON MARS?
THERE ISN'T-- MAYBE CENTURIES AGO, BUT THEY'RE EXTINCT. I RECOGNIZE THEIR DESCRIPTION FROM REPORTS ON OTHER REALITIES...
...GUY NAMED KILLRAVEN HAD A LOT TO SAY ON THE MATTER.
WONDER HOW LONG HE'S BEEN HERE LIVING AMONGST US AS A HUMAN BEING?
I'VE HAD AN INQUIRING WORD WITH SOME OF DAGMAR'S LACKEYS. THEY THOUGHT HIM HUMAN.
MY QUESTIONING WAS...TO THE POINT. I DOUBT I WAS LIED TO.
HOW DO WE KNOW THEY'RE NOT MARTIANS TOO?

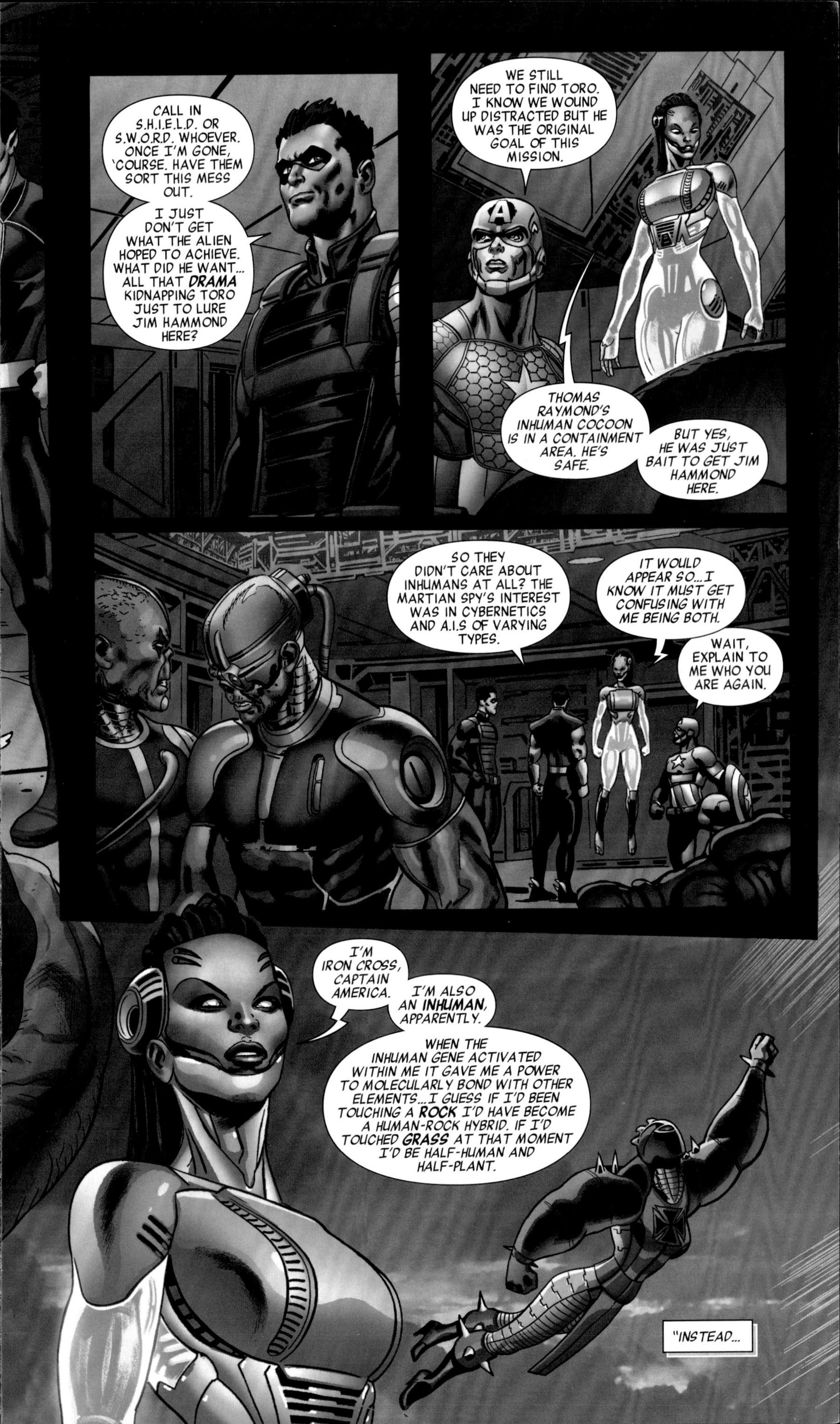
CALL IN S.H.I.E.L.D. OR S.W.O.R.D. WHOEVER. ONCE I'M GONE, 'COURSE. HAVE THEM SORT THIS MESS OUT.
I JUST DON'T GET WHAT THE ALIEN HOPED TO ACHIEVE. WHAT DID HE WANT... ALL THAT DRAMA KIDNAPPING TORO JUST TO LURE JIM HAMMOND HERE?
WE STILL NEED TO FIND TORO. I KNOW WE WOUND UP DISTRACTED BUT HE WAS THE ORIGINAL GOAL OF THIS MISSION.
THOMAS RAYMOND'S INHUMAN COCOON IS IN A CONTAINMENT AREA. HE'S SAFE.
BUT YES, HE WAS JUST BAIT TO GET JIM HAMMOND HERE.
SO THEY DIDN'T CARE ABOUT INHUMANS AT ALL? THE MARTIAN SPY'S INTEREST WAS IN CYBERNETICS AND A.I.S OF VARYING TYPES.
IT WOULD APPEAR SO...I KNOW IT MUST GET CONFUSING WITH ME BEING BOTH.
WAIT, EXPLAIN TO ME WHO YOU ARE AGAIN.
I'M IRON CROSS, CAPTAIN AMERICA.
I'M ALSO AN INHUMAN, APPARENTLY.
WHEN THE INHUMAN GENE ACTIVATED WITHIN ME IT GAVE ME A POWER TO MOLECULARLY BOND WITH OTHER ELEMENTS...I GUESS IF I'D BEEN TOUCHING A ROCK I'D HAVE BECOME A HUMAN-ROCK HYBRID. IF I'D TOUCHED GRASS AT THAT MOMENT I'D BE HALF-HUMAN AND HALF-PLANT.
"INSTEAD...

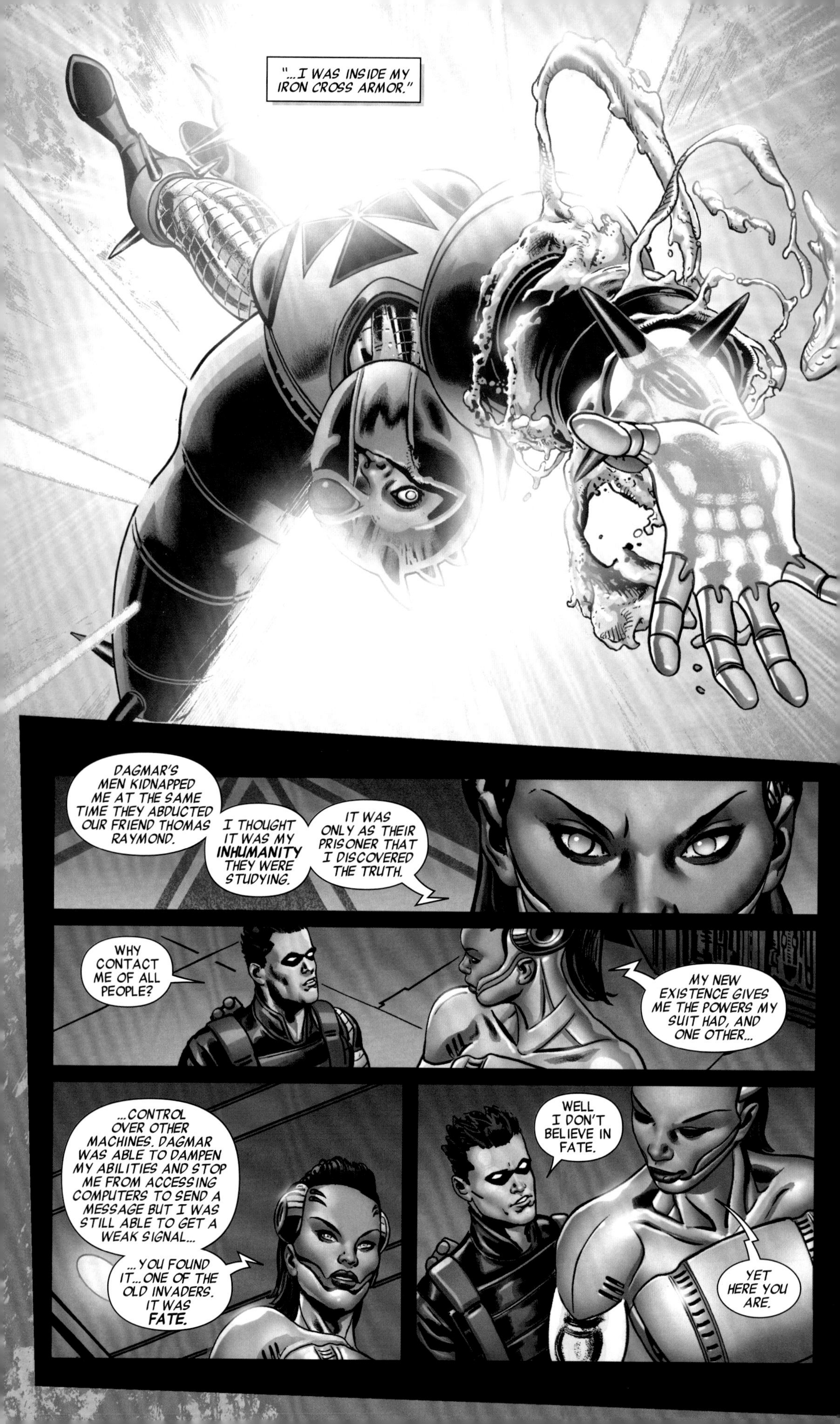

"...I WAS INSIDE MY IRON CROSS ARMOR."
DAGMAR'S MEN KIDNAPPED ME AT THE SAME TIME THEY ABDUCTED OUR FRIEND THOMAS RAYMOND.
I THOUGHT IT WAS MY **INHUMANITY** THEY WERE STUDYING.
IT WAS ONLY AS THEIR PRISONER THAT I DISCOVERED THE TRUTH.
WHY CONTACT ME OF ALL PEOPLE?
MY NEW EXISTENCE GIVES ME THE POWERS MY SUIT HAD, AND ONE OTHER...
...CONTROL OVER OTHER MACHINES. DAGMAR WAS ABLE TO DAMPEN MY ABILITIES AND STOP ME FROM ACCESSING COMPUTERS TO SEND A MESSAGE BUT I WAS STILL ABLE TO GET A WEAK SIGNAL...
...YOU FOUND IT...ONE OF THE OLD INVADERS. IT WAS **FATE.**
WELL I DON'T BELIEVE IN FATE.
YET HERE YOU ARE.

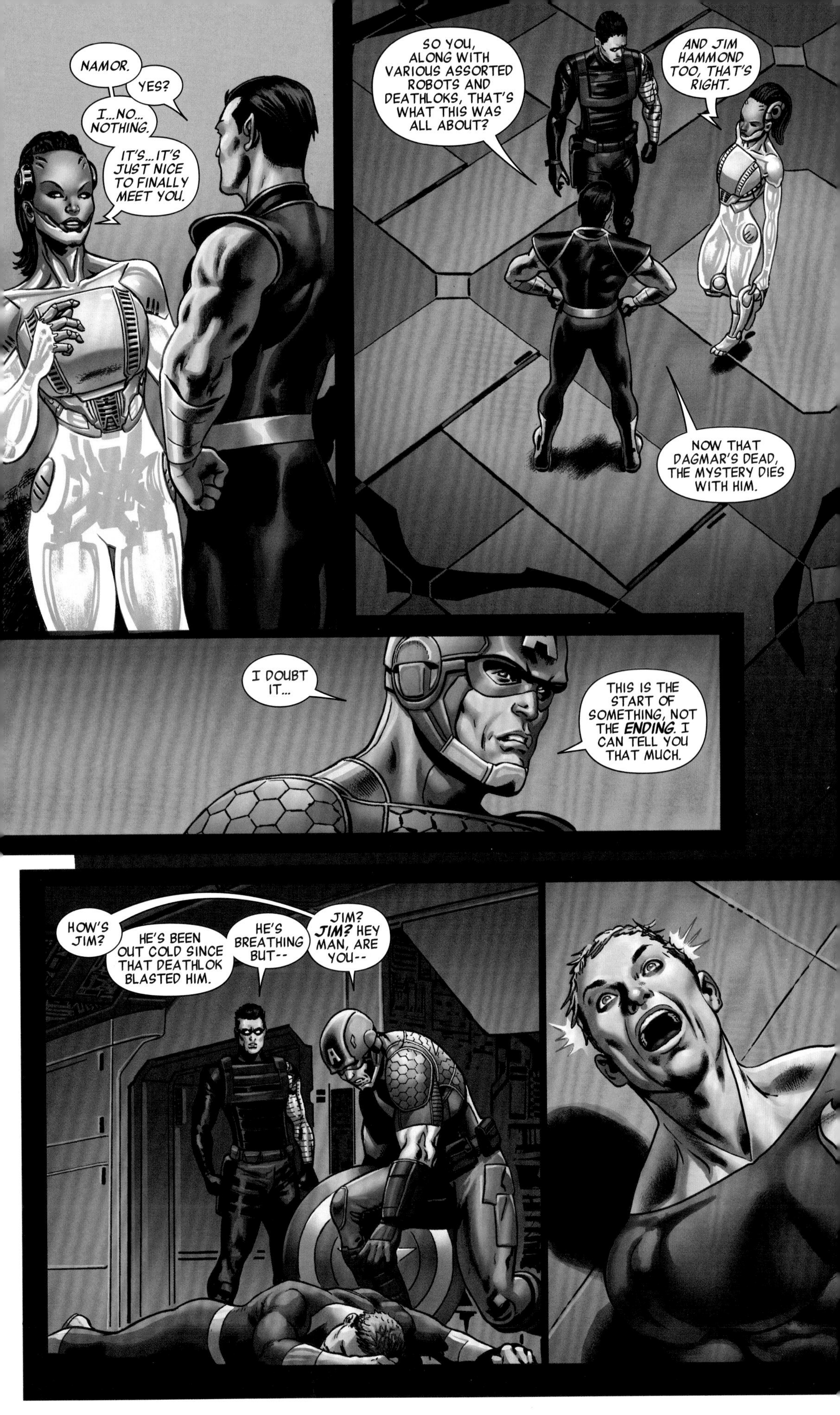
NAMOR.
YES?
I...NO... NOTHING.
IT'S...IT'S JUST NICE TO FINALLY MEET YOU.
SO YOU, ALONG WITH VARIOUS ASSORTED ROBOTS AND DEATHLOKS, THAT'S WHAT THIS WAS ALL ABOUT?
AND JIM HAMMOND TOO, THAT'S RIGHT.
NOW THAT DAGMAR'S DEAD, THE MYSTERY DIES WITH HIM.
I DOUBT IT...
THIS IS THE START OF SOMETHING, NOT THE ENDING. I CAN TELL YOU THAT MUCH.
HOW'S JIM?
HE'S BEEN OUT COLD SINCE THAT DEATHLOK BLASTED HIM.
HE'S BREATHING BUT--
JIM? JIM? HEY MAN, ARE YOU--

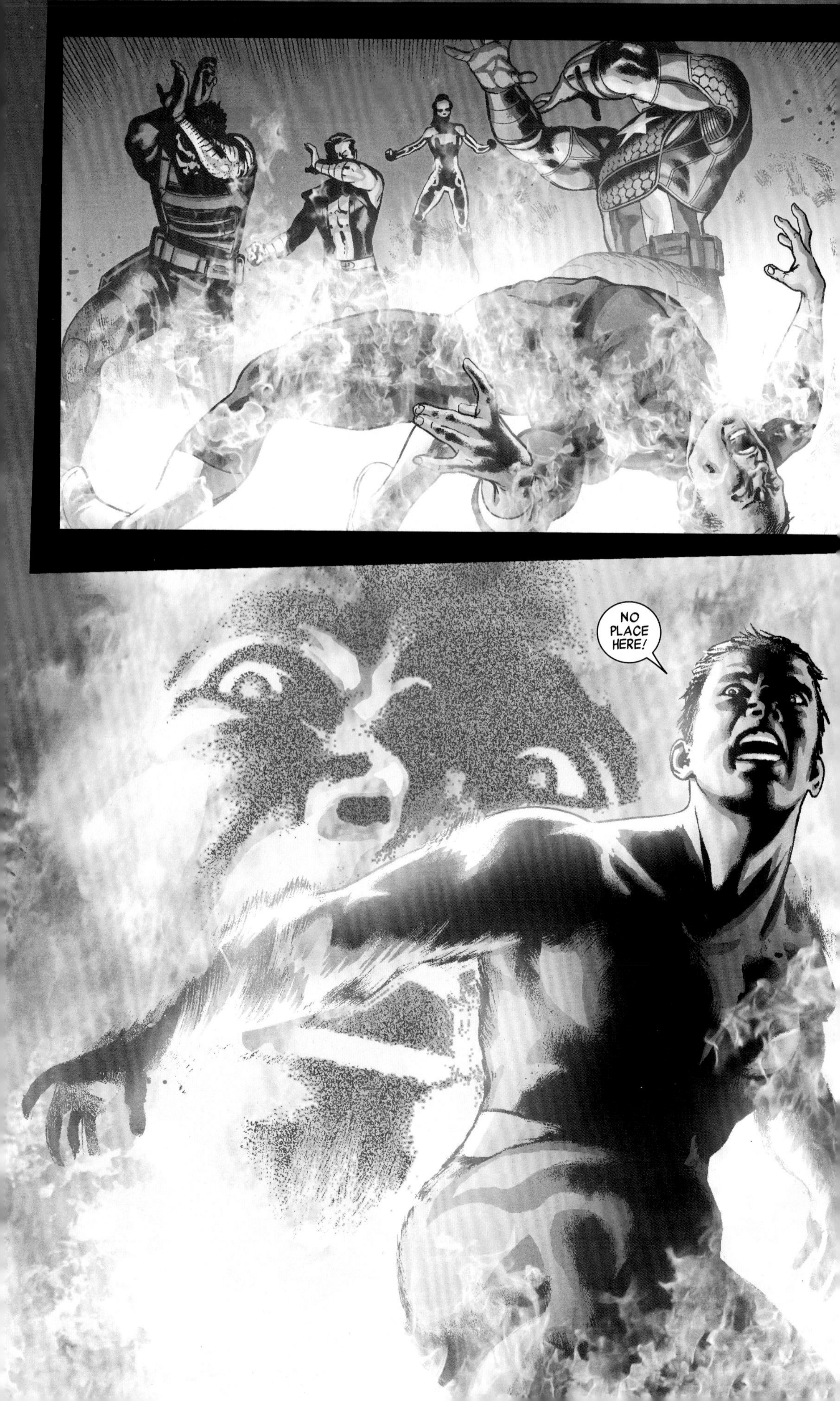
NO PLACE HERE!

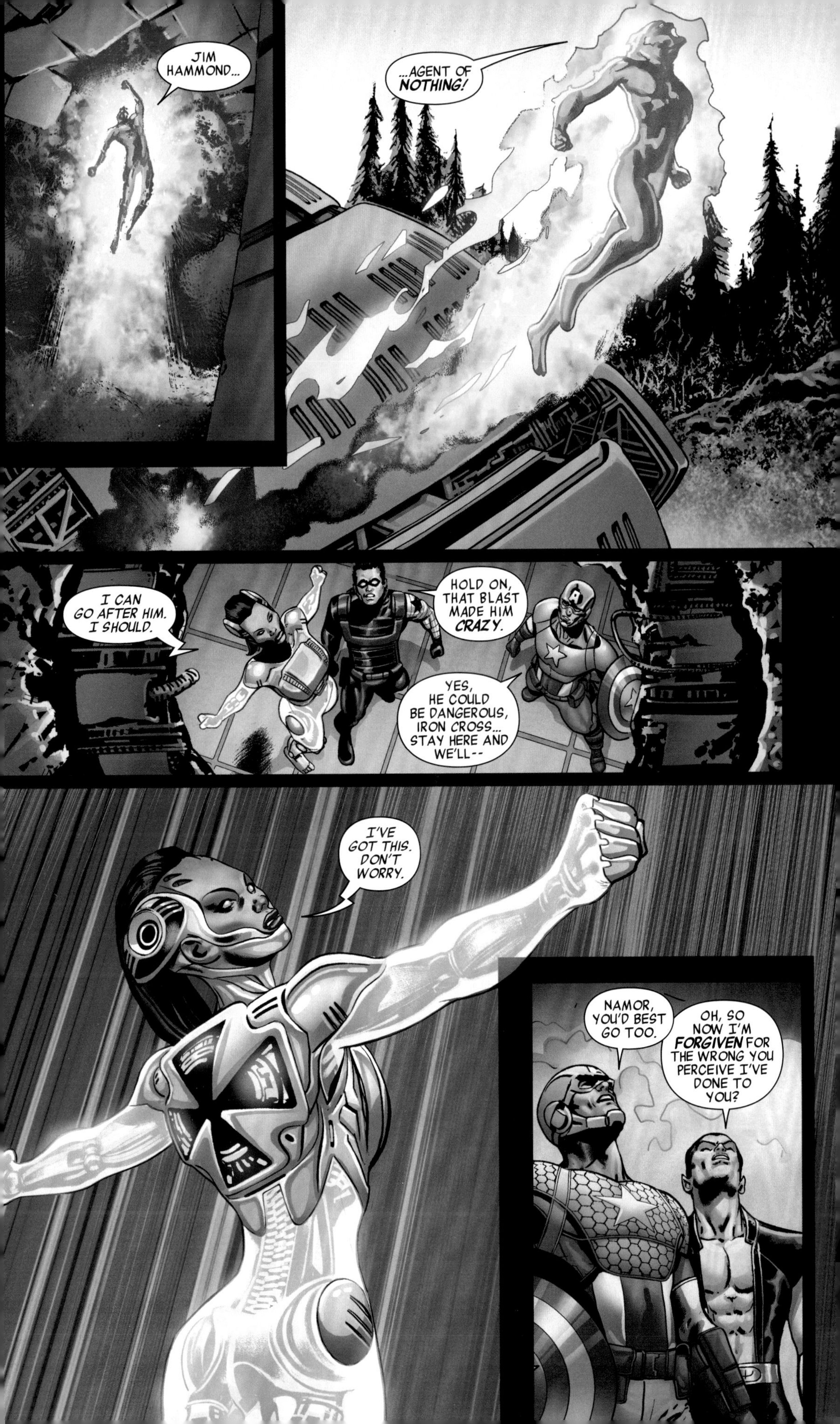

JIM HAMMOND...
...AGENT OF NOTHING!
I CAN GO AFTER HIM. I SHOULD.
HOLD ON, THAT BLAST MADE HIM CRAZY.
YES, HE COULD BE DANGEROUS, IRON CROSS... STAY HERE AND WE'LL--
I'VE GOT THIS. DON'T WORRY.
NAMOR, YOU'D BEST GO TOO.
OH, SO NOW I'M FORGIVEN FOR THE WRONG YOU PERCEIVE I'VE DONE TO YOU?

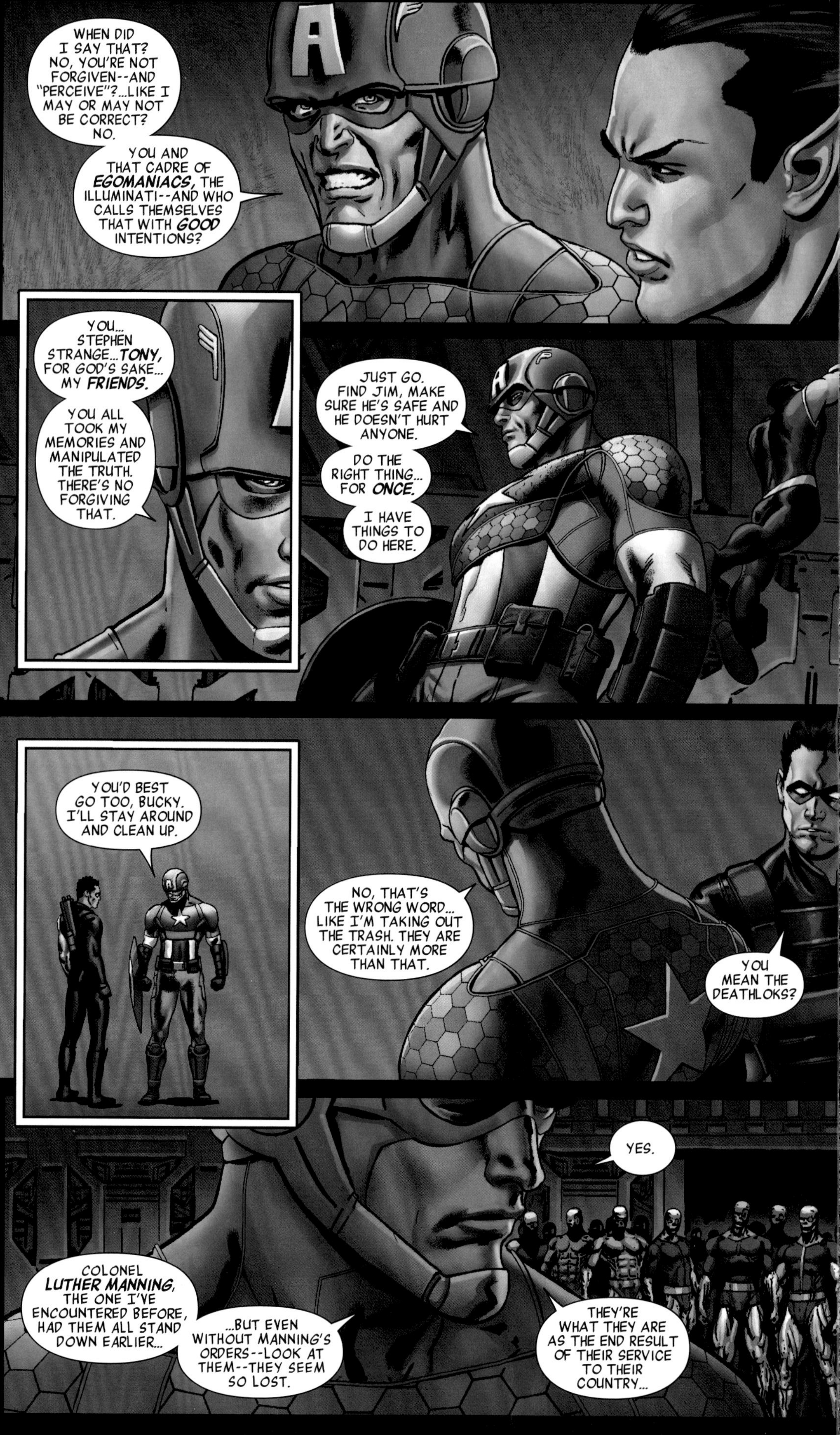
WHEN DID I SAY THAT? NO, YOU'RE NOT FORGIVEN--AND "PERCEIVE"?...LIKE I MAY OR MAY NOT BE CORRECT? NO.
YOU AND THAT CADRE OF **EGOMANIACS,** THE ILLUMINATI--AND WHO CALLS THEMSELVES THAT WITH **GOOD** INTENTIONS?
YOU... STEPHEN STRANGE...**TONY,** FOR GOD'S SAKE... MY **FRIENDS.**
YOU ALL TOOK MY MEMORIES AND MANIPULATED THE TRUTH. THERE'S NO FORGIVING THAT.
JUST GO. FIND JIM, MAKE SURE HE'S SAFE AND HE DOESN'T HURT ANYONE.
DO THE RIGHT THING... FOR **ONCE.**
I HAVE THINGS TO DO HERE.
YOU'D BEST GO TOO, BUCKY. I'LL STAY AROUND AND CLEAN UP.
NO, THAT'S THE WRONG WORD... LIKE I'M TAKING OUT THE TRASH. THEY ARE CERTAINLY MORE THAN THAT.
YOU MEAN THE DEATHLOKS?
YES.
COLONEL **LUTHER MANNING,** THE ONE I'VE ENCOUNTERED BEFORE, HAD THEM ALL STAND DOWN EARLIER...
...BUT EVEN WITHOUT MANNING'S ORDERS--LOOK AT THEM--THEY SEEM SO LOST.
THEY'RE WHAT THEY ARE AS THE END RESULT OF THEIR SERVICE TO THEIR COUNTRY...

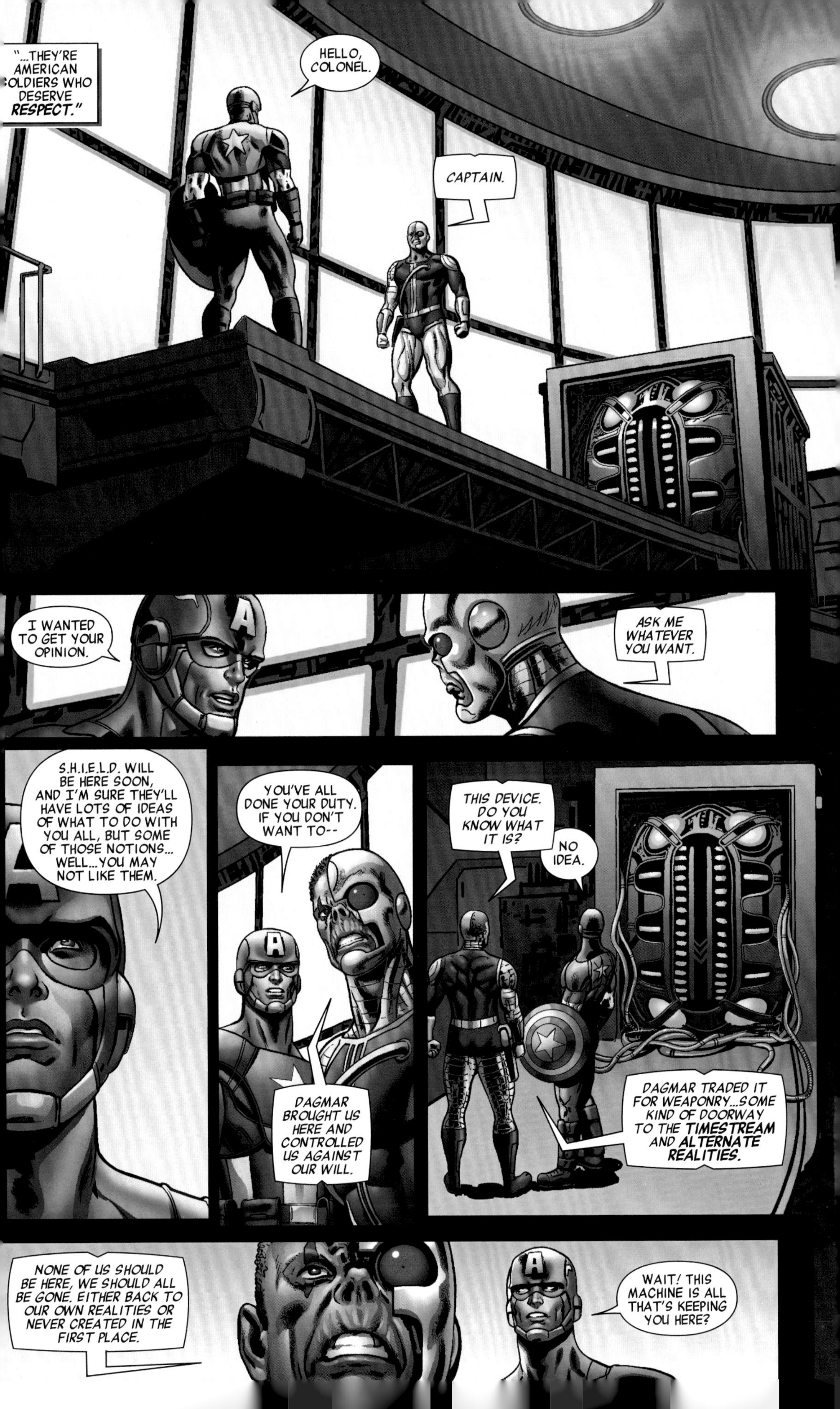
"...THEY'RE AMERICAN SOLDIERS WHO DESERVE RESPECT."
HELLO, COLONEL.
CAPTAIN.
I WANTED TO GET YOUR OPINION.
ASK ME WHATEVER YOU WANT.
S.H.I.E.L.D. WILL BE HERE SOON, AND I'M SURE THEY'LL HAVE LOTS OF IDEAS OF WHAT TO DO WITH YOU ALL, BUT SOME OF THOSE NOTIONS... WELL...YOU MAY NOT LIKE THEM.
YOU'VE ALL DONE YOUR DUTY. IF YOU DON'T WANT TO--
DAGMAR BROUGHT US HERE AND CONTROLLED US AGAINST OUR WILL.
THIS DEVICE. DO YOU KNOW WHAT IT IS?
NO IDEA.
DAGMAR TRADED IT FOR WEAPONRY...SOME KIND OF DOORWAY TO THE TIMESTREAM AND ALTERNATE REALITIES.
NONE OF US SHOULD BE HERE, WE SHOULD ALL BE GONE. EITHER BACK TO OUR OWN REALITIES OR NEVER CREATED IN THE FIRST PLACE.
WAIT! THIS MACHINE IS ALL THAT'S KEEPING YOU HERE?

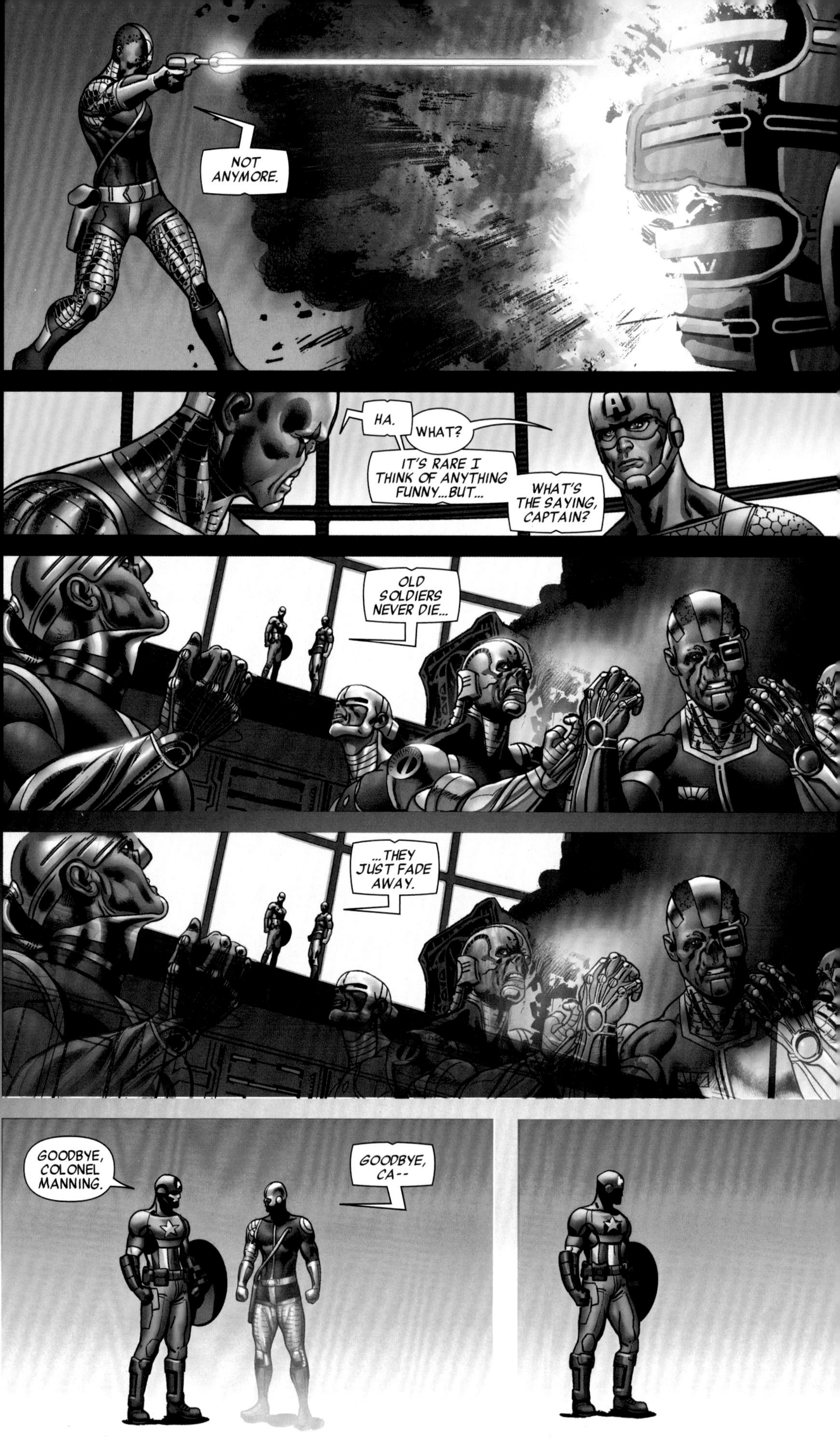
NOT ANYMORE.
HA.
WHAT?
IT'S RARE I THINK OF ANYTHING FUNNY...BUT...
WHAT'S THE SAYING, CAPTAIN?
OLD SOLDIERS NEVER DIE...
...THEY JUST FADE AWAY.
GOODBYE, COLONEL MANNING.
GOODBYE, CA--

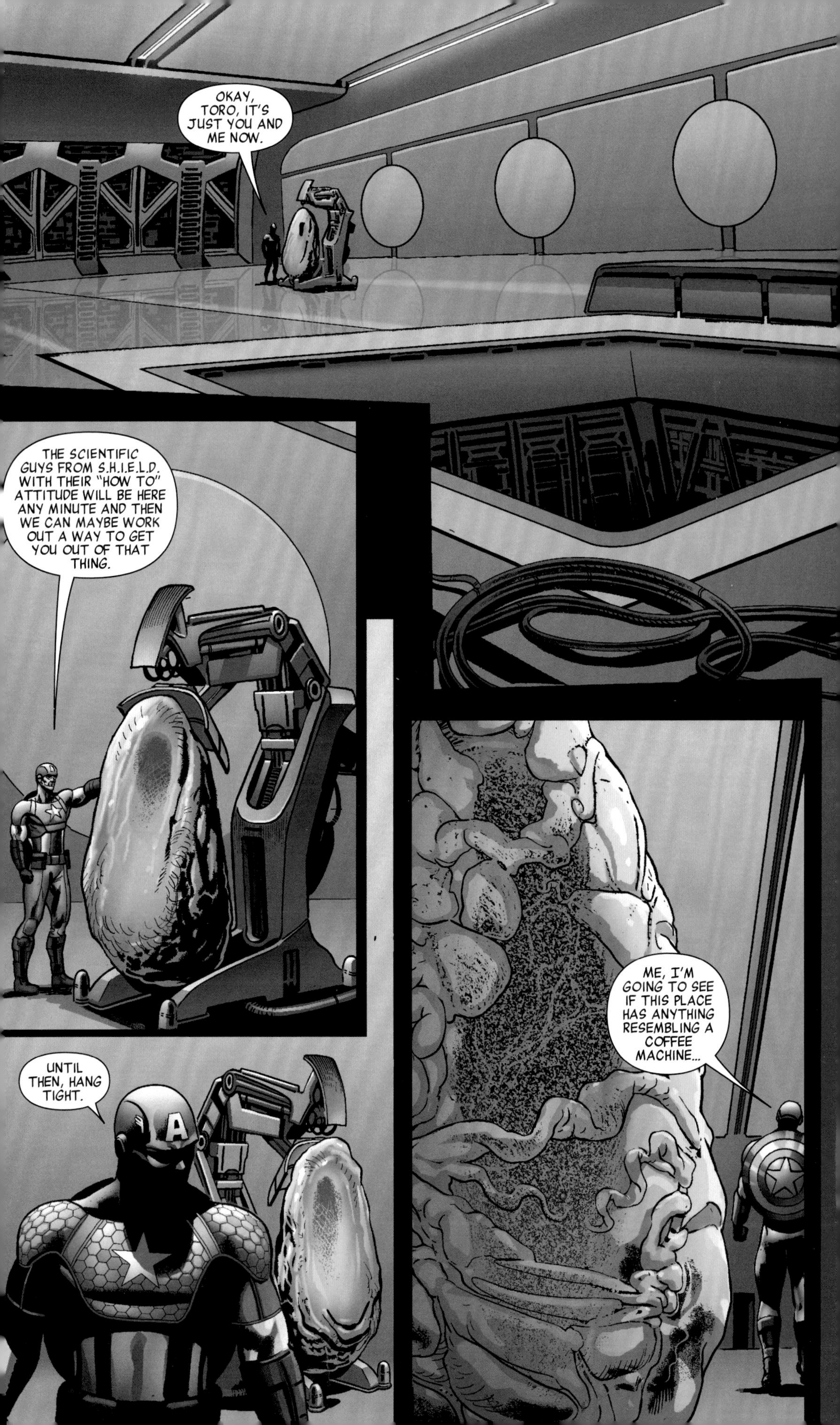
OKAY, TORO, IT'S JUST YOU AND ME NOW.
THE SCIENTIFIC GUYS FROM S.H.I.E.L.D. WITH THEIR "HOW TO" ATTITUDE WILL BE HERE ANY MINUTE AND THEN WE CAN MAYBE WORK OUT A WAY TO GET YOU OUT OF THAT THING.
UNTIL THEN, HANG TIGHT.
ME, I'M GOING TO SEE IF THIS PLACE HAS ANYTHING RESEMBLING A COFFEE MACHINE...

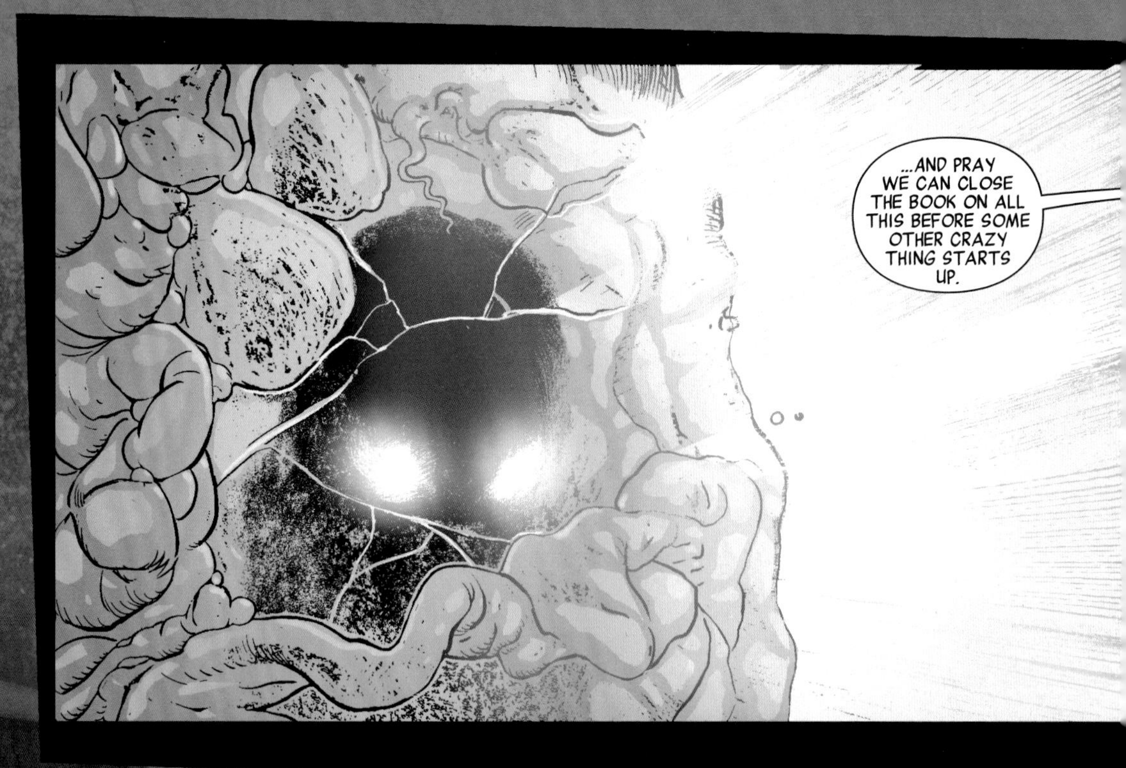
...AND PRAY WE CAN CLOSE THE BOOK ON ALL THIS BEFORE SOME OTHER CRAZY THING STARTS UP.

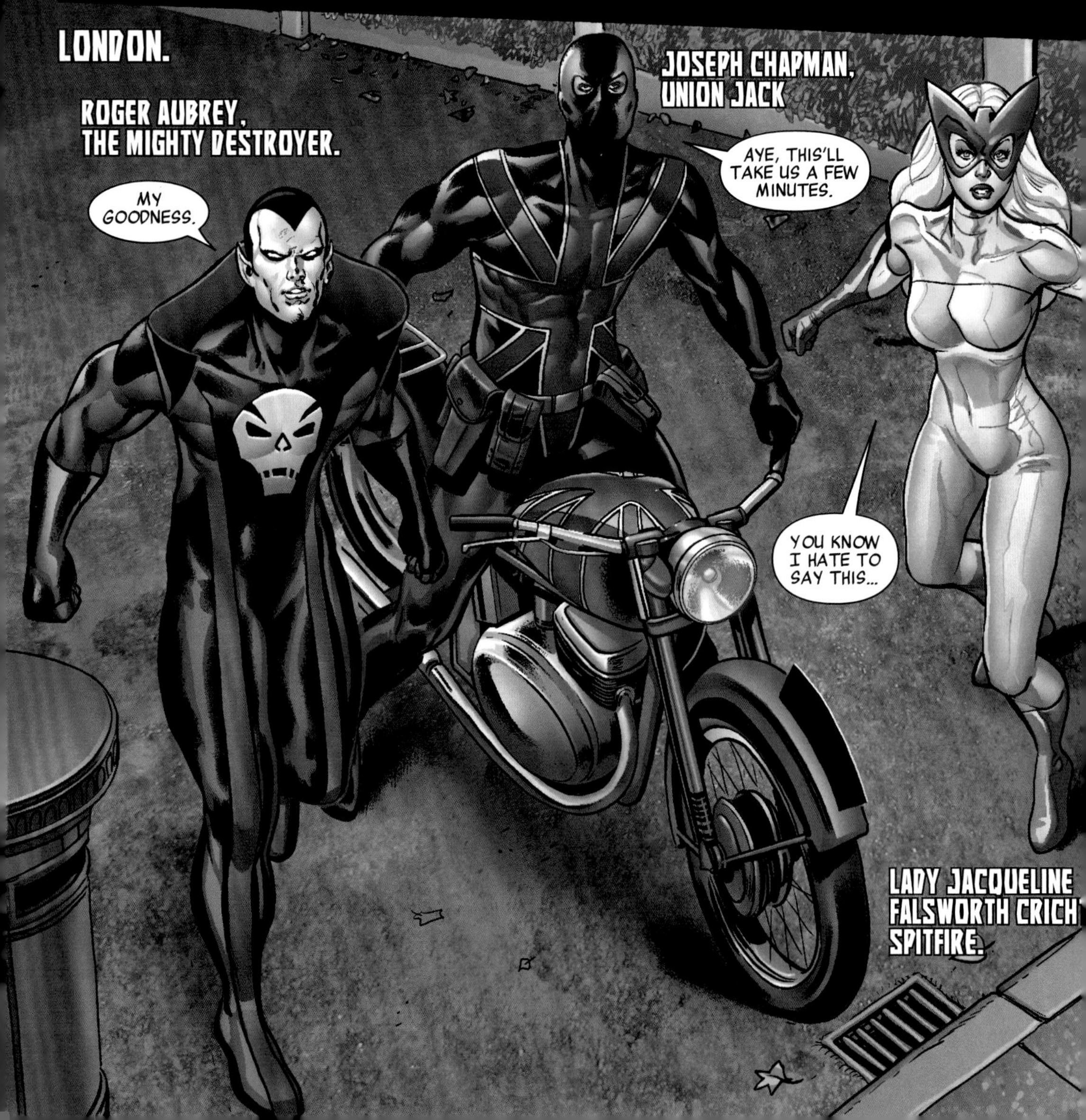
LONDON.
ROGER AUBREY, THE MIGHTY DESTROYER.
JOSEPH CHAPMAN, UNION JACK
LADY JACQUELINE FALSWORTH CRICHTON, SPITFIRE.
MY GOODNESS.
AYE, THIS'LL TAKE US A FEW MINUTES.
YOU KNOW I HATE TO SAY THIS...

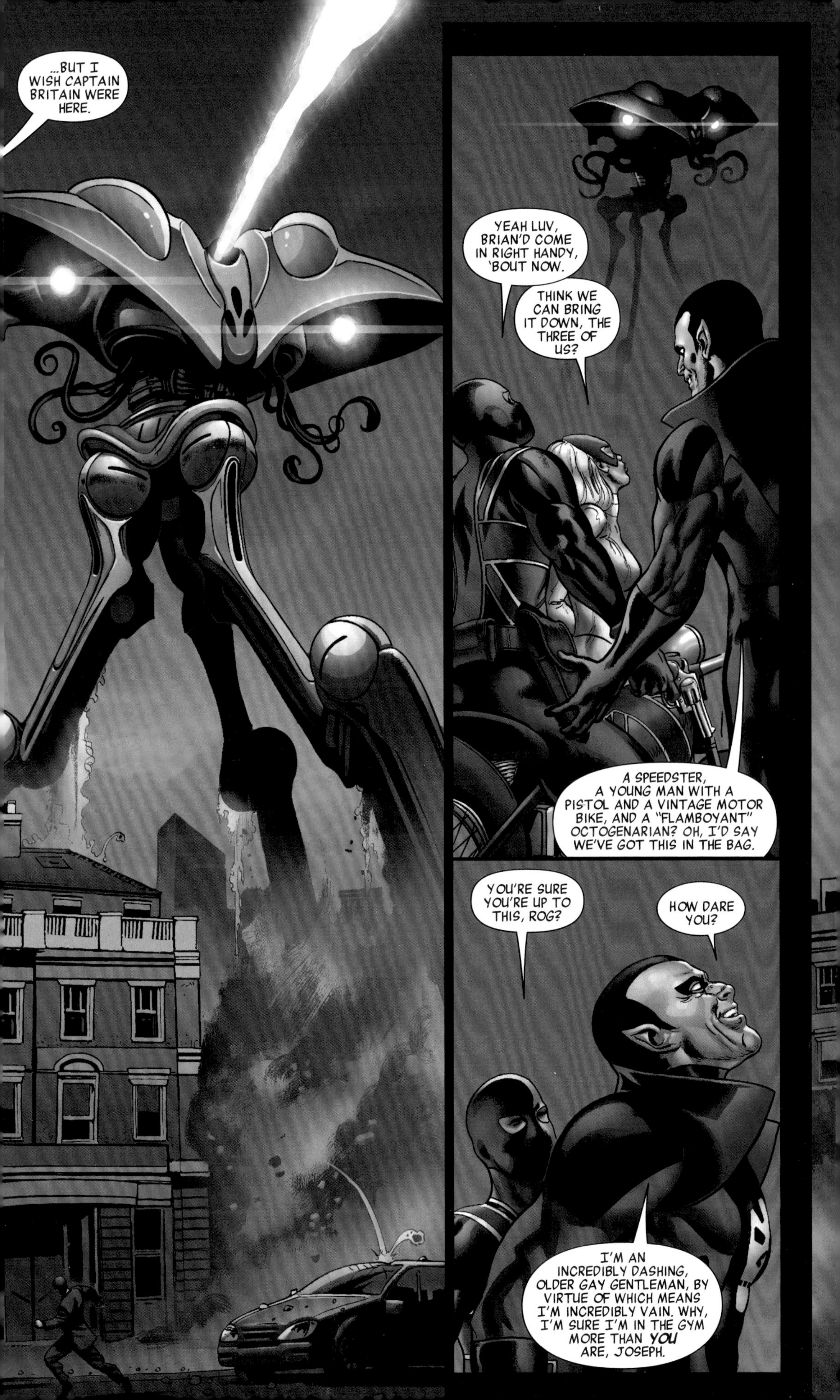
...BUT I WISH CAPTAIN BRITAIN WERE HERE.
YEAH LUV, BRIAN'D COME IN RIGHT HANDY, 'BOUT NOW.
THINK WE CAN BRING IT DOWN, THE THREE OF US?
A SPEEDSTER, A YOUNG MAN WITH A PISTOL AND A VINTAGE MOTOR BIKE, AND A "FLAMBOYANT" OCTOGENARIAN? OH, I'D SAY WE'VE GOT THIS IN THE BAG.
YOU'RE SURE YOU'RE UP TO THIS, ROG?
HOW DARE YOU?
I'M AN INCREDIBLY DASHING, OLDER GAY GENTLEMAN, BY VIRTUE OF WHICH MEANS I'M INCREDIBLY VAIN. WHY, I'M SURE I'M IN THE GYM MORE THAN YOU ARE, JOSEPH.

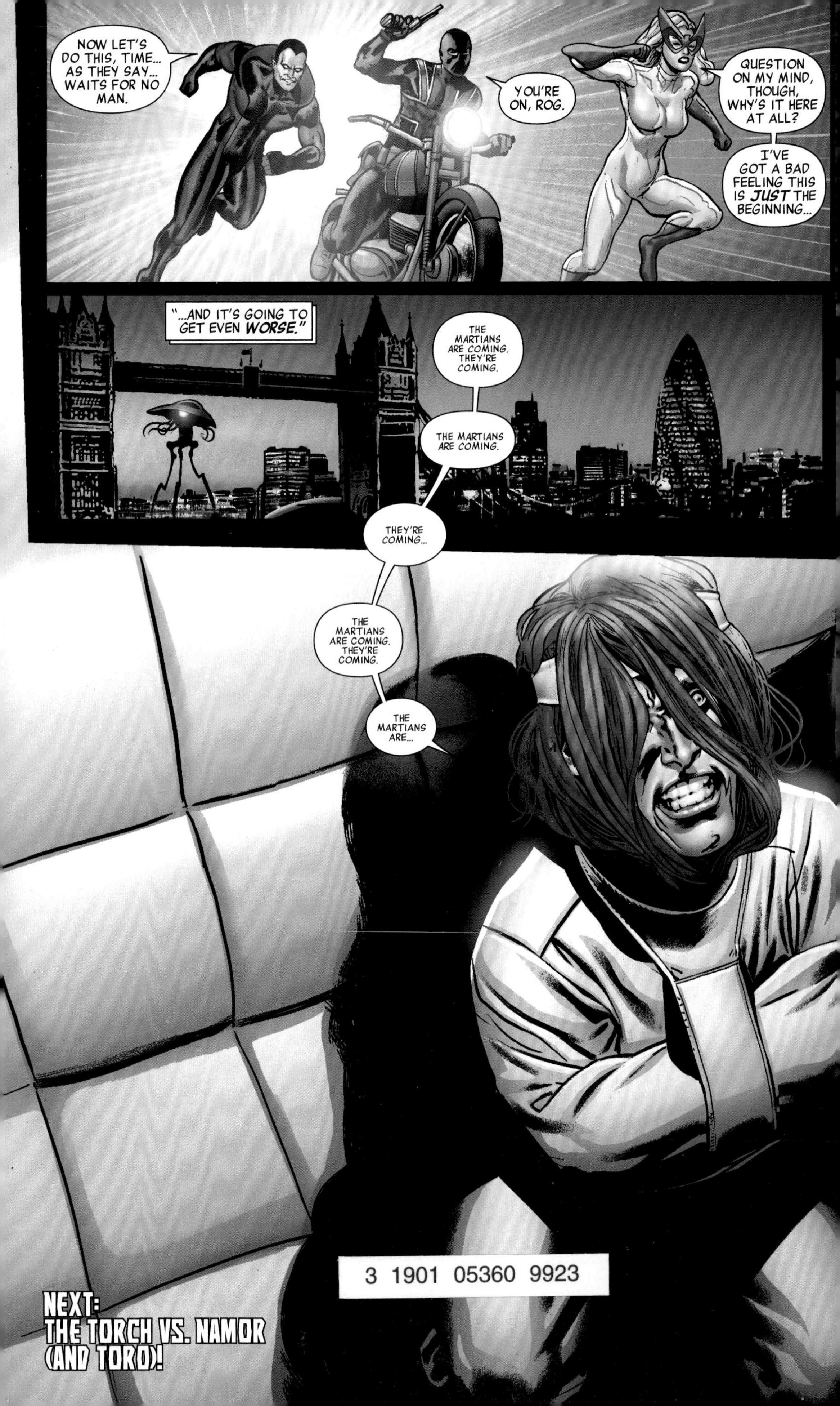
NOW LET'S DO THIS, TIME... AS THEY SAY... WAITS FOR NO MAN.
YOU'RE ON, ROG.
QUESTION ON MY MIND, THOUGH, WHY'S IT HERE AT ALL?
I'VE GOT A BAD FEELING THIS IS JUST THE BEGINNING...
"...AND IT'S GOING TO GET EVEN WORSE."
THE MARTIANS ARE COMING. THEY'RE COMING.
THE MARTIANS ARE COMING.
THEY'RE COMING...
THE MARTIANS ARE COMING. THEY'RE COMING.
THE MARTIANS ARE...
NEXT:
THE TORCH VS. NAMOR (AND TORO)!